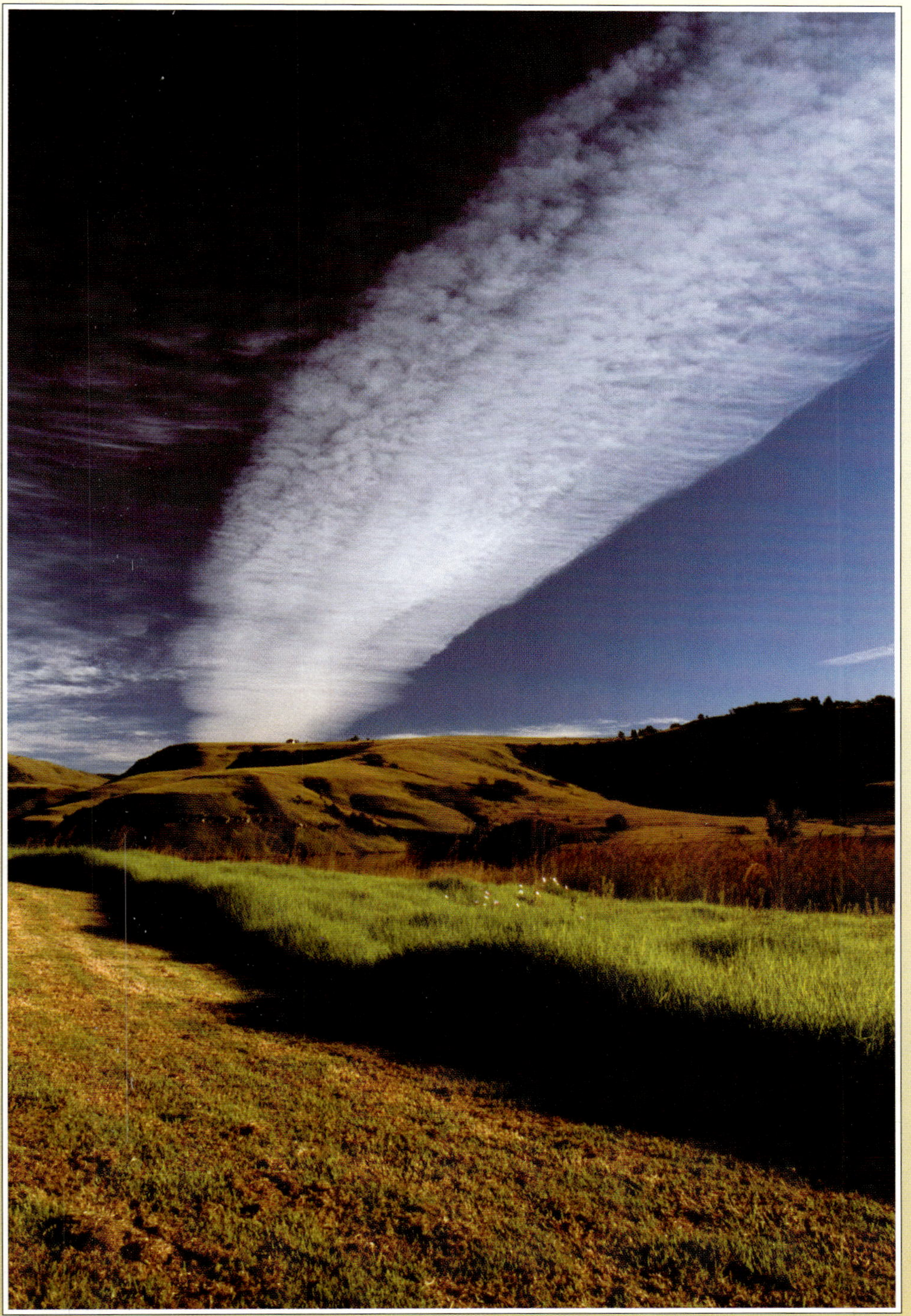

Around South Africa in Eighteen Days

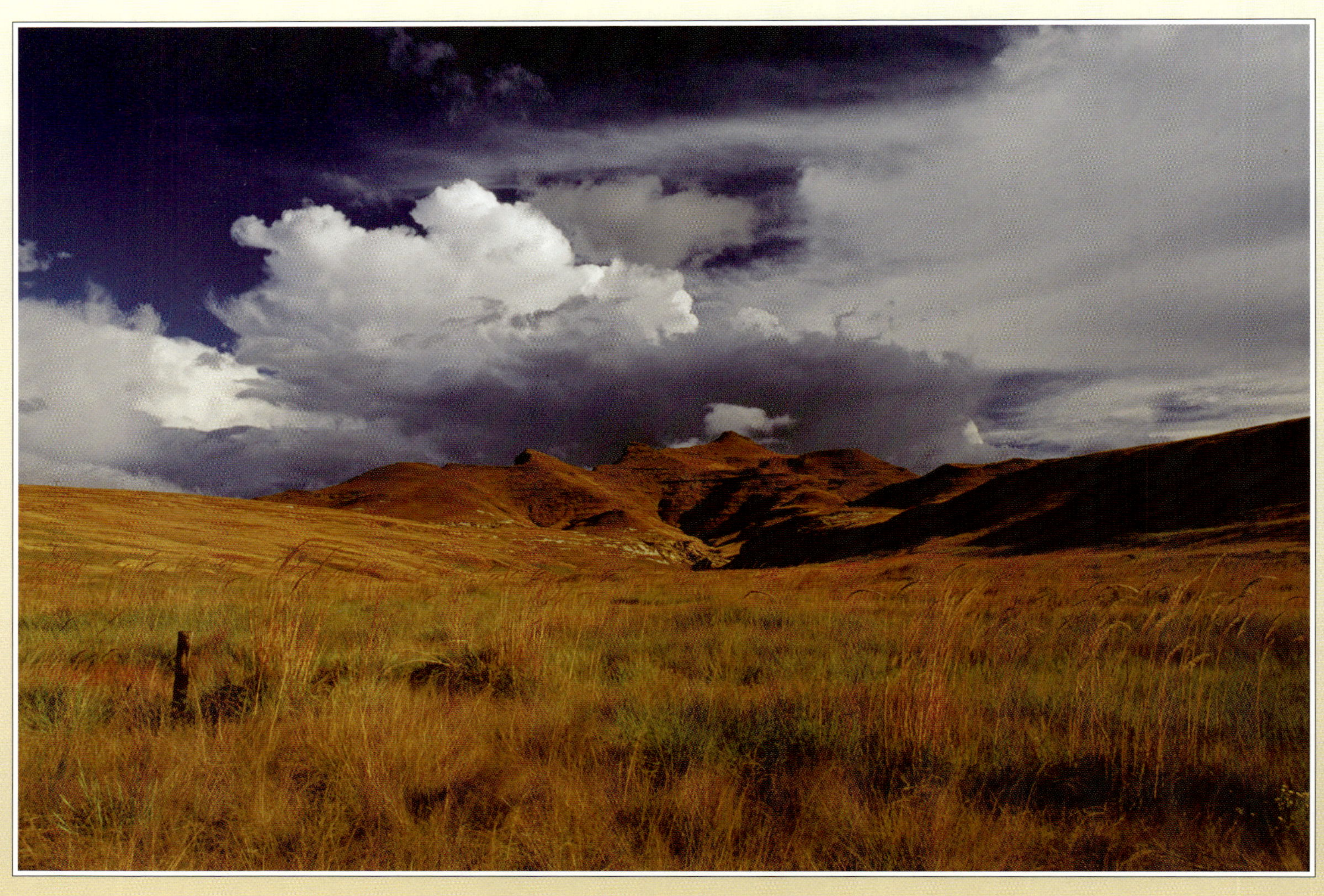

AROUND SOUTH AFRICA IN EIGHTEEN DAYS

A photographic journey

MIKE JOHNSON

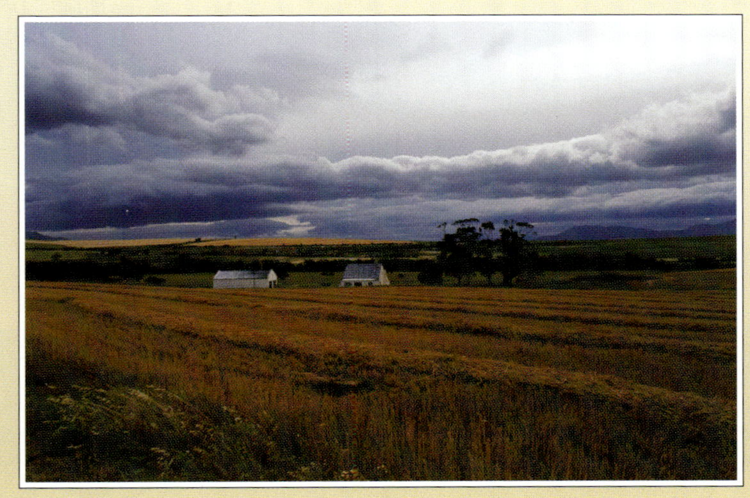

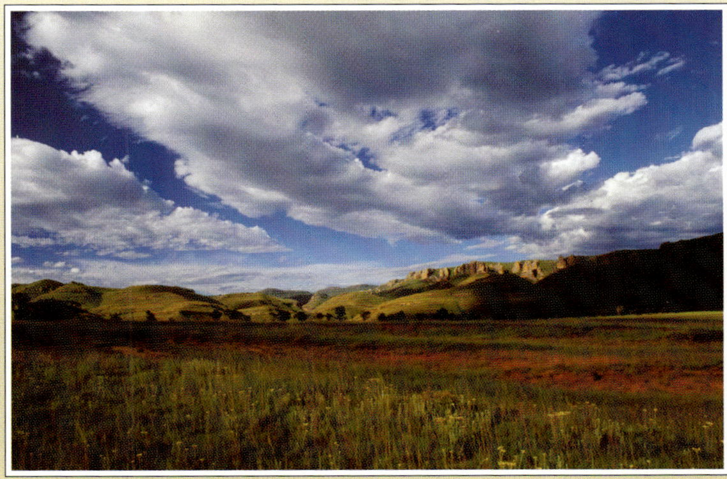

Protea Book House
Pretoria
2008

First editon, first impression in 2008 by Protea Book House
PO Box 35110, Menlo Park, 0102
1067 Burnett Street, Hatfield, Pretoria
8 Minni Street, Clydesdale, Pretoria
protea@intekom.co.za
www.proteaboekhuis.co.za
Editor: Karen Horn
Cover design: Elrene Jones, Discover Design & Photography
Cover image: Mike Johnson
Set in Bell on 11.5 pt by Elrene Jones
Printed and bound by Mills Litho, Maitland

ISBN: 978-1-86919-235-8

CONTENTS

INTRODUCTION

"Photographers talk about 'creating' images, but I'm not certain that anybody has ever created anything with a camera. Perhaps it is more accurate to say that God creates, and that some human beings discover." *Freeman Patterson—PHOTOGRAPHY FOR THE JOY OF IT.*

As the title (with apologies to Jules Verne) suggests, the collection of photographs in this book were all taken along a broadly circular route which, for most of the way, stays near the outer circumference of South Africa. Starting in Pretoria (or Johannesburg), this circuit will take us via Upington in the Northern Cape to Namaqualand, then down the West Coast to Cape Town and along the southern coastline as far as East London. After that we head northwards past the Drakensberg escarpment and through the northeastern Free State back to our starting point, with a short detour into Lesotho along the way (see map on p. 142). Our journey will generally stay "far from the madding crowd" and the bright city lights, with most of the images reflecting the quiet and peace of South Africa's countryside and seaside, its small towns and villages, its mountains, rivers and natural vegetation. For those travellers with photographic interests that lean towards places rather than people or even fauna and flora, i.e., landscape photography in the broad sense, this book will give a glimpse of the kind of picture-taking opportunities that abound along this particular route.

As in most classical landscape paintings, legitimate ingredients of landscape photographs include sky, land, water, vegetation, domestic animals, buildings, (traditional) means of transport—and even people on occasion! The South African sky can be infinitely varied in its moods, ranging from the brilliant blue of a clear midday to the bright reds and oranges or more pastel shades of pink at sunrise and sunset, the sombre greys of menacing storm clouds or the pale uniformity of rain, mist or falling snow. The mountains and hills compete with the valleys and kloofs, sometimes bare, but more usually covered with grass, trees, wild flowers or crops to which each season lends its own distinctive character. Quiet lakes and dams contrast with rushing waterfalls, calm seas with wild waves. Sheep and cattle will reinforce a pastoral mood, while buildings, roads and bridges lend form and substance to the scenes of which they form a part. Boats and trains (especially the steam variety) are leisurely means of transport that occupy an acceptable place in landscape photographs. Aircraft and motor vehicles, on the other hand, are uncomfortable reminders of today's hectic lifestyle—even if they are the usual means of reaching our getaways!

Like the landscape artist, the landscape photographer seeks to combine these various elements into a harmonious whole that is visually pleasing, making appropriate use of colour and lighting to enhance the overall effect. There is an important difference between the two mediums, however, in that the artist potentially has unlimited freedom when it comes to deciding what to include in the picture, how to arrange these components, what colours to use and how to handle the lighting. Photographers, on the other hand, have always had to do the best they could by finding a suitable vantage point and choosing the appropriate lens that would combine to maximise the aesthetic possibilities of a given scene—and then, if necessary, waiting patiently for the clouds to move or the light to improve! Of course, with the advent of digital manipulation these distinctions are no longer quite that clear cut, but even so (apart from certain special applications such as advertising) most people would consider a landscape "photograph" created on a computer by combining various elements such as mountains, clouds, buildings and trees from unrelated scenes to be inherently meaningless. This is because we normally assume that the photographer is sharing with others something unique that he or she saw and experienced in a particular place at a specific moment in time.

Clearly, a premeditated landscape photograph will always be more satisfying than a so-called "record shot", a technically correct portrayal in which the same elements are present but without any serious thought having been given to their arrangement within the scene or to the kind of lighting, for example, that would have set them off to best advantage. Providing aesthetic pleasure similar to that which would be evoked by a well-executed painting of the same scene is, of course, the ultimate aim of all landscape photographers. Which, if any, of the photographs in this collection have succeeded in attaining such a lofty goal is for the reader to judge. Hopefully, at least some of these photographs will make readers long to visit the places in question, and perhaps even recall Alan Paton's memorable (if ironically intended) book title, *Ah, but your land is beautiful*. South Africa has long been recognised as a scenically magnificent part of the world that for sheer variety has few equals in any other country of similar size. Our land is indeed beautiful, and my hope is that these images will not only help in some small way to reinforce this claim, but will also stimulate others to experience the joys of landscape photography for themselves.

The book is organised in the form of a single eighteen-day round trip that includes most of the areas that I, and many others as well, have found photographically rewarding. While some may wish to follow the itinerary exactly (see details on p. 143), most will probably need to adapt it to suit their own needs. With one or two exceptions, none of the photographs has involved straying very far from roads that are suitable for normal cars, nor did any require a long hike.

In planning an actual trip, the seasonal nature of some of the subjects (autumn colours, snow scenes, spring flowers) needs to be taken into account, and more than one trip will obviously be needed to do justice to all the seasons. Nevertheless, for those with around eighteen days at their disposal, I am convinced that the suggested route would be hard to beat for photographic opportunities at any time of the year.

DAY 1

Pretoria to Upington

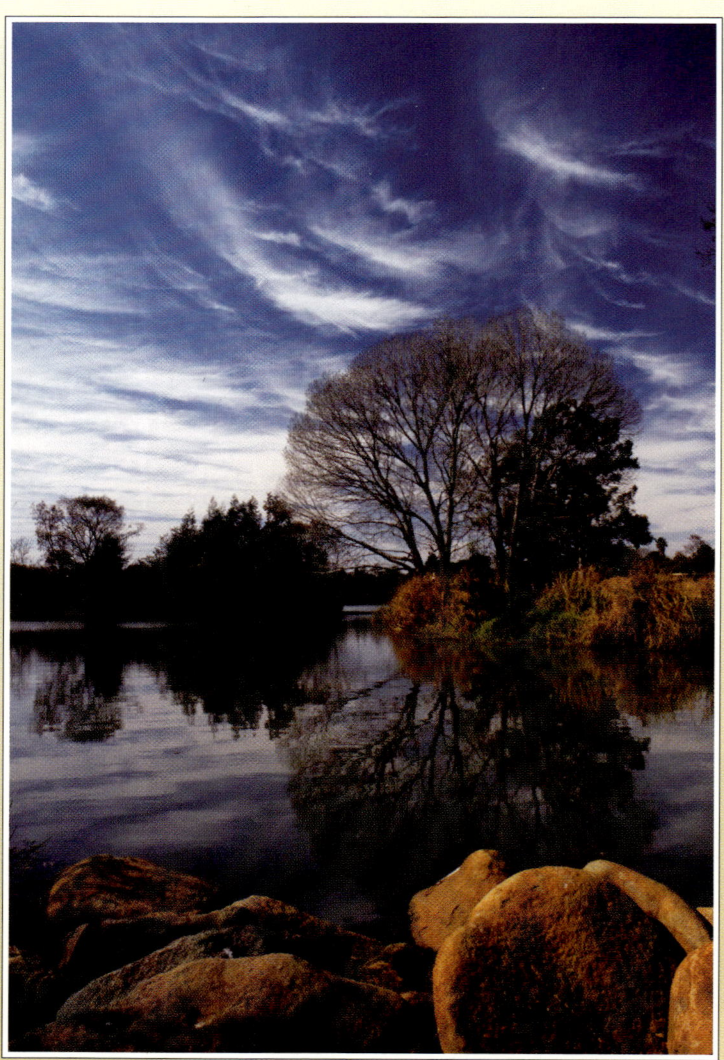

The Struben Dam and its surroundings afford a tranquil haven for the residents of Pretoria's eastern suburbs.

Our journey commences in South Africa's capital where—as in most cities—there are various spots to which one can escape for a time of peace and tranquillity such as the Pretoria National Botanical Garden in Silverton, the Struben Dam in the quiet suburb of Lynnwood Glen, and the Irene Dairy Farm and Smuts House in Irene. These places should preferably be visited for possible photos during the afternoon preceding the commencement of our eighteen-day journey proper, since the first leg involves a fairly long (800 km) drive from Pretoria to Upington and will not allow much time for photography. Although the generally flat and featureless terrain traversed by this stretch of road contains few obvious scenic attractions to tempt the landscape photographer, interesting cloud formations can often be effectively combined with groups of trees, rows of crops or other suitable foreground material. If a really early start is made, a detour via the Witsand Nature Reserve south of Olifantshoek is highly recommended as this unique area of white sand dunes has many photographic possibilities.

Upington, where Day 1 ends, is a quiet, pleasant town on the banks of the Orange River, although it can get uncomfortably hot in summer. There are some attractive churches and other old buildings worth photographing, while time should be allowed for a walk or drive along the main bridge across the Orange River (the Louisvale road) in the late afternoon in case a dramatic evening sky develops. But be sure not to arrive at the bridge without a camera as I once did and missed recording the most spectacular sunset that I have ever witnessed!

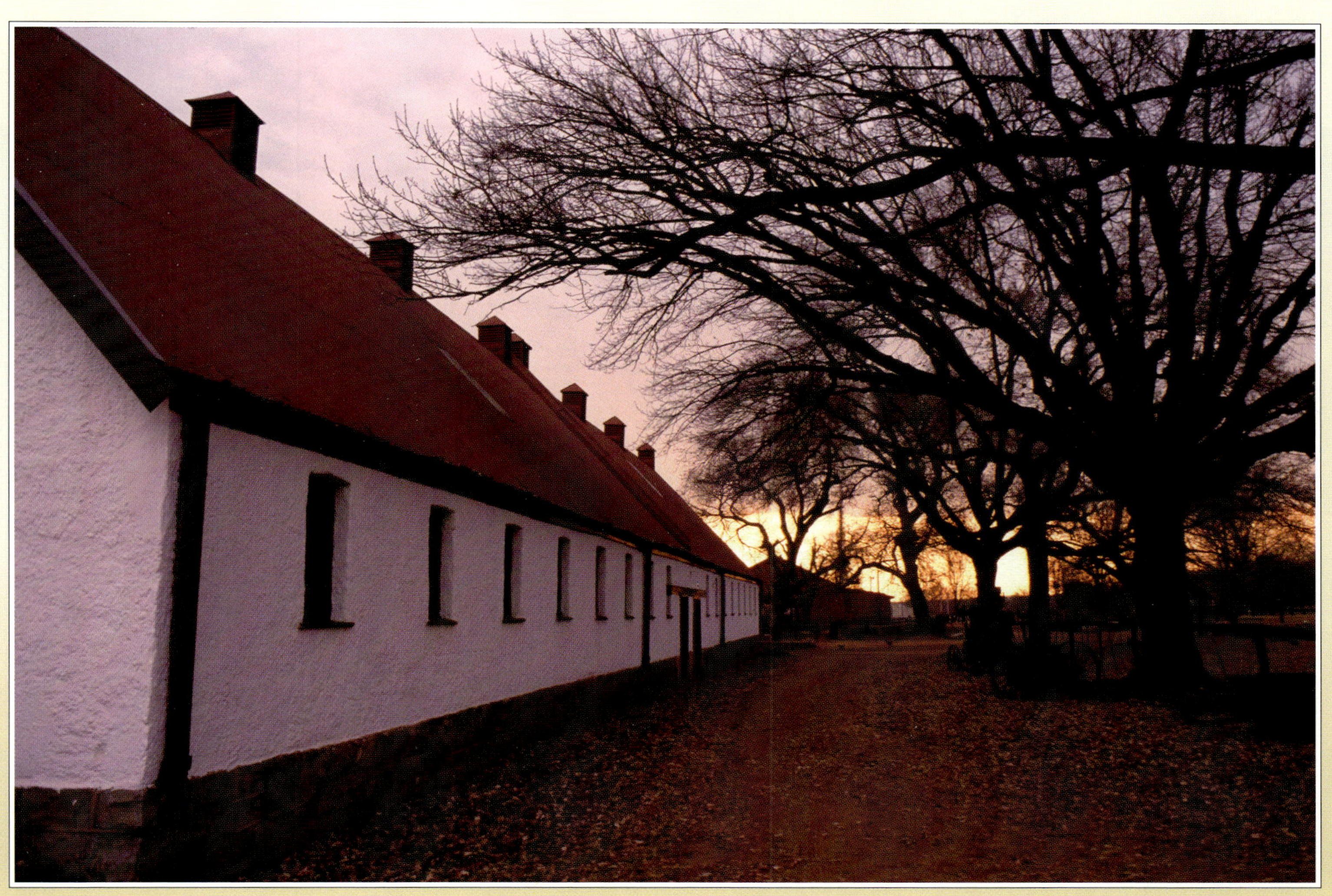

The Irene Dairy Farm in Irene retains its rural atmosphere, even though this particular barn has now been converted to a restaurant.

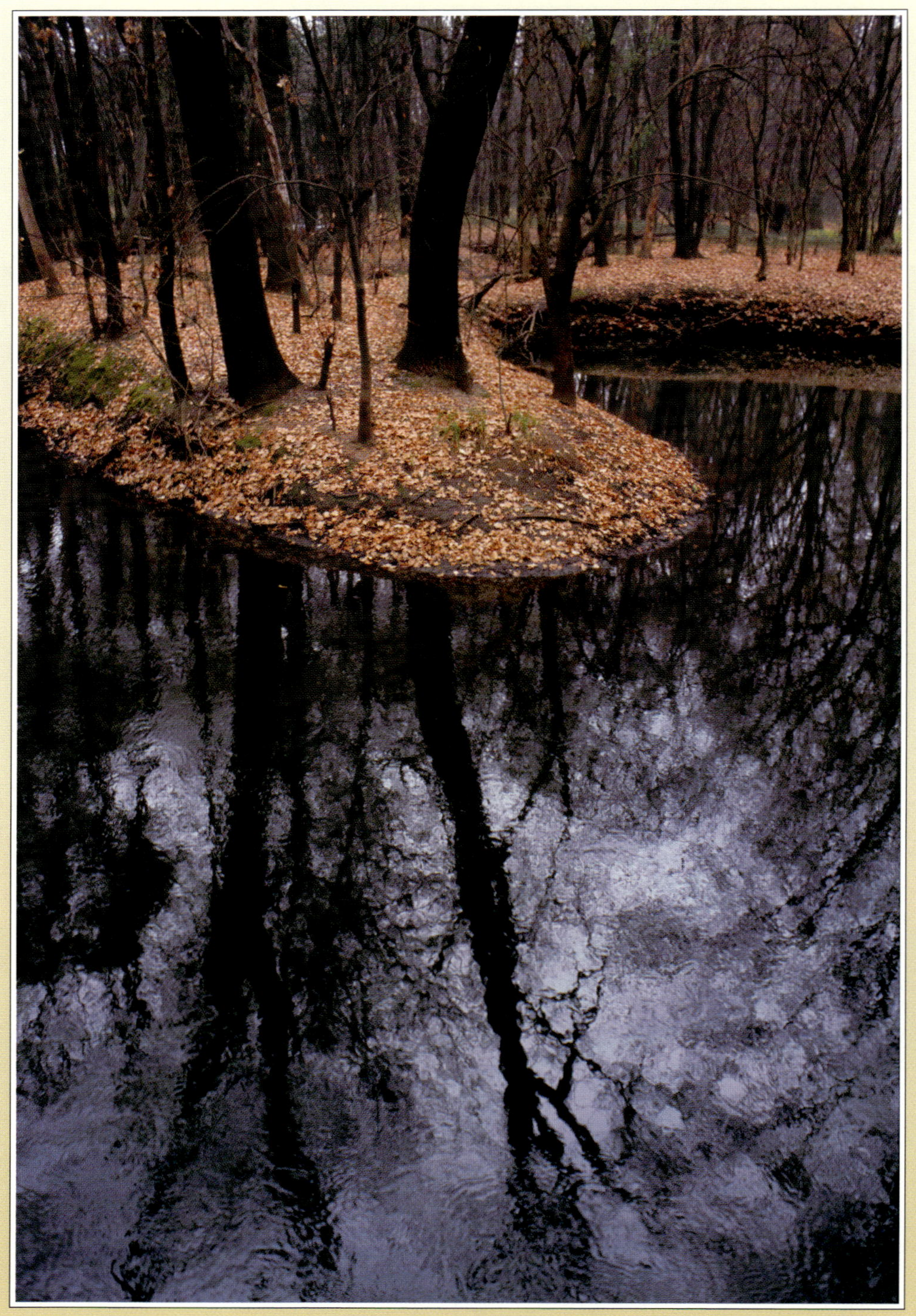

An autumn scene alongside the road to the home of General Smuts in Irene, which has been preserved in its original state as a museum.

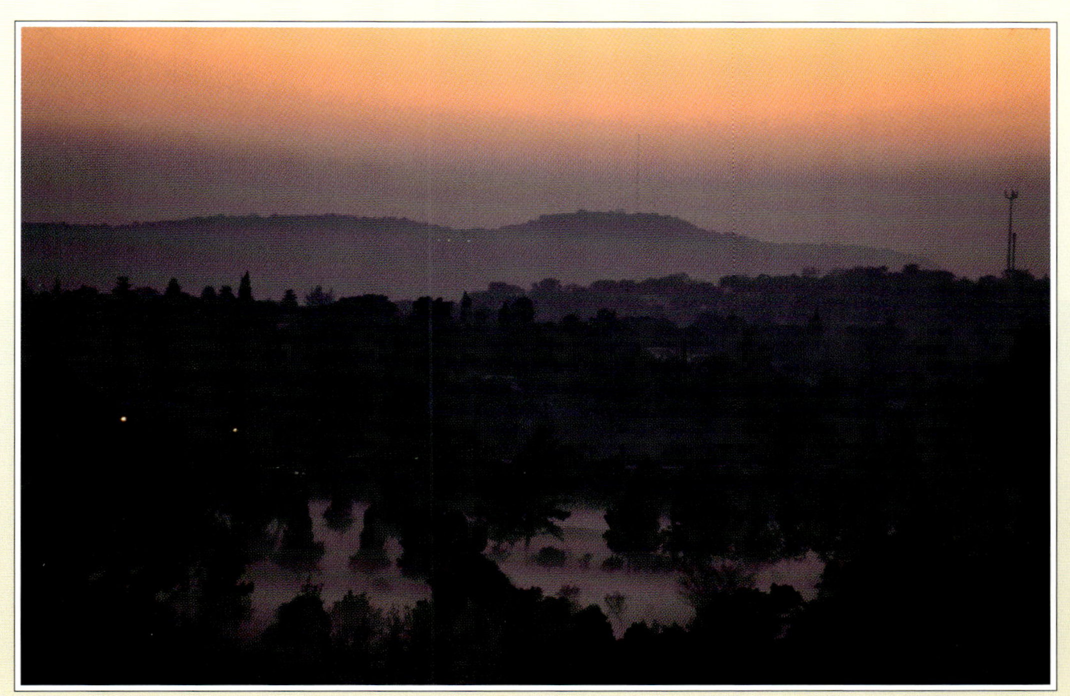

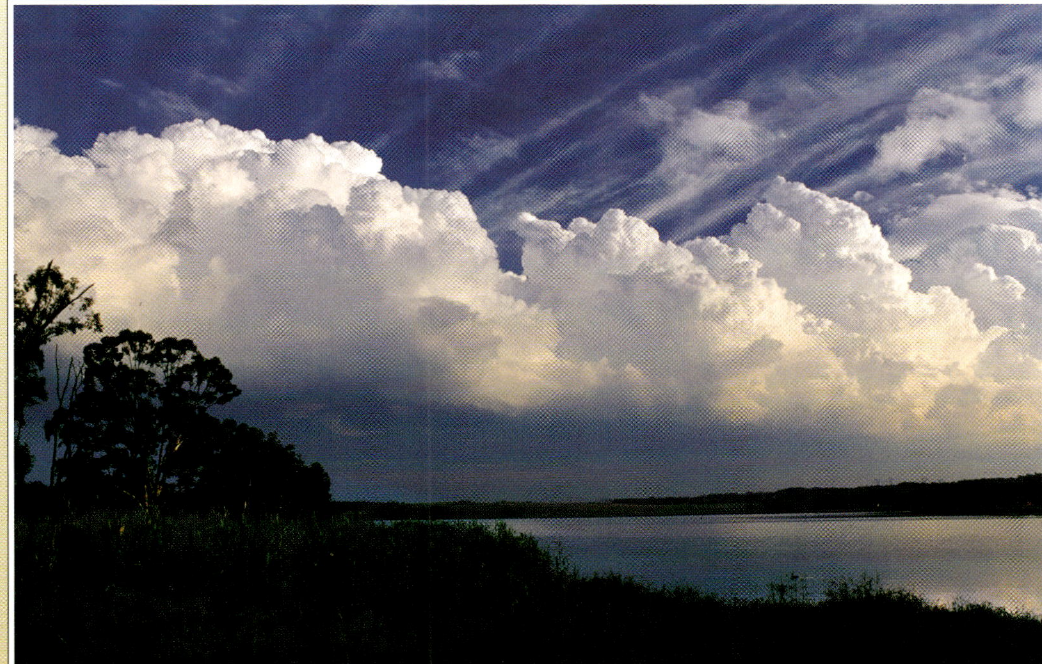

Top:
Early morning mist blankets the golf course at the prestigious Pretoria Country Club in the suburb of Waterkloof.

Bottom:
Storm clouds gather over the Rietvlei Dam south of Pretoria.

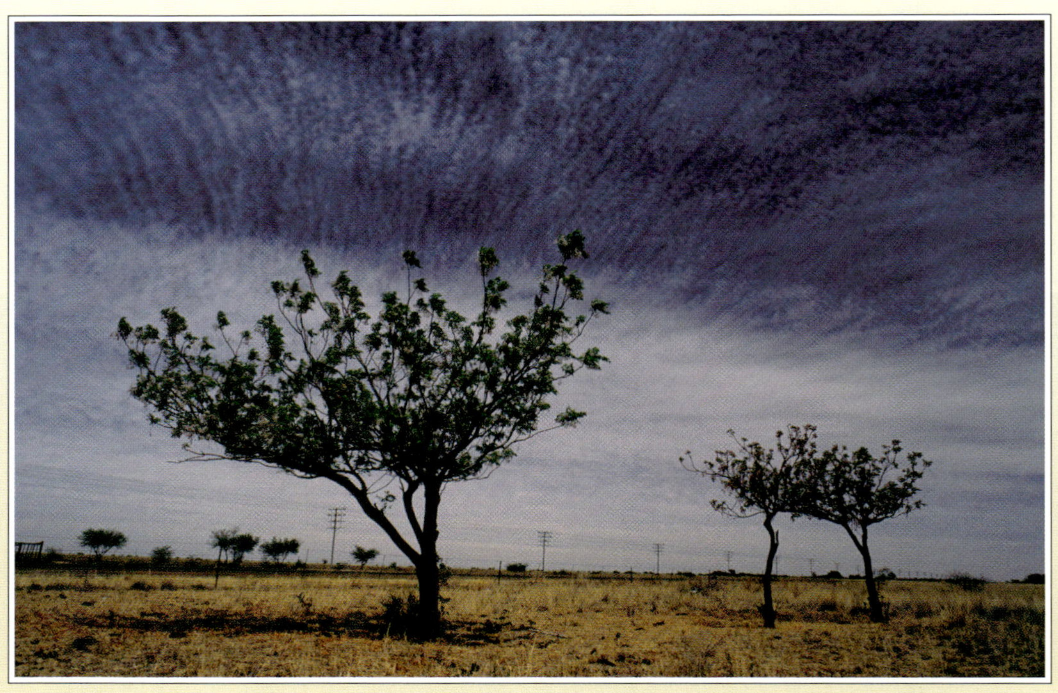

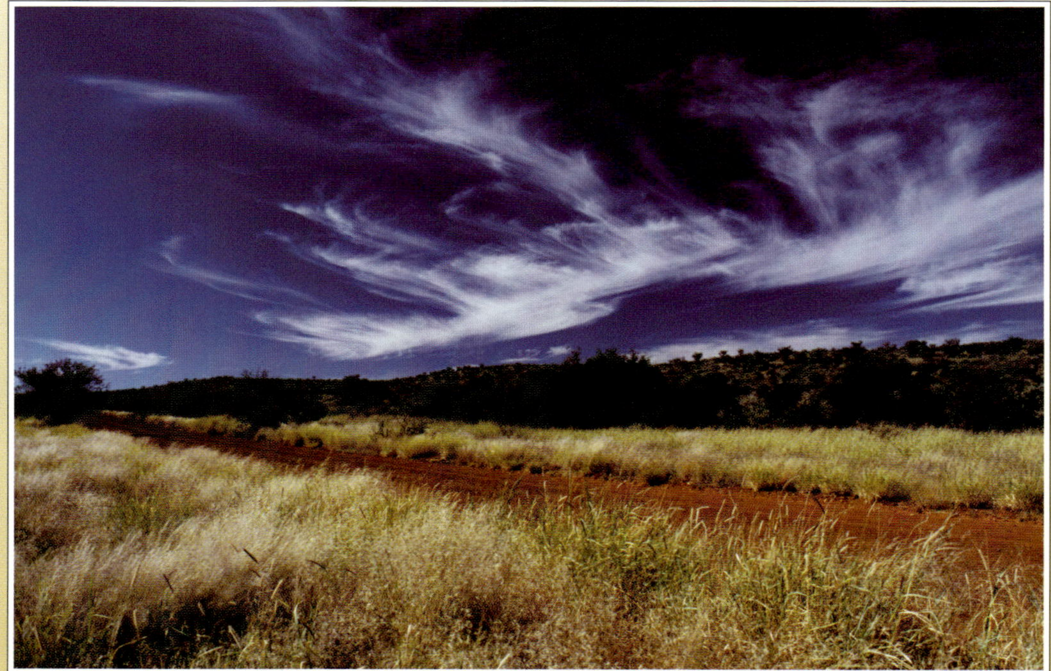

In the absence of more traditional landscape subjects, photogenic cloud patterns can help relieve the monotony of the long stretch of road between Vryburg and Upington.

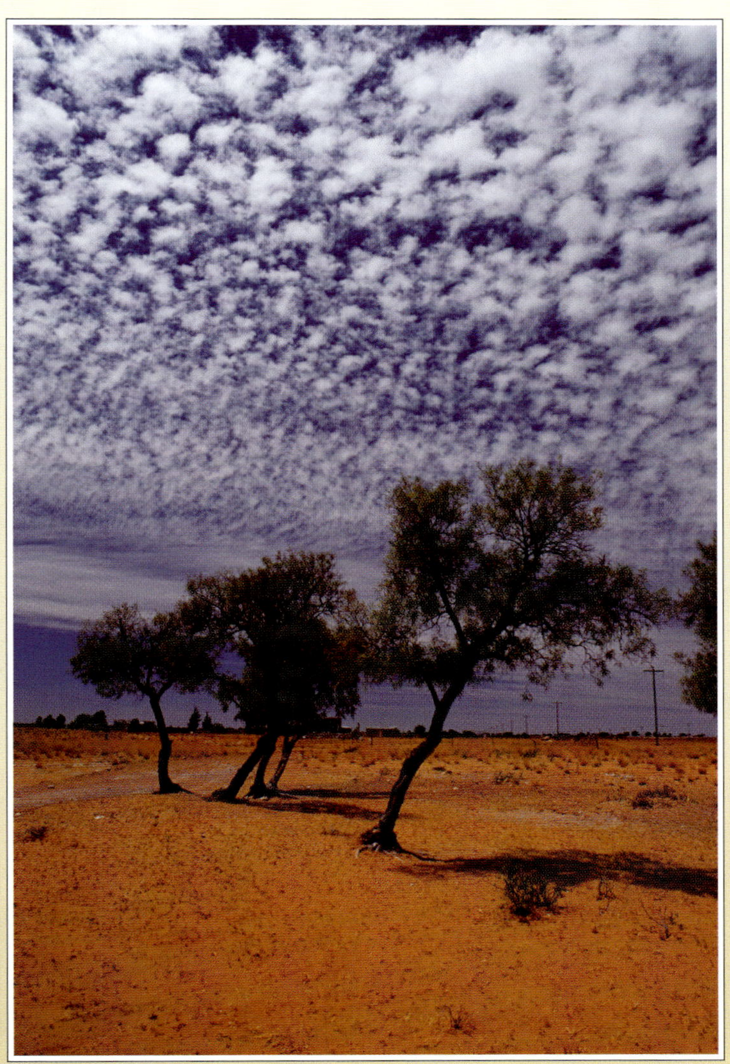

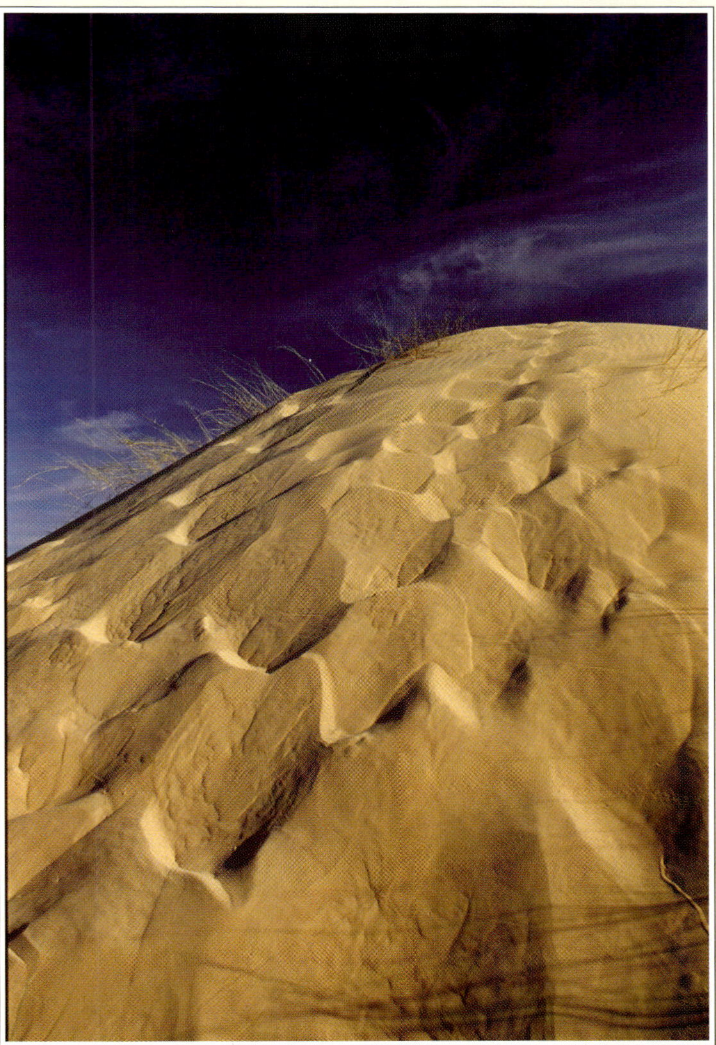

The typical red Kalahari soil of the Northern Cape (left) provides a contrast with the light-coloured sand that makes the dunes of the Witsand Nature Reserve south of Postmasburg (right) so unique in this area.

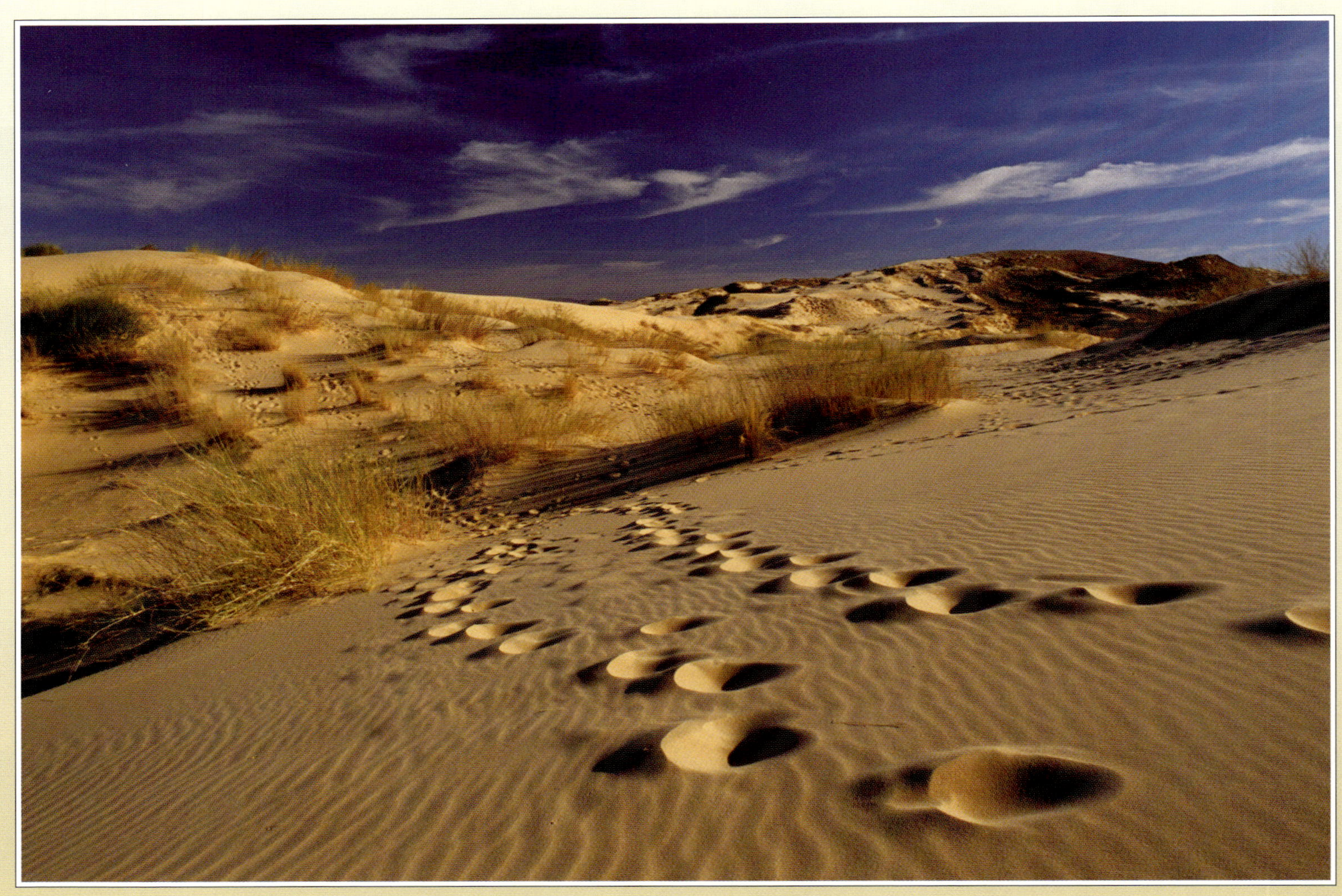

The so-called "roaring sands" (Afrikaans: "brulsand") in the Witsand Nature Reserve owe their name to the distinctive sound emanating from them at certain times.

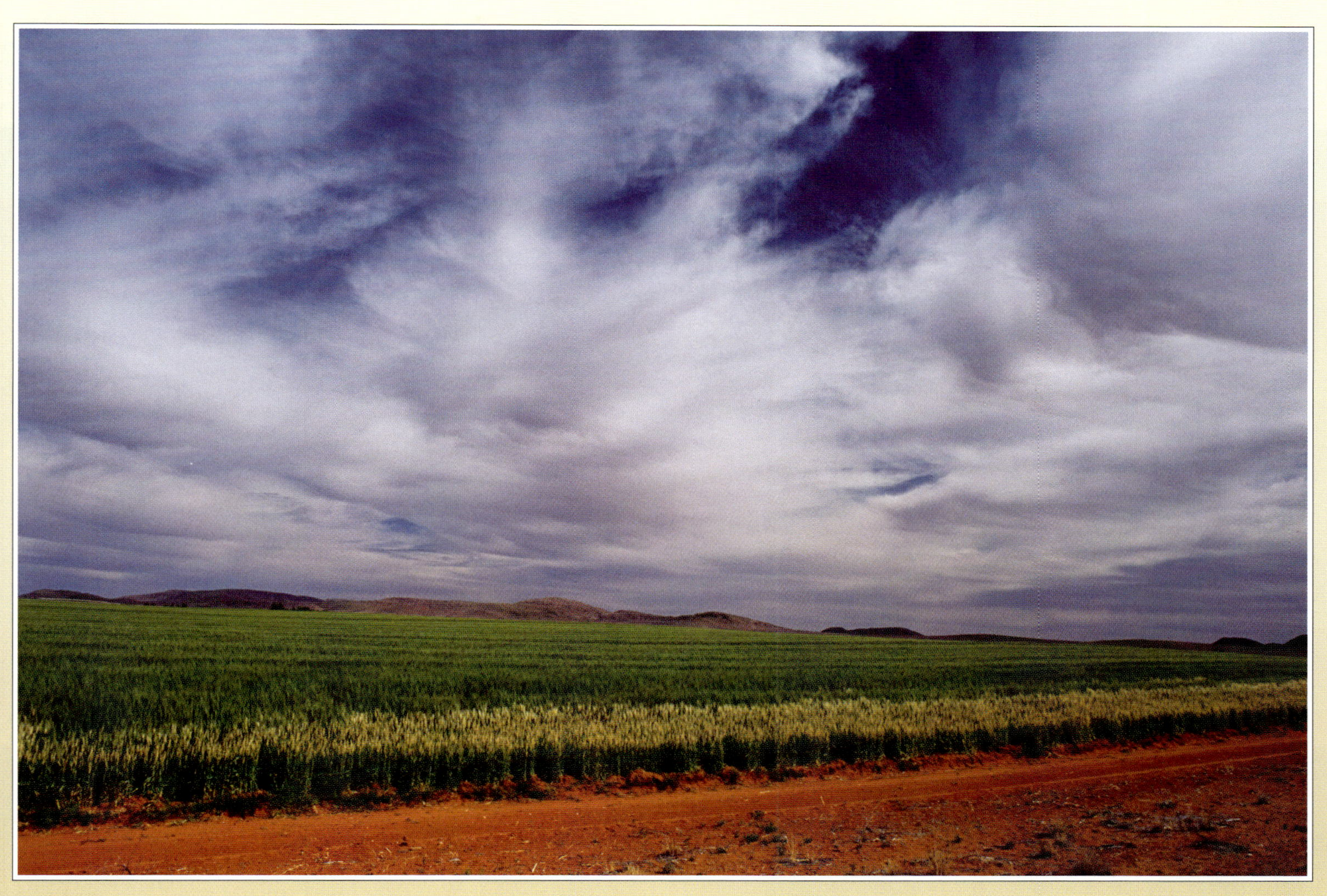

The bright red soil, the green field and the unusual sky made for a mandatory photo-stop close to Upington.

DAY 2

Namaqualand

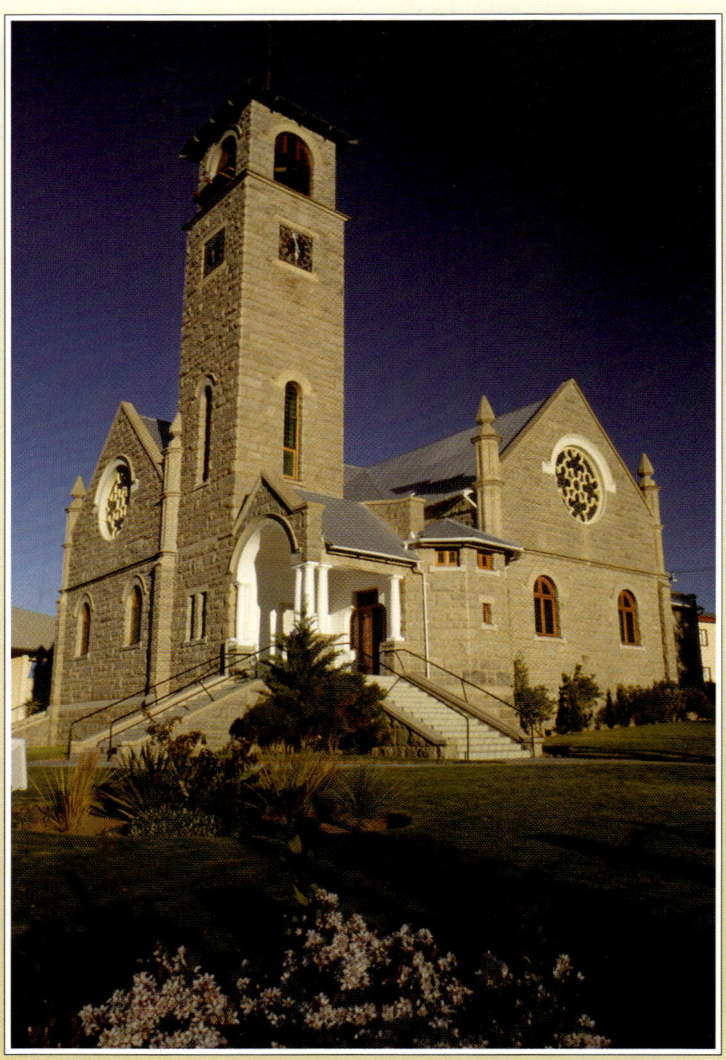

The handsome "Klipkerk" ("stone church") in Springbok, was built with local material and completed in 1921.

The second day takes us through the stark, barren Namaqualand landscape. Barren, that is, except for a few glorious months in spring when this semi-desert area comes alive with flower displays that have attracted photographers from all over the world. In fact, annual workshops held in the small village of Kamieskroon by Canadian photographer Freeman Patterson and his associates have become established institutions. The months of August to October normally constitute the flower season. Particularly prolific localities include the Goegap Nature Reserve near Springbok, the Skilpad Section of the Namaqua National Park near Kamieskroon, the Nababeep area north of Springbok and the gravel road from Kamieskroon to Garies via Leliefontein. The relative merits of each area, and the overall quality of the annual spectacle, will vary from year to year, depending on the distribution and abundance of the winter rains on which this whole phenomenon relies.

Outside the flower season there is still the rugged beauty of the bare, rocky hills rising from the surrounding plains, often with scattered "kokerbome" ("quiver trees"). In places, lines of sand dunes form reddish-coloured ridges snaking across the countryside. Because of the sparse grazing, domestic animals such as sheep are a relatively uncommon sight. Not surprisingly, towns are few and far between.

In Springbok, the main centre, there are a number of churches that have been declared national monuments. The small towns of Nababeep and Okiep to the north enjoyed greater prosperity in the past when copper mining flourished.

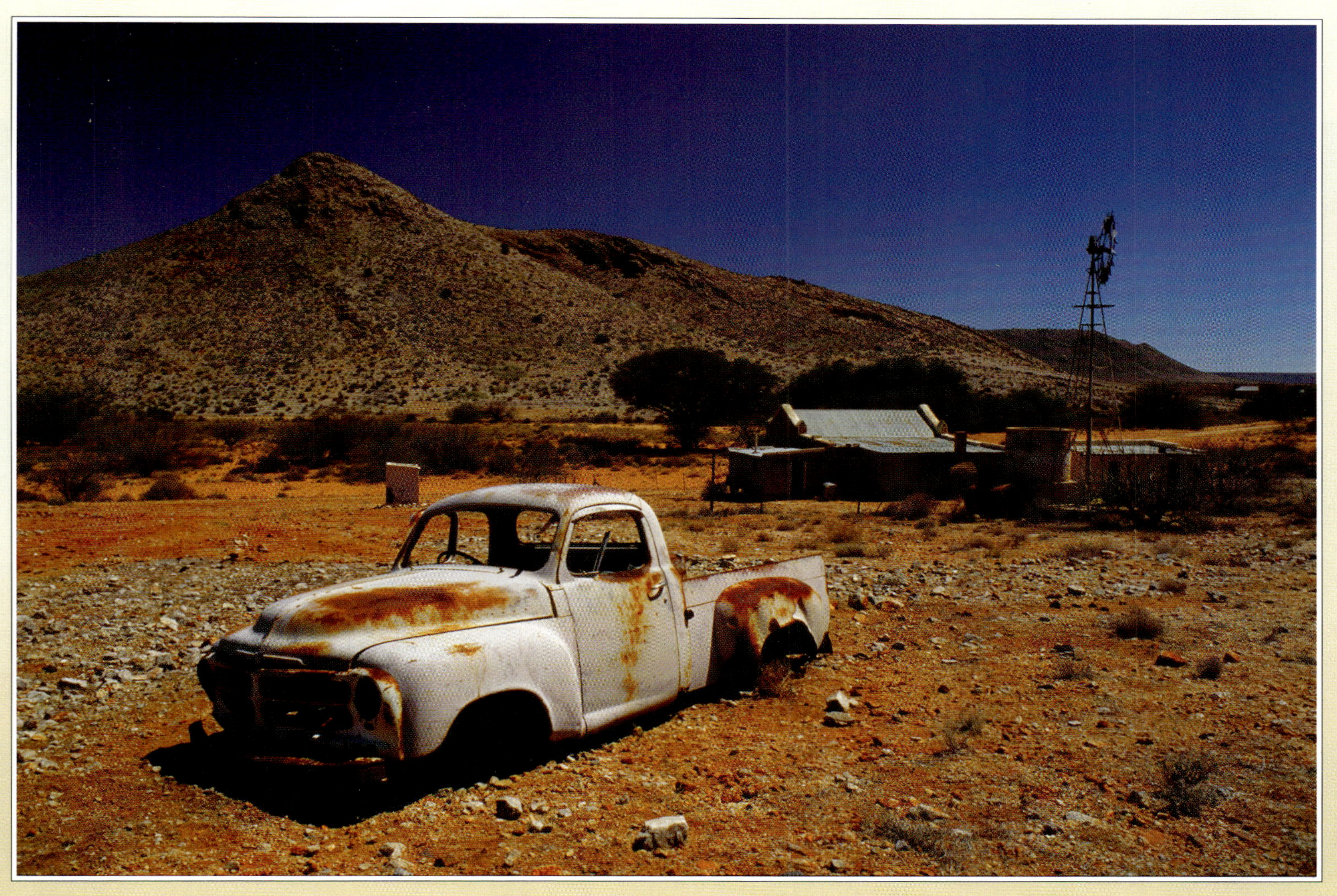

A rusty, abandoned vehicle and a run-down homestead bear eloquent testimony to the harshness of farming conditions in Namaqualand.

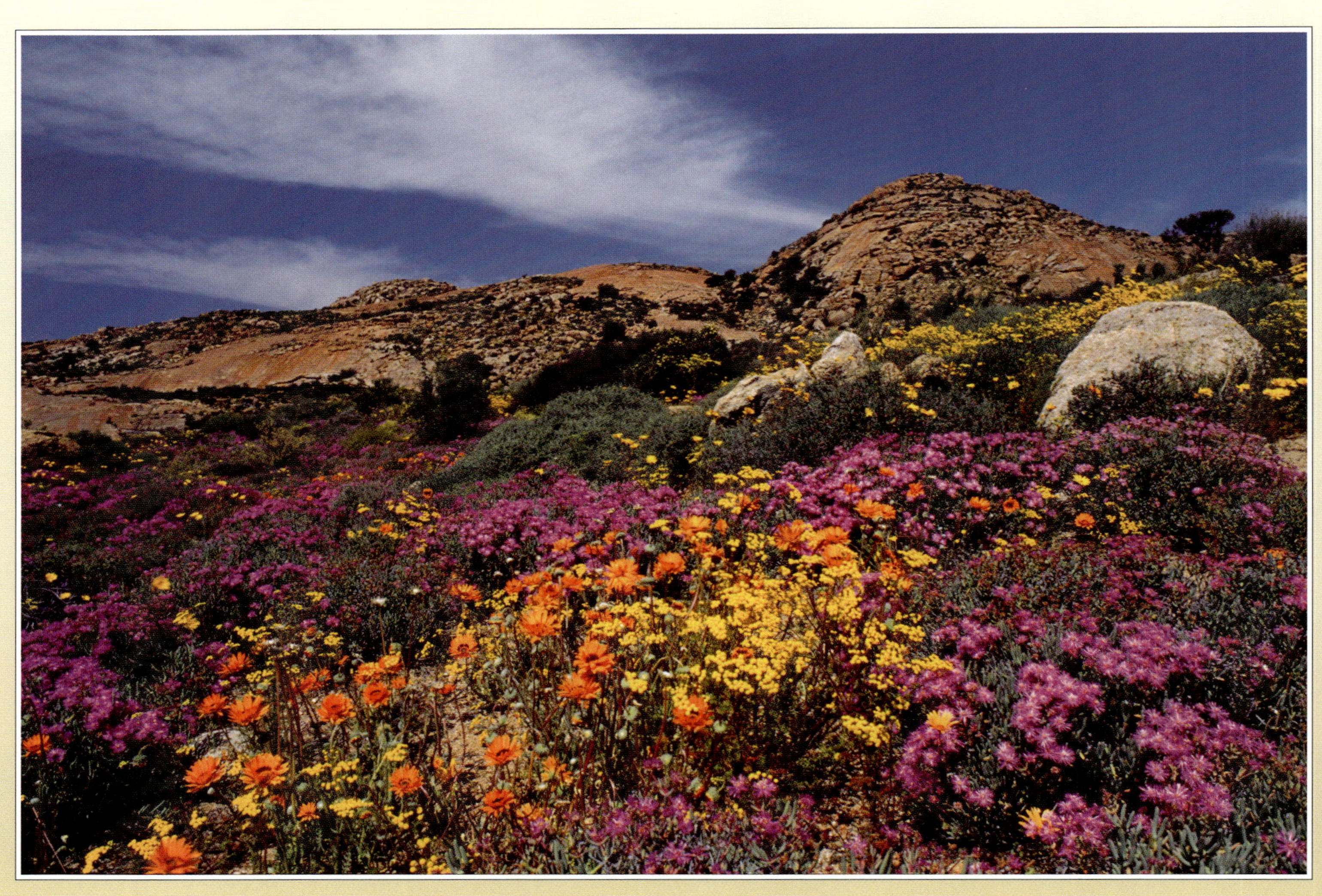

A colourful natural rock garden in the Goegap Nature Reserve.

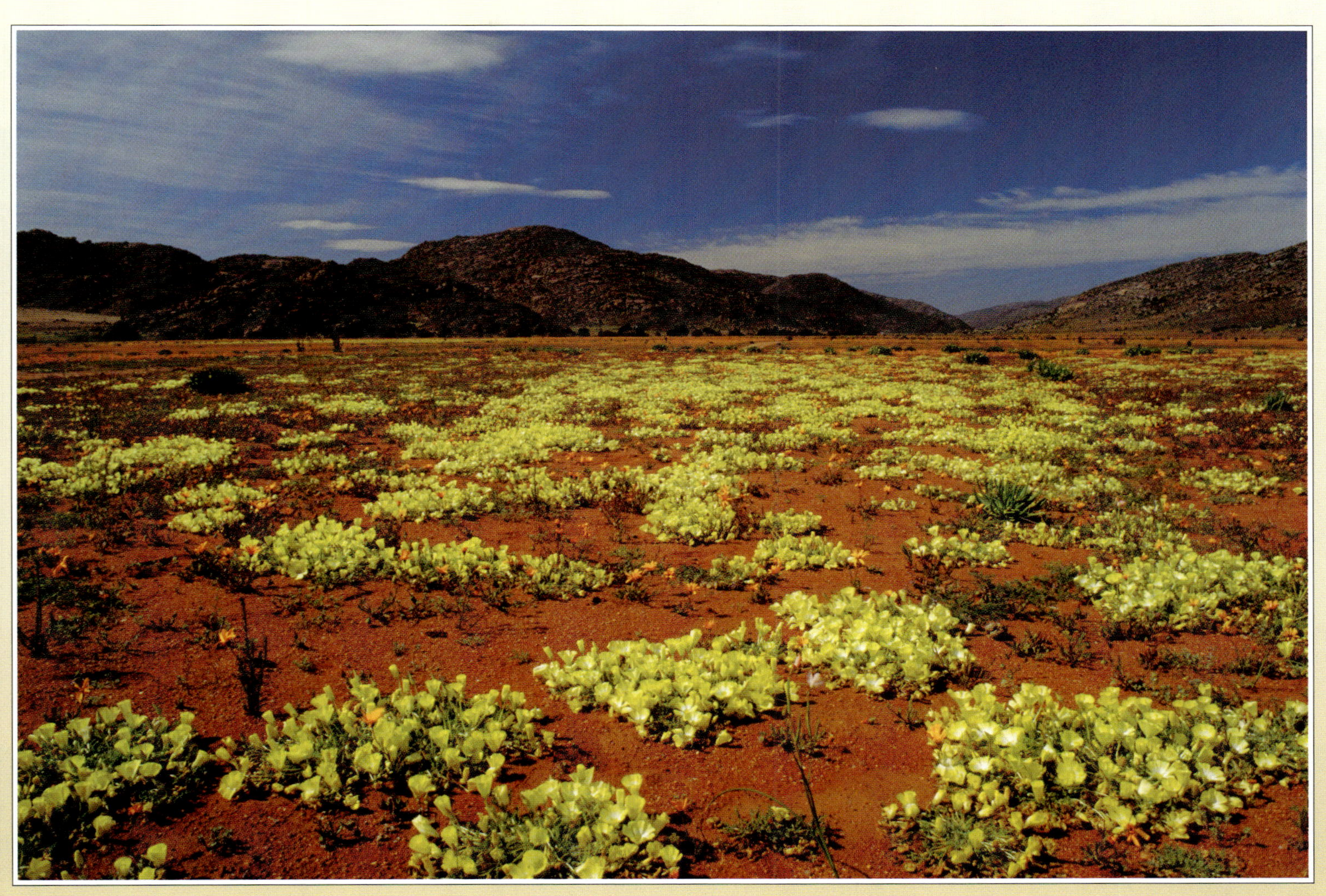

A carpet of cheerful yellow Grielum flowers somewhere between Klein-Nourivier and Leliefontein.

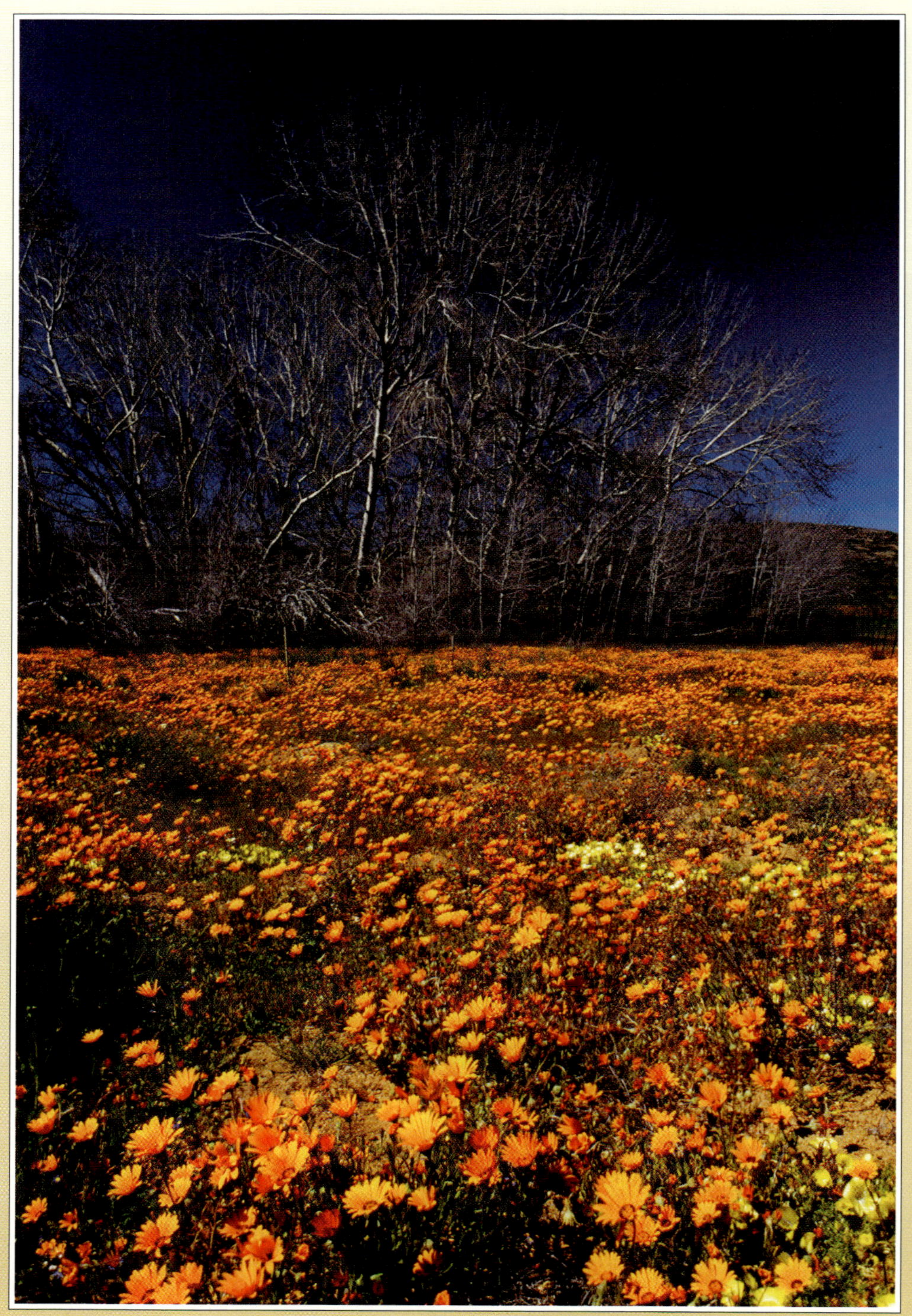

Although the flower season is already in full swing, this stand of bare poplars on a farm near Kamieskroon shows no sign of emerging from winter's grip.

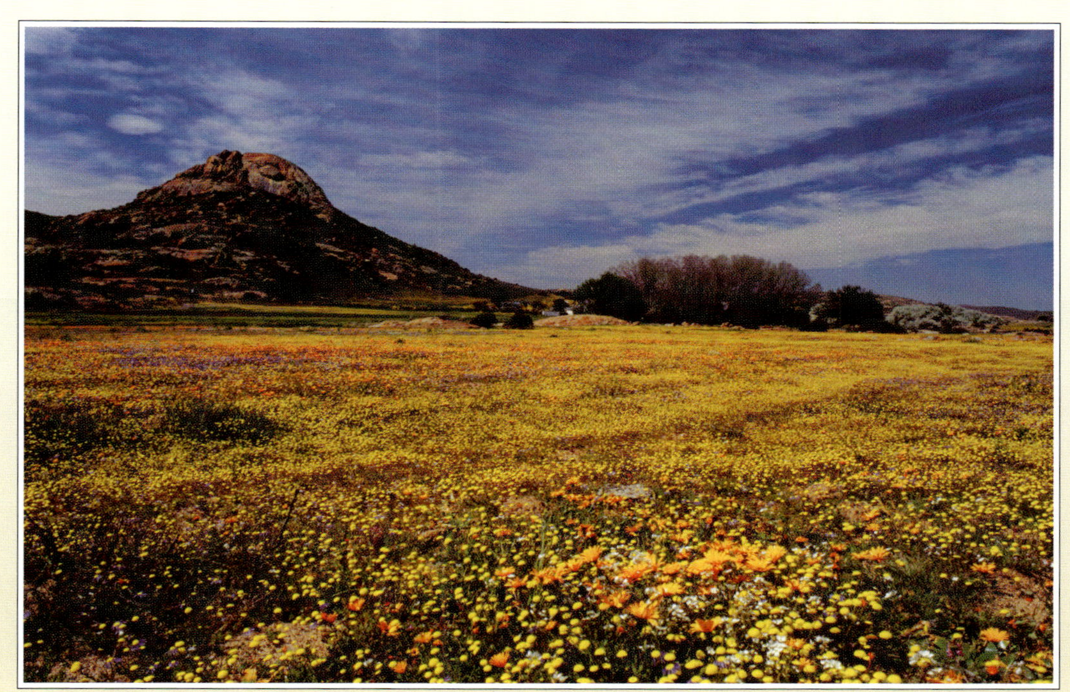

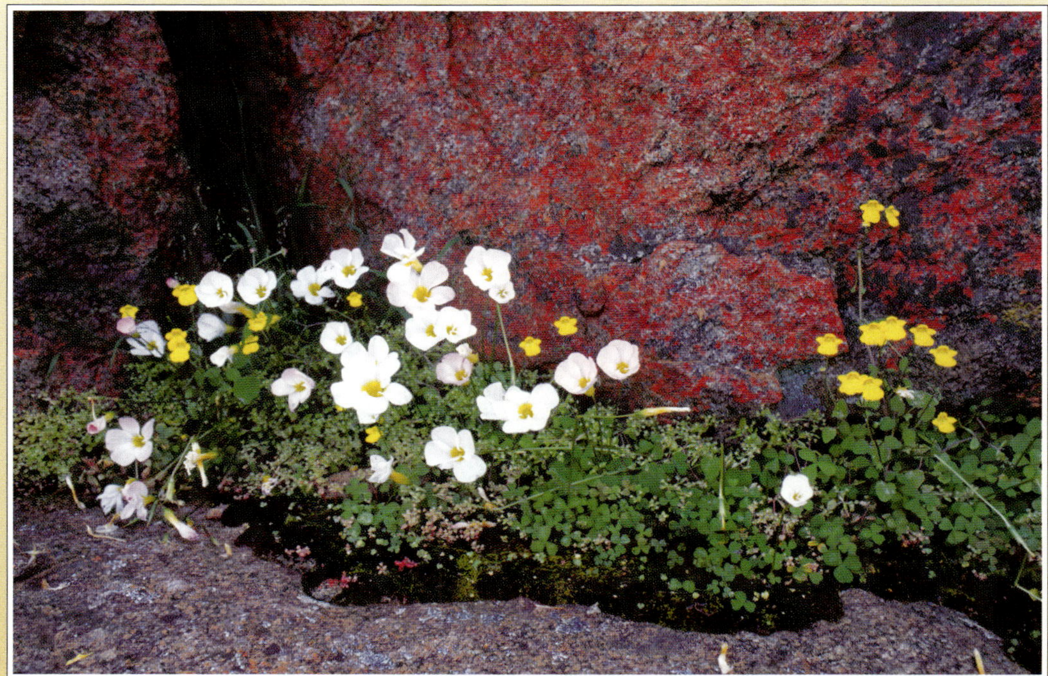

Top:
Yellow Cotula *flowers dominate the spring display in this field between Leliefontein and Garies.*

Bottom:
Rocky overhangs provide shelter from the harsh sun for clumps of Oxalis *in the granite hills east of Kamieskroon.*

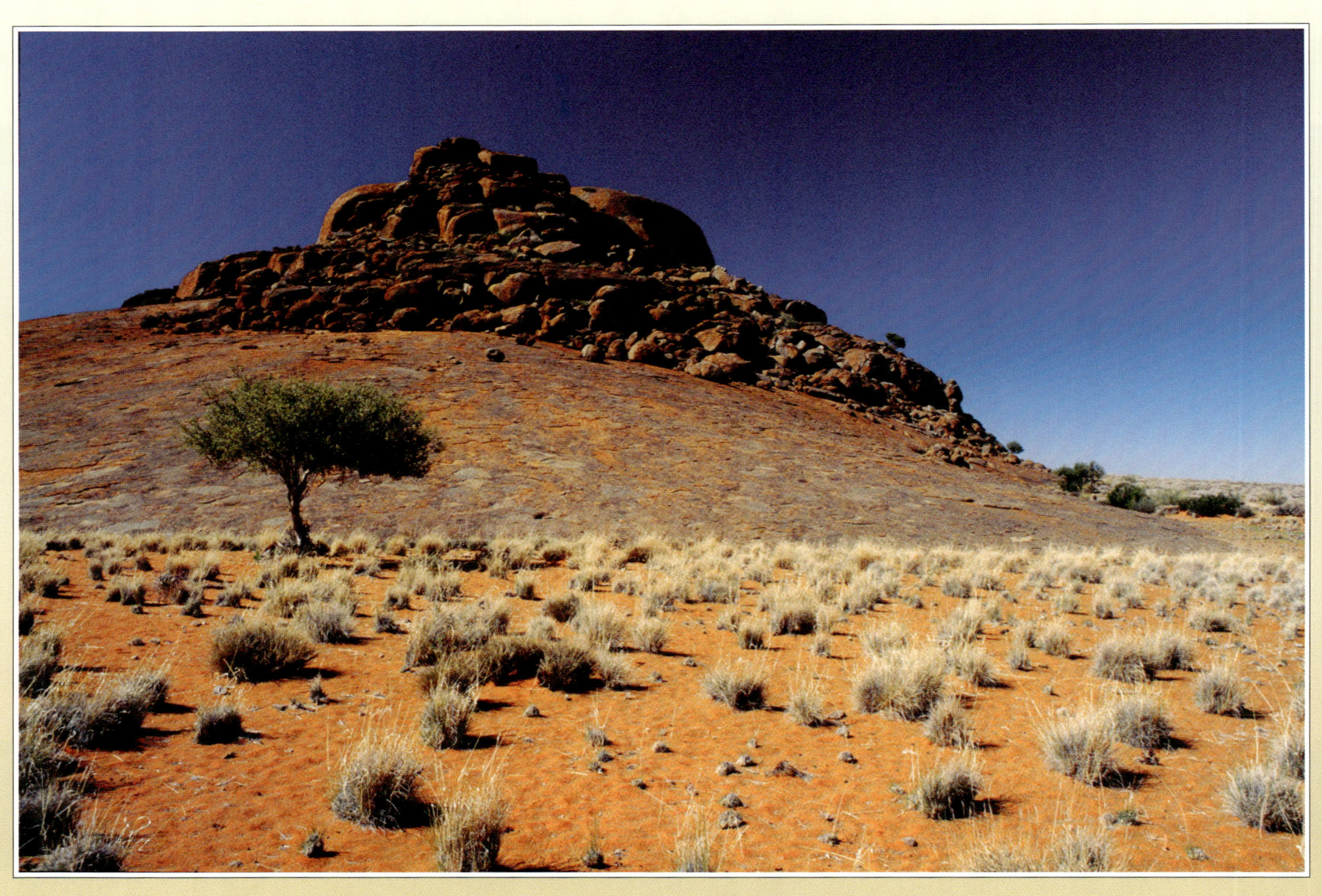

Outcrops of barren rock, surrounded by red sandy soil and sparse vegetation, are typical of large areas of Namaqualand.

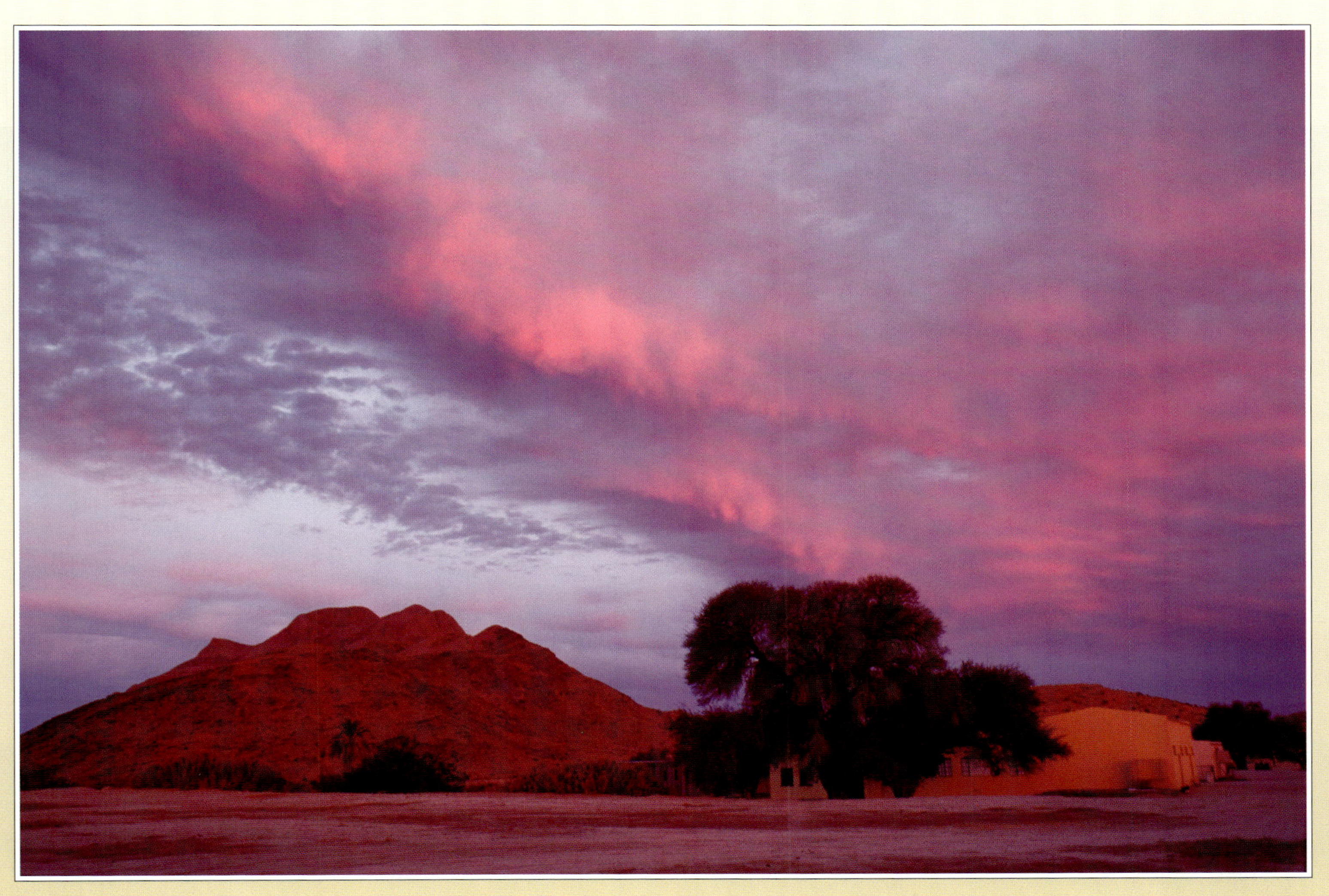

Dramatic sunsets, such as this one at Klein-Pella west of Pofadder, occasionally light up the Namaqualand skies.

DAY 3

West Coast

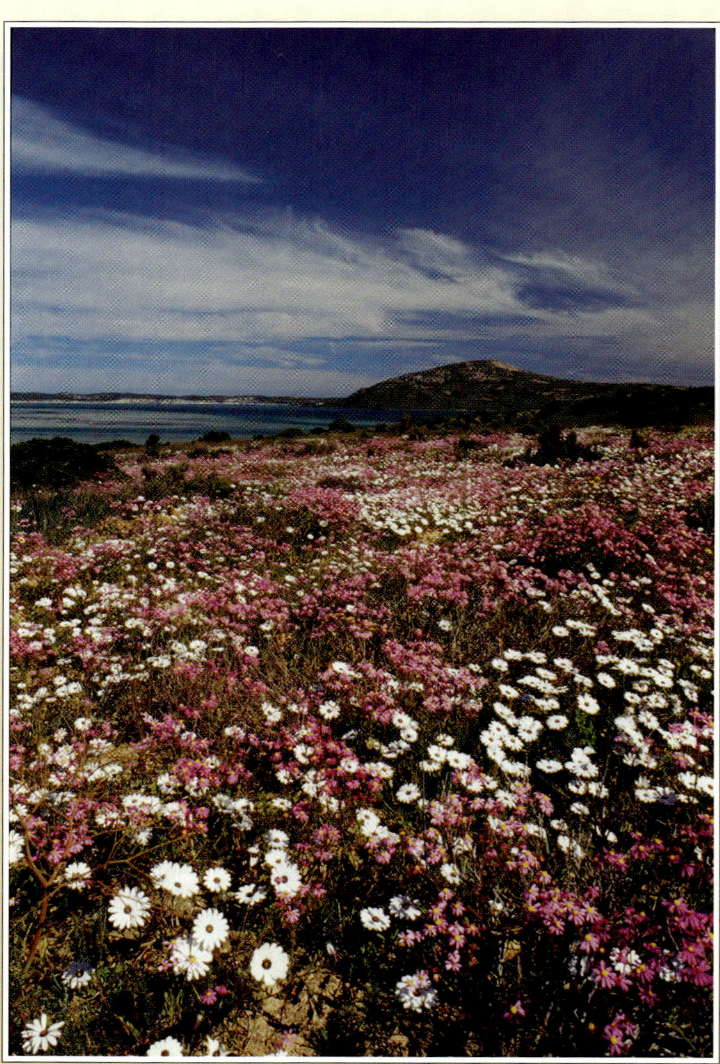

Spring flowers south of Langebaan, with the lagoon just visible in the background.

The "West Coast" is generally taken to refer to the coastline between Strandfontein or Lambert's Bay and Cape Town as well as the adjacent flat-lying coastal plain, extending inland (according to some) to also embrace Clanwilliam, Citrusdal and Piketberg. It is an area of contrasts, with fishing villages and towns such as Lambert's Bay, Laaiplek, St. Helena Bay, Paternoster and Saldanha co-existing with up-market holiday resorts and residential areas like Langebaan, Club Mykonos, Jacobsbaai, Shelly Beach and Port Owen. The Saldanha steelworks and ore terminal are counter-balanced by the West Coast National Park to the south, which contains the ecologically important Langebaan Lagoon as well as the former Postberg flower reserve.

Photographic possibilities are endless. Fishing boats are always photogenic, especially when the frequent mists roll in from the sea and create a soft, ethereal atmosphere. Traditional fishermen's cottages at Paternoster and elsewhere have often been photographed, but finding really good specimens is easier said than done. The spring flowers compete with those of Namaqualand, not only in the Postberg area but in many inland areas as well, with smaller patches of colour also adding interest to most of the coastline. The quiet waters of Langebaan Lagoon contrast with the wild Atlantic waves that often lash the coast exposed to the open sea. Sheltered bays and coves are interspersed among long stretches of rugged granite outcrops. A number of lighthouses, such as the one at Cape Columbine, have a long history behind them and are well worth investigating.

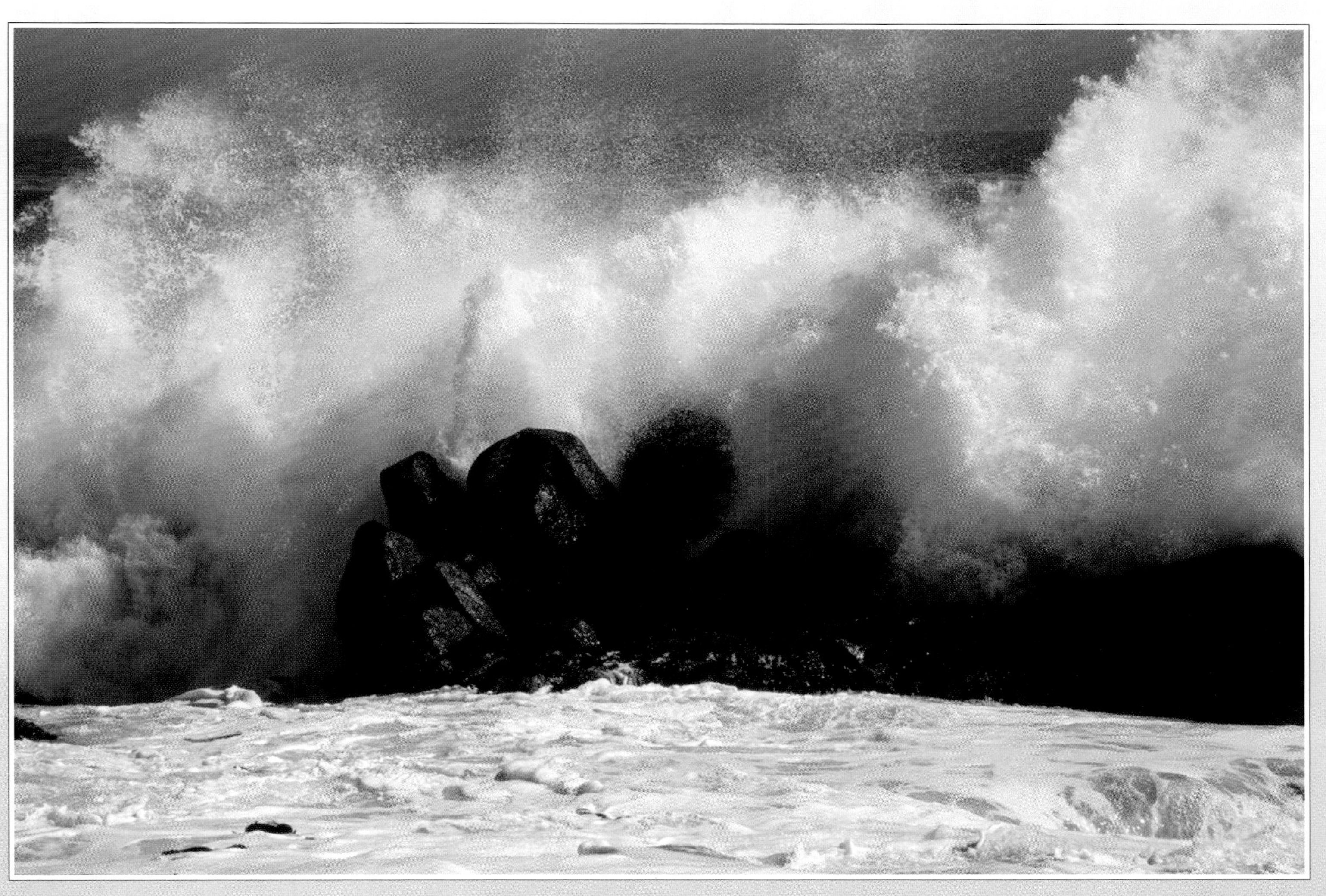

The West Coast shoreline is often pounded by massive waves following several days of strong northwesterly winds.

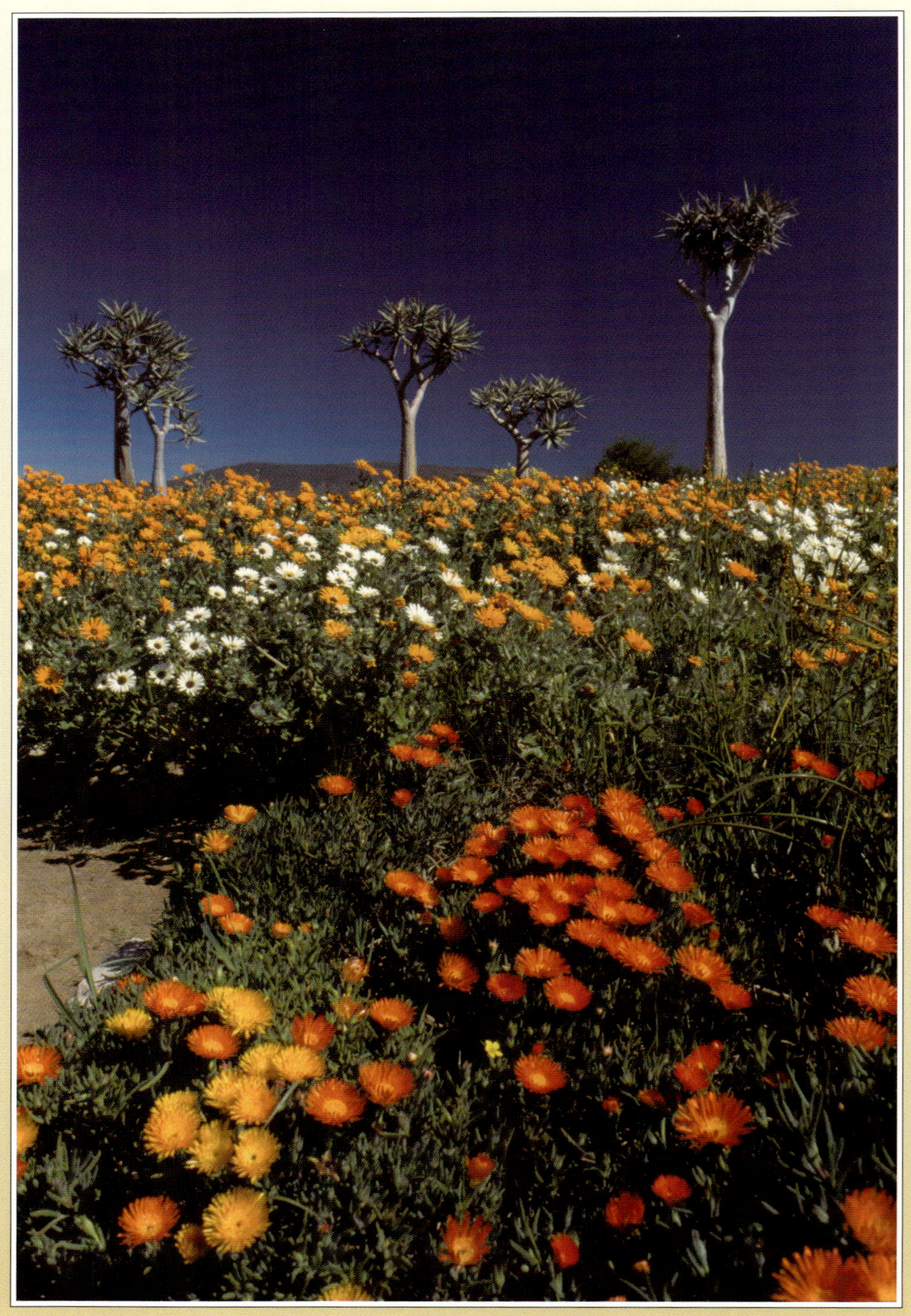

A group of "kokerbome" ("quiver trees") look onto a colourful display of daisies and mesembryanthemums in the Ramskop Wild Flower Reserve at Clanwilliam.

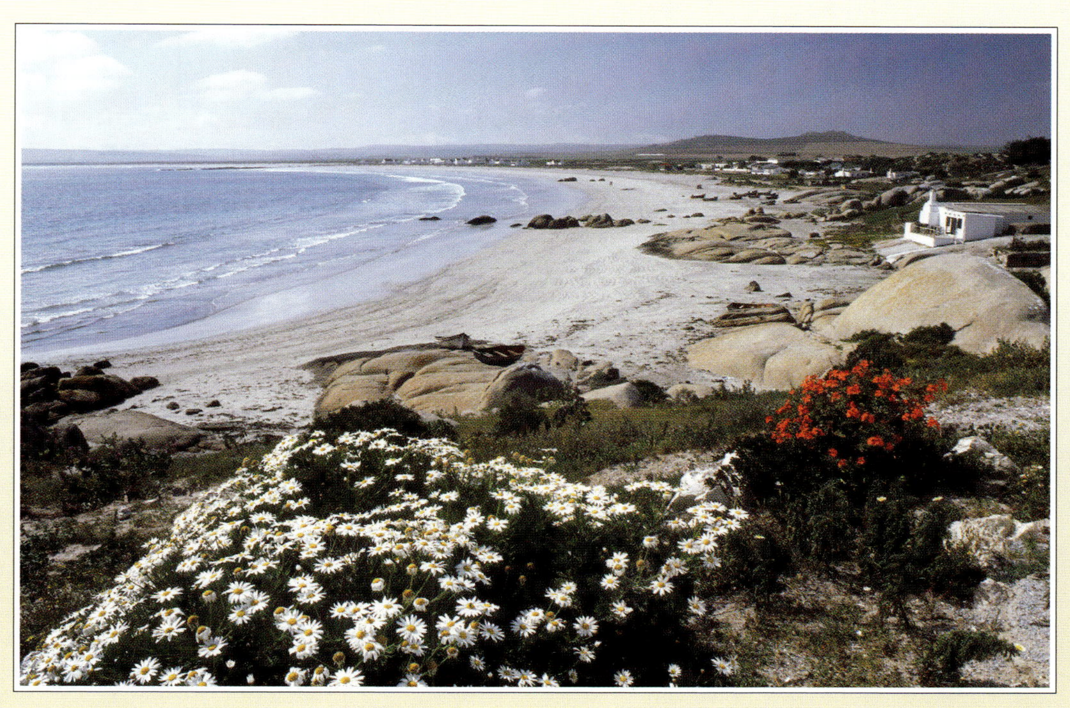

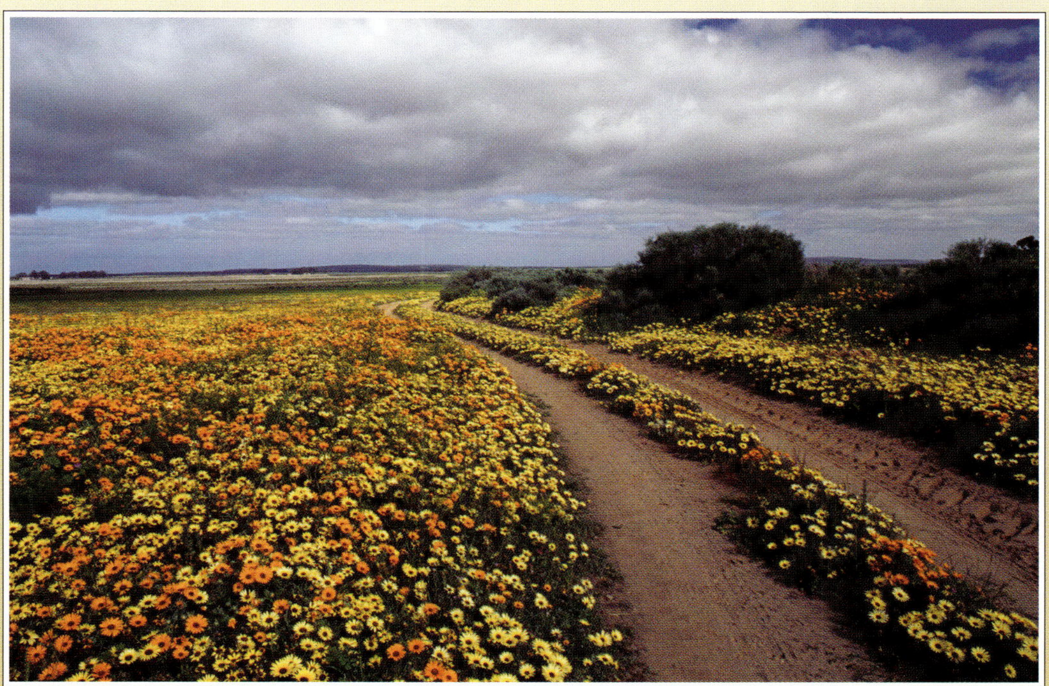

Top:
Simple fishermen's cottages now exist side by side with expensive holiday homes in the picturesque village of Paternoster.

Bottom:
An old field on a guest farm along the Berg River near Velddrif puts on a flower display rivalling those of the more famous localities.

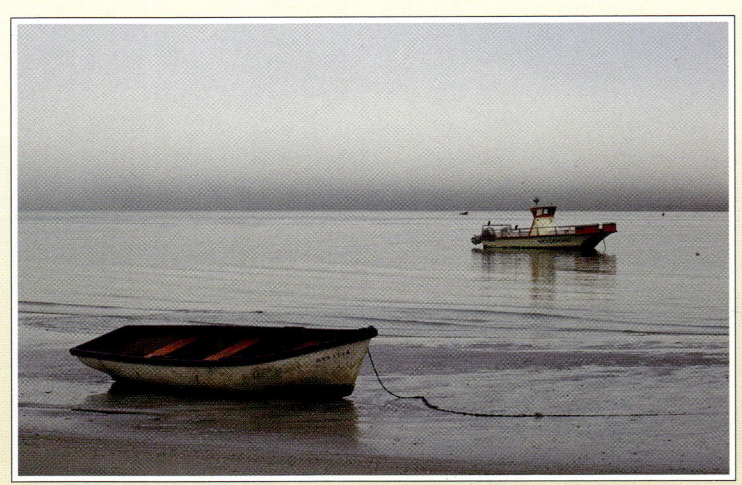

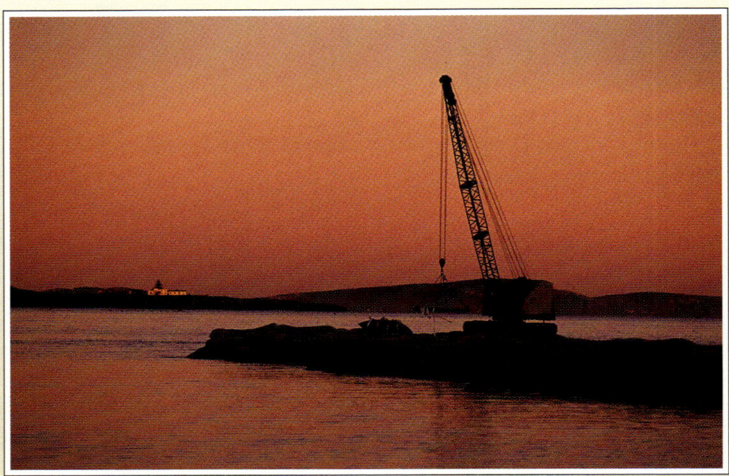

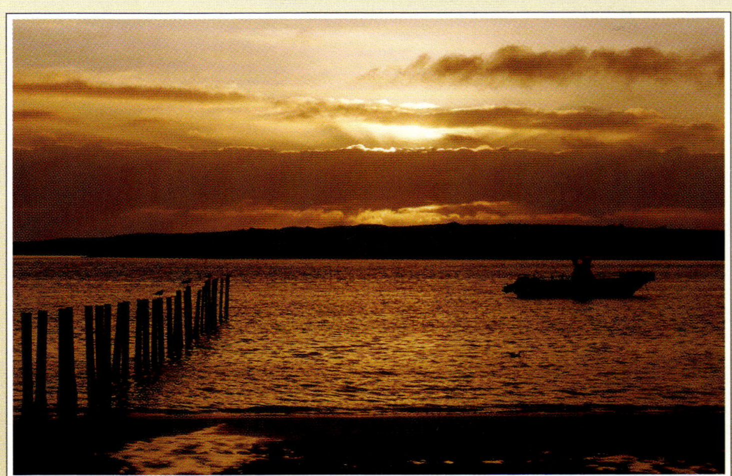

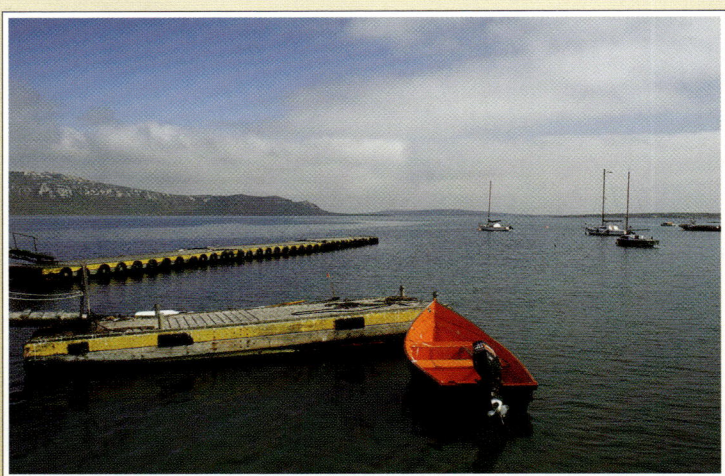

The many moods of Langebaan Lagoon range from the brilliant blue of a cloudless day to the bleak greys of an overcast, rainy one, with the subtle pinks and oranges of sunrise and sunset adding yet more variety for the photographer to enjoy.

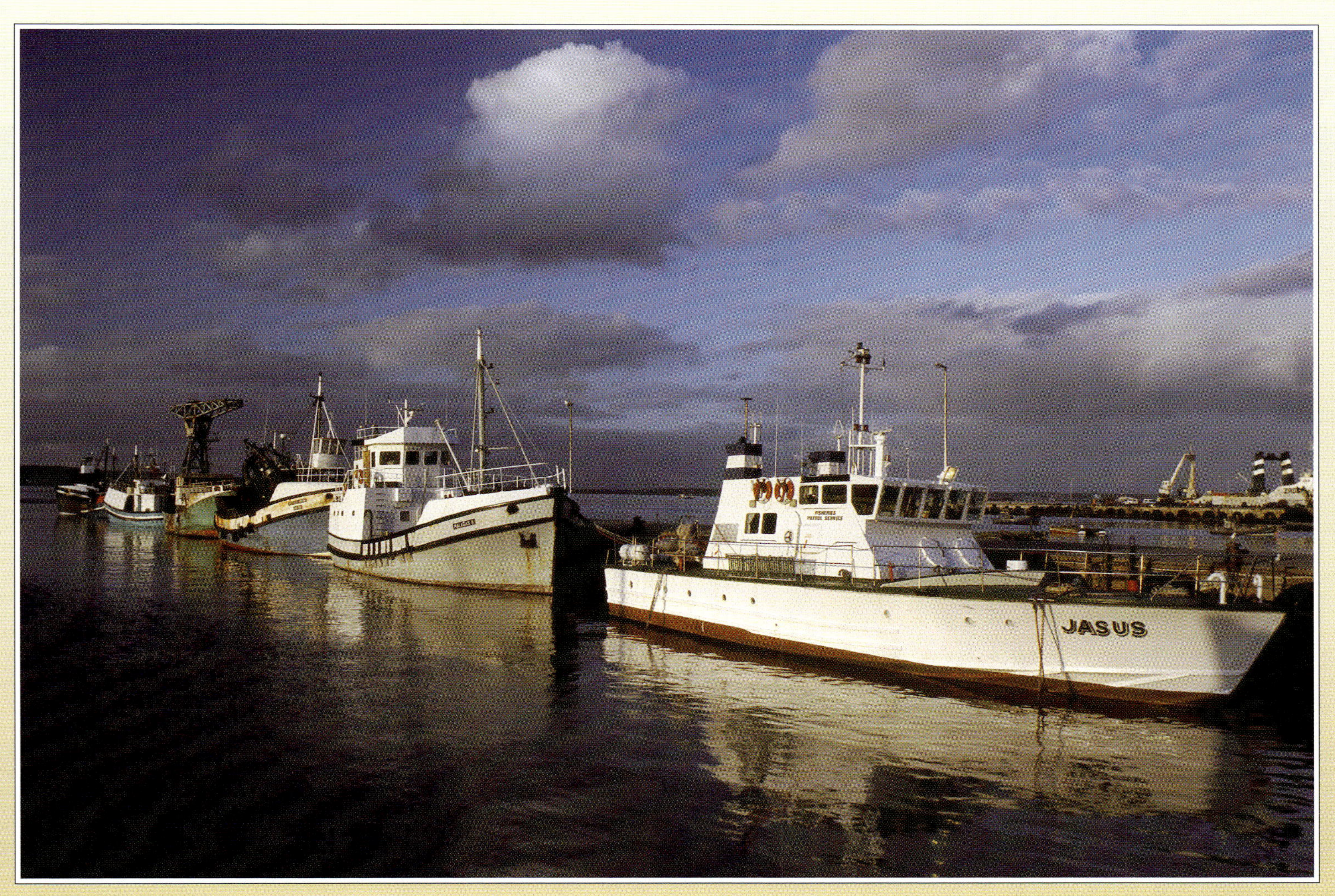

Saldanha Bay offers protection from angry West Coast storms to ships sheltering in the harbour.

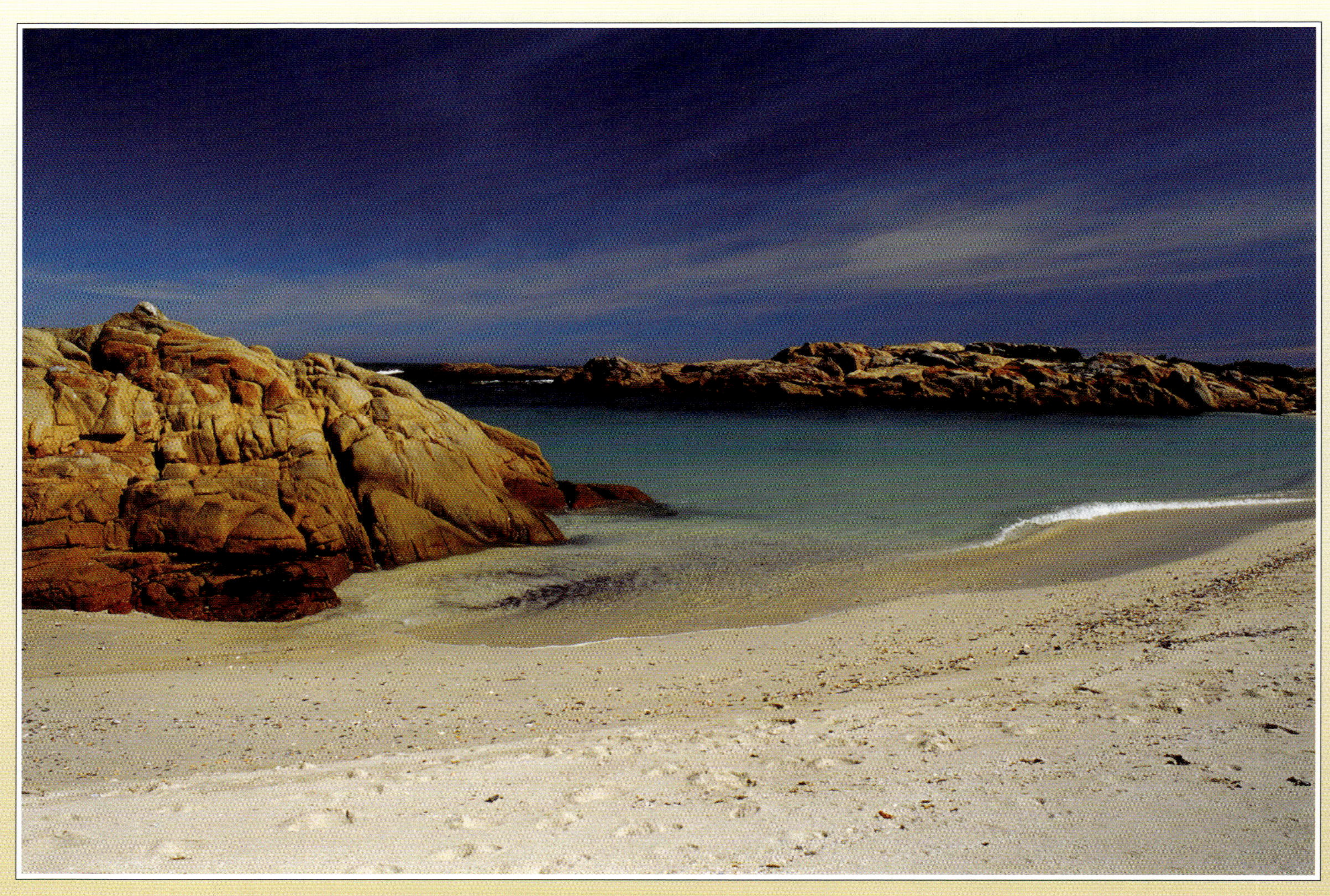

Beyond Paternoster, the gravel road heading southward past the Cape Columbine lighthouse hugs the coast and provides access to delightful coves such as Tieties Bay.

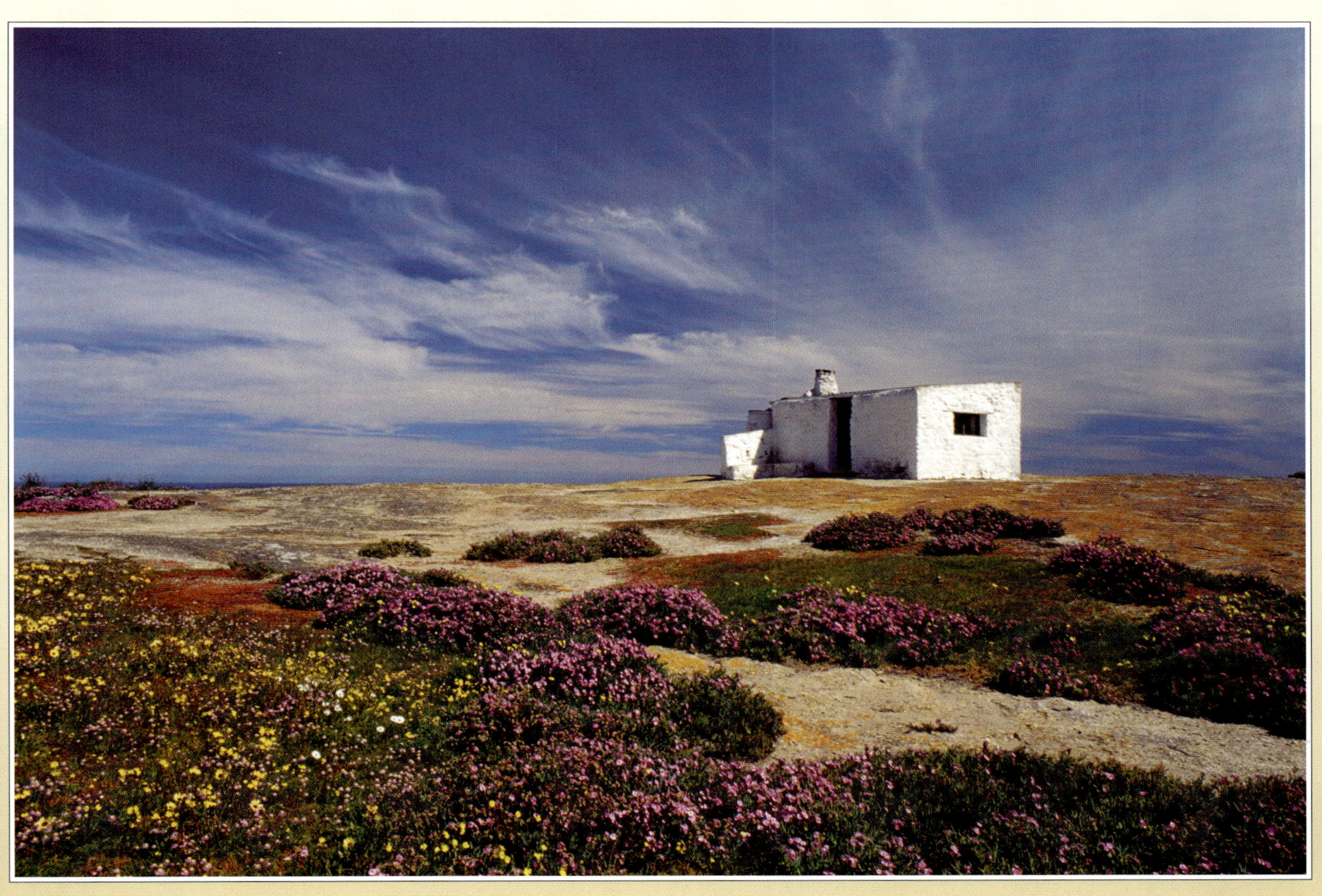

Seeberg hill, overlooking the lagoon south of Langebaan, boasts a one-room "house built on the rock".

DAY 4

Cape Peninsula

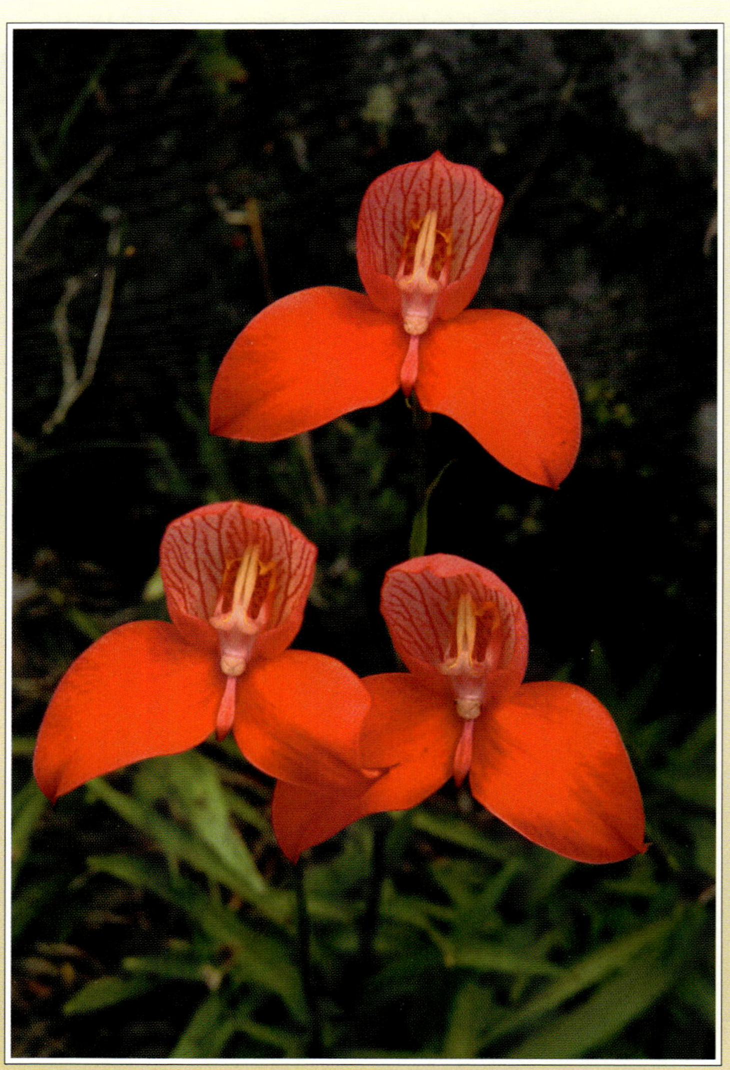

Bright red disas (Disa uniflora) are common alongside the small streams on the top of Table Mountain.

The Cape Peninsula is one of South Africa's premier tourist destinations, not just for local holidaymakers but for overseas visitors as well. And no wonder, when one considers what is on offer. There is Cape Town itself, with its harbour and the popular Alfred and Victoria Waterfront, its historic buildings, which include Groot Constantia, Groote Schuur, the Castle and the University of Cape Town campus, and its secluded beaches such as Clifton and Llandudno. Then there is the rugged grandeur of Table Mountain itself, now a World Heritage Site, with the world-famous Kirstenbosch Botanical Gardens on its eastern flank.

Further south, Muizenberg and Kommetjie beaches, the fishing harbours of Hout Bay in the west and Kalk Bay in the east, and the naval base at Simonstown offer quieter alternatives compared with Cape Town itself. All of these places are embraced by an incomparable circular scenic route that includes the famous Chapman's Peak Drive between Hout Bay and Noordhoek. Finally, the unspoilt southernmost part of the Peninsula, which now forms part of the Cape of Good Hope Nature Reserve, represents a stark but welcome contrast to the heavily developed northern and central parts of the Peninsula.

With such as a variety on offer, the photographer should experience no shortage of suitable material. Fishing boats and naval vessels, beaches, the fynbos vegetation (either cultivated in Kirstenbosch Botanical Gardens or growing naturally in the Cape of Good Hope Nature Reserve and elsewhere), the old buildings and the mountain itself are all worthy subjects.

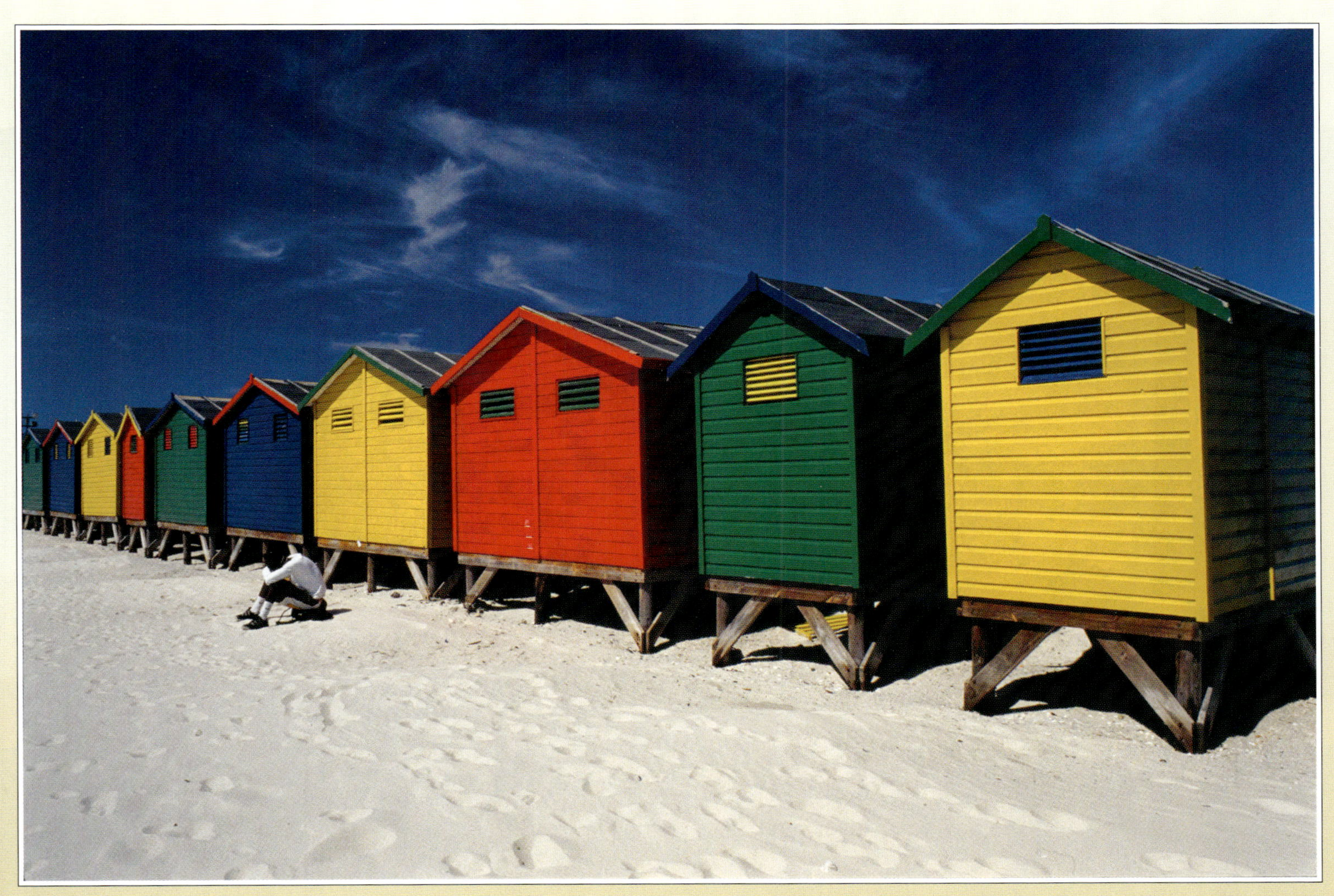

The colourful beach houses at Muizenberg are always worth photographing, especially if one is lucky enough to find them freshly painted.

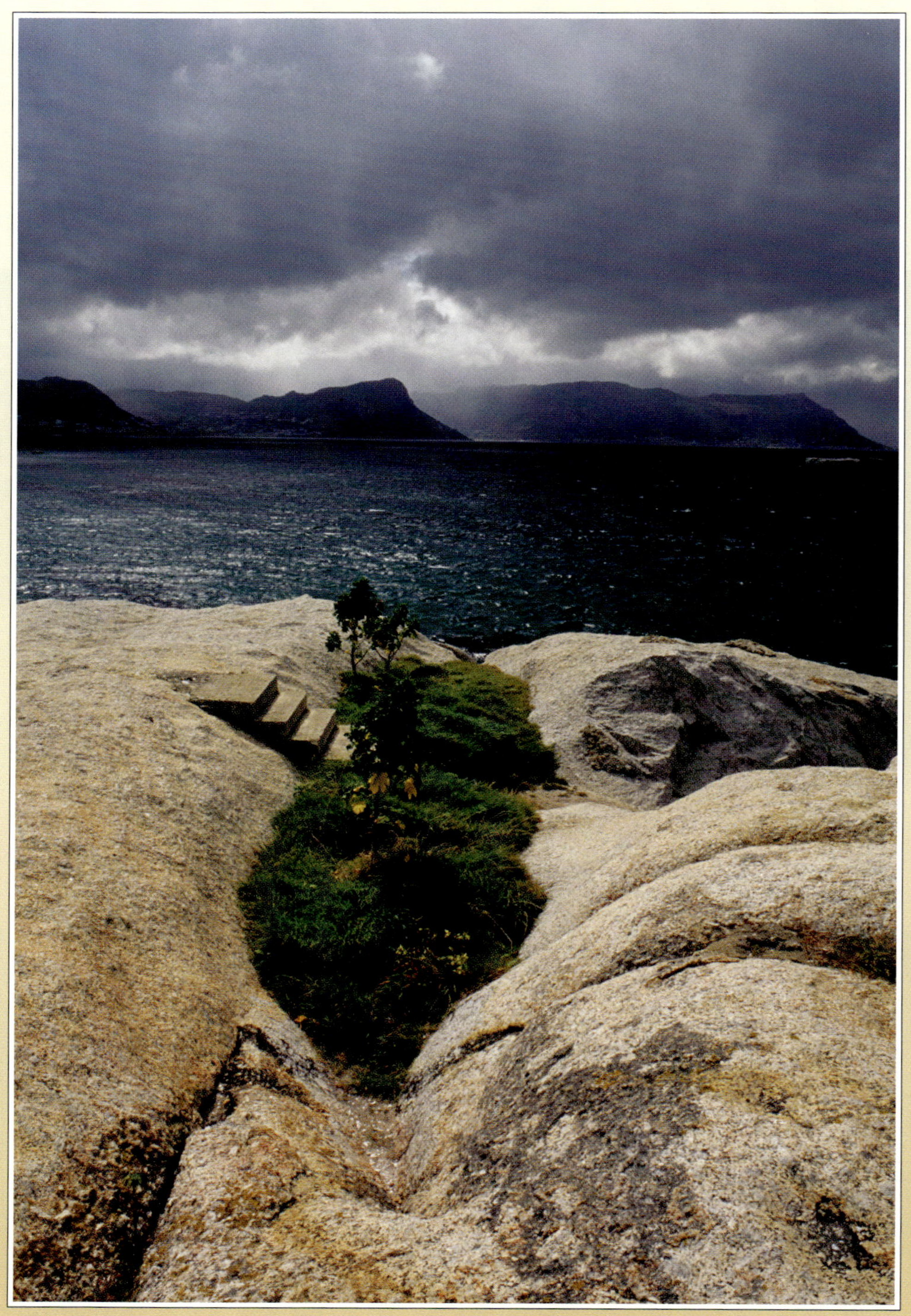

Distant showers threaten to advance towards the granite outcrops at "The Boulders" near Simon's Town on the False Bay coast.

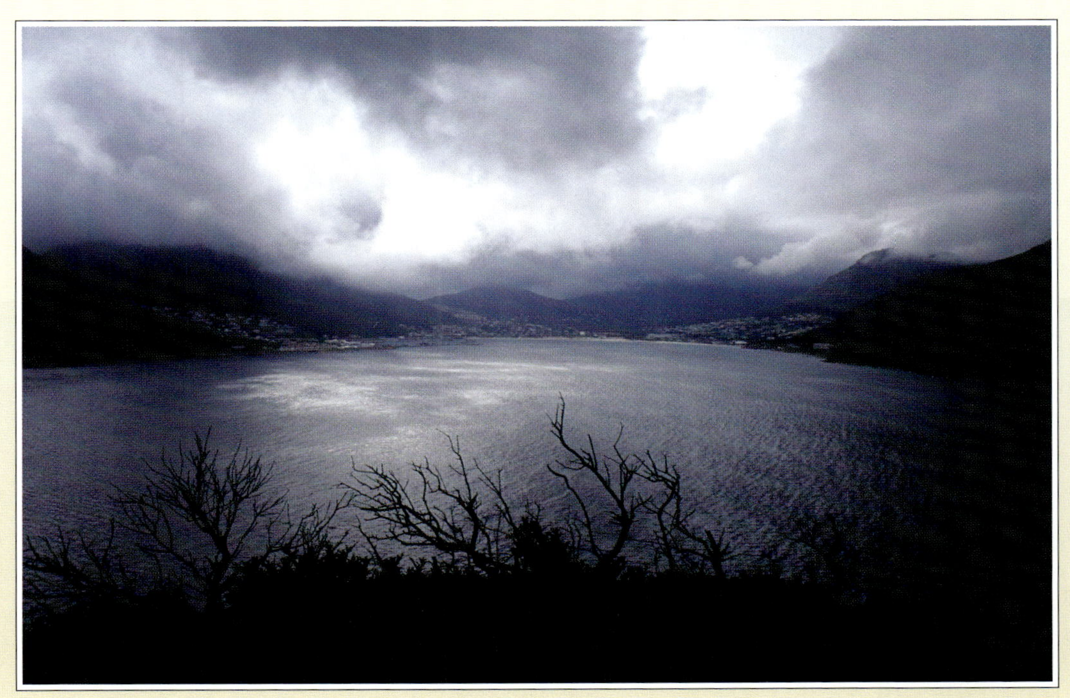

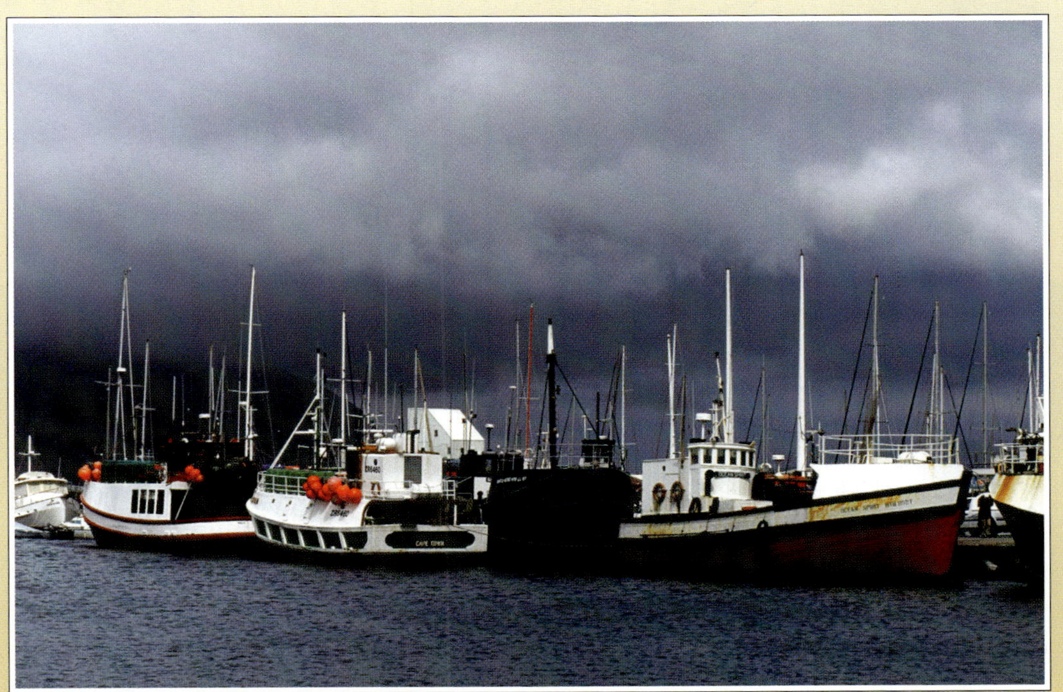

Top:
Rain clouds close in on Hout Bay, here viewed from Chapman's Peak Drive.

Bottom:
Part of the fishing fleet based in Hout Bay harbour, a safe haven in this part of the "Cape of Storms".

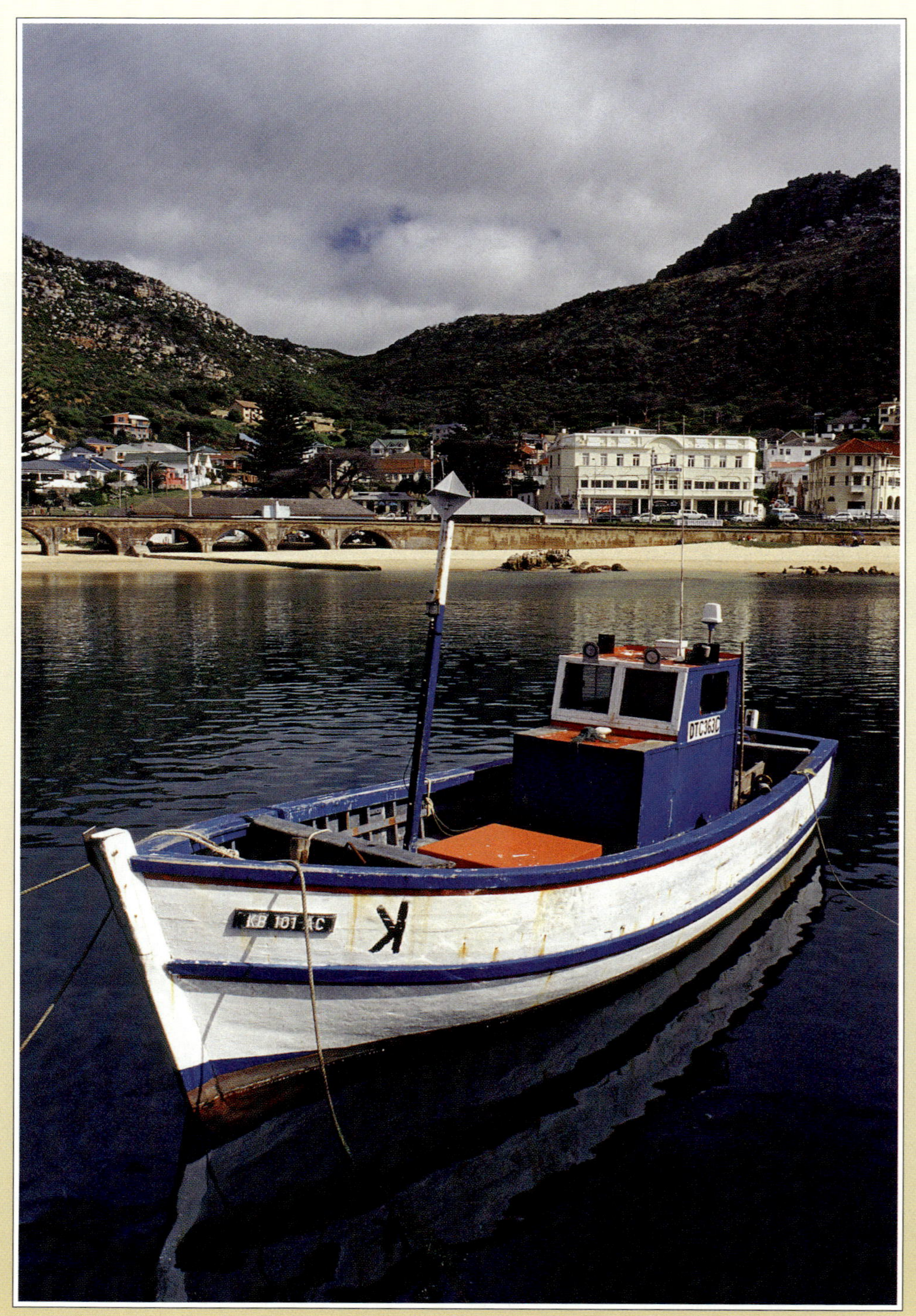

Kalk Bay harbour north of Simon's Town is home to fishing boats of various shapes and sizes.

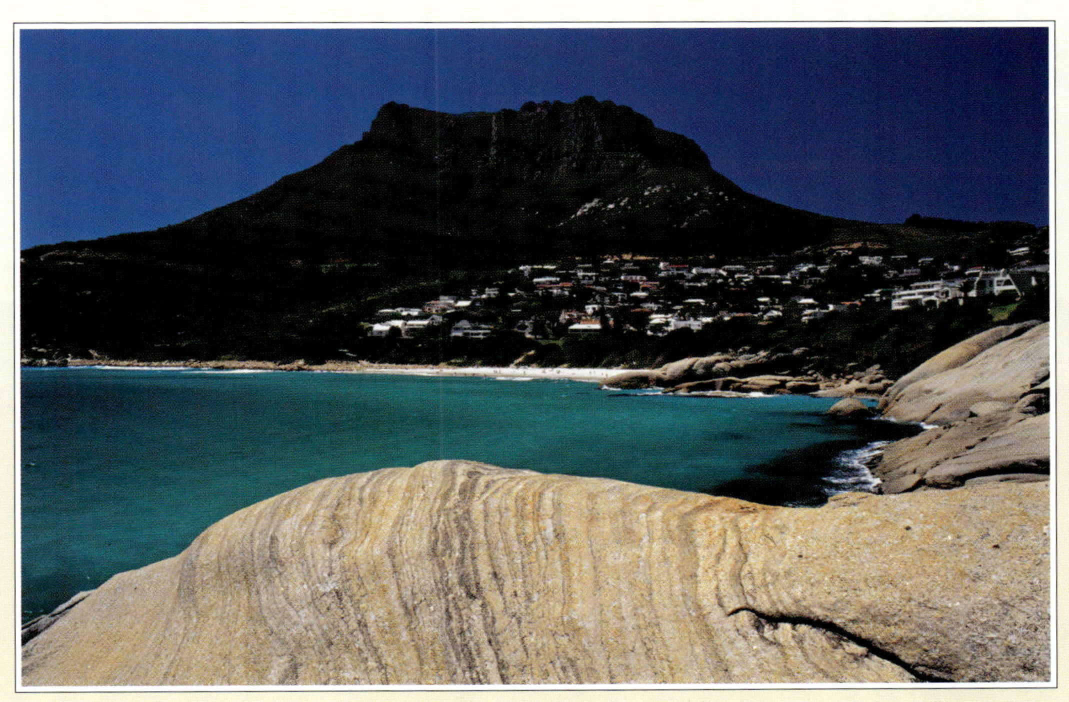

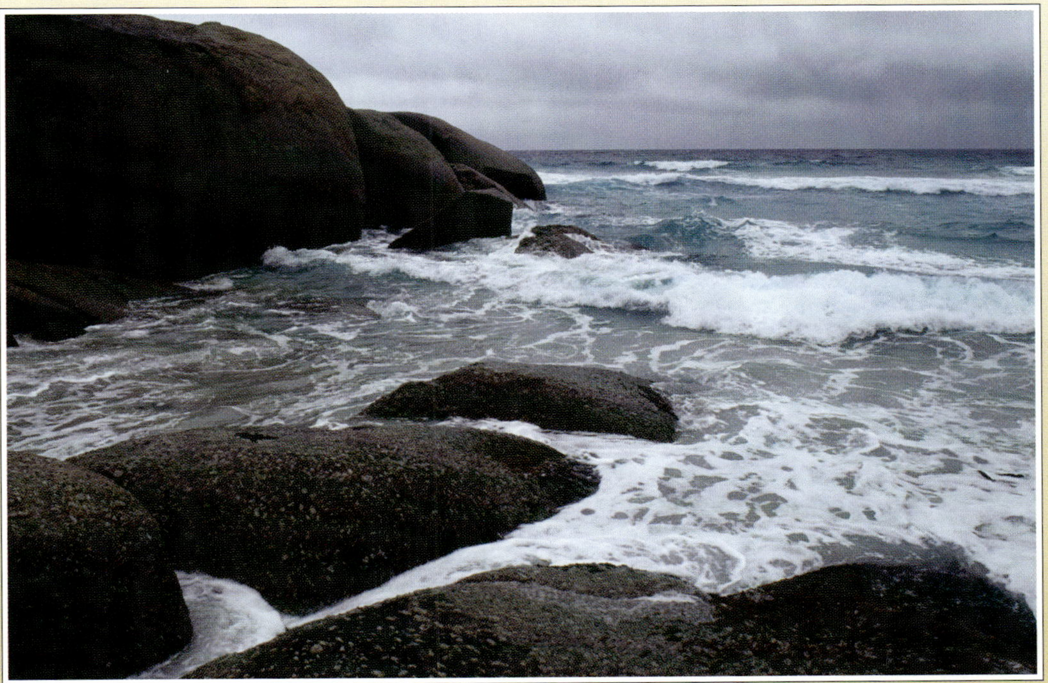

Top:
The residents of Llandudno have a magnificent view of the turquoise Atlantic Ocean below.

Bottom:
An overcast day, and the rocks at Llandudno beach are now dark and sombre in a sea that has been drained of nearly all colour.

DAY 5

Stellenbosch

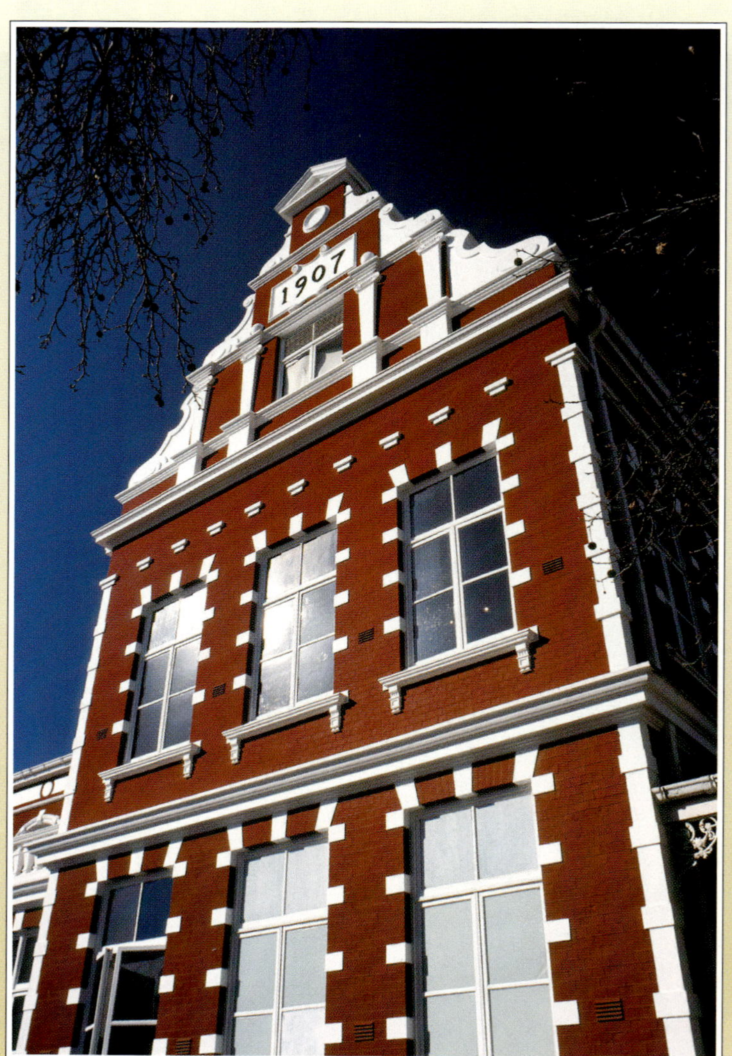

The old Bloemhof School for Girls, completed in 1907, now functions as an art centre and museum.

Founded by Simon van der Stel in 1679, the picturesque university town of Stellenbosch is famous for its oak-lined streets and its many old buildings that have qualified as national monuments. It is a focal point for the wine industry, with many well-known wine estates and "wine routes" being located in the surrounding area. Spier Estate, situated a short distance from the town on the banks of the Eerste River, comprises a particularly attractive complex of buildings and is widely known for the various prestigious cultural events it hosts during the year. The beautiful Jonkershoek valley, to the south of Stellenbosch, is served by a road that winds between magnificent stands of oaks and poplars bordering a clear mountain stream, with rugged mountain peaks surrounding the valley on three sides. At the end of the road a nature reserve contains an attractive dam surrounded by fynbos vegetation. A recommended scenic drive is that over Helshoogte Pass to Franschhoek, another historic town that is well worth visiting. The road to Somerset West, which lies to the southeast of Stellenbosch, passes through vineyards interspersed with the occasional wheat fields or green pastures dotted with cows and sheep.

Photographers will find much to keep themselves busy. The most obvious subjects are the various old buildings, but the majestic mountains, the vineyards, orchards and fields and the tree-lined avenues and valleys are all equally photogenic. The southeaster bringing white clouds tumbling over the mountain crests and the occasional morning mists adding romance to the pastoral scenes are always photo-enhancing bonuses.

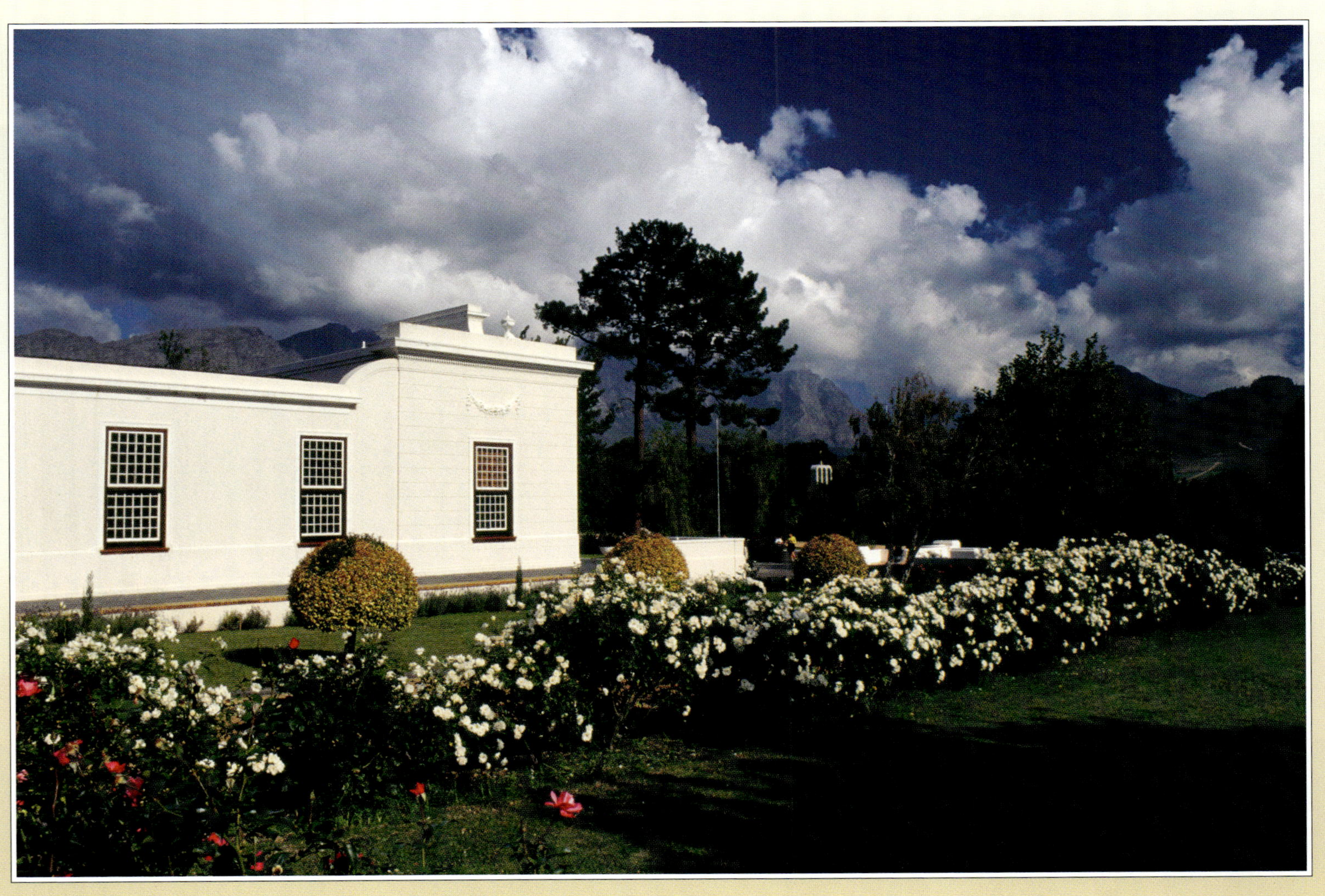

The Huguenot Memorial Museum in Franschhoek is a replica of the Cape Town home of Baron Pieter van Oudtshoorn, which was built in 1791.

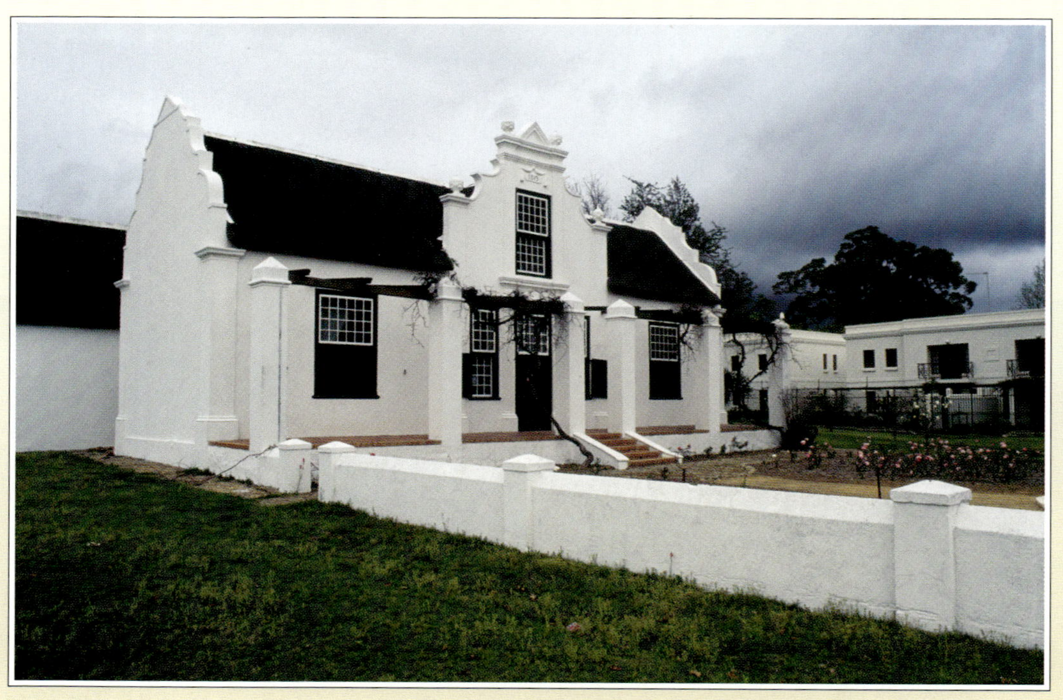

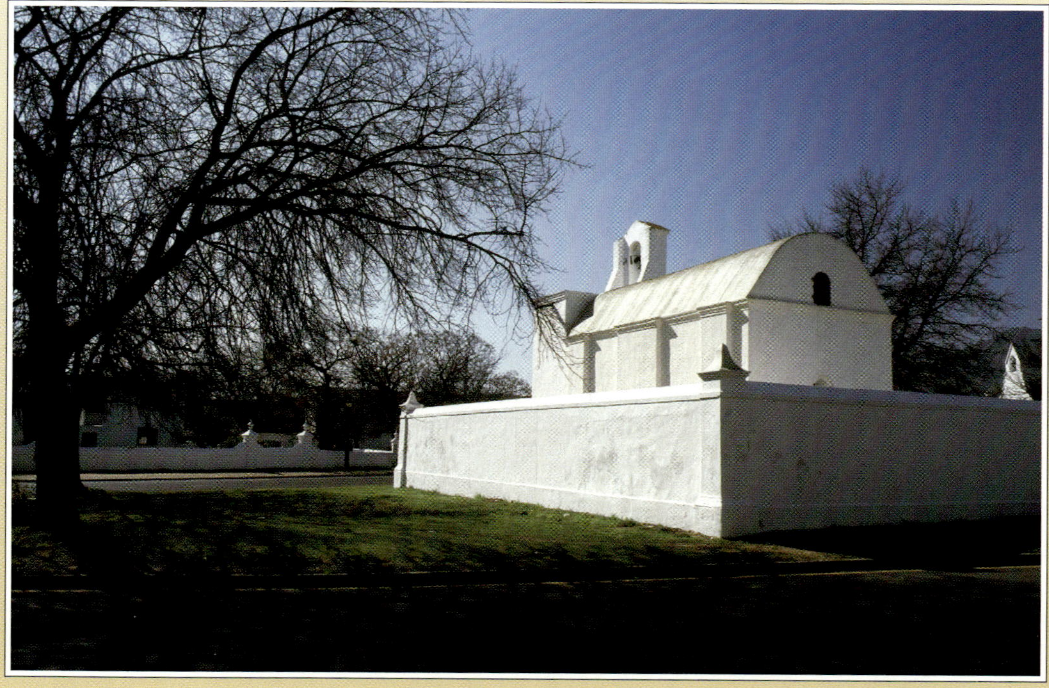

Top:
The Rhenish Parsonage, dated 1815, forms part of the Rhenish Complex of restored buildings.

Bottom:
The "Kruithuis" ("powder magazine") was built in 1777 to house "cannons, flintlocks, powder and other ammunition".

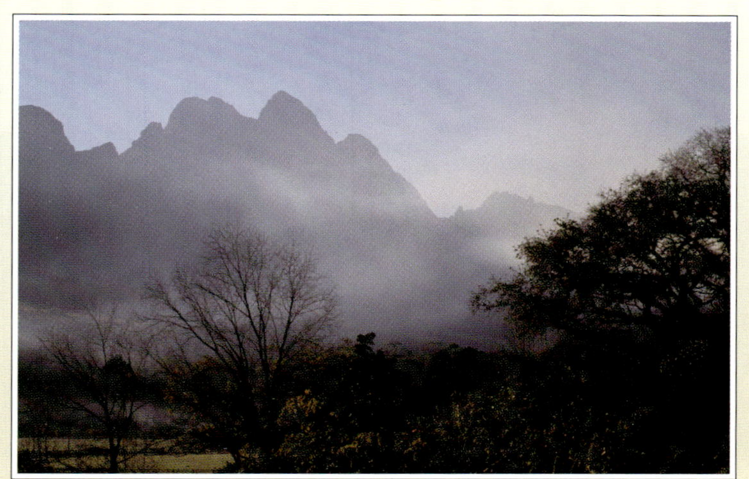

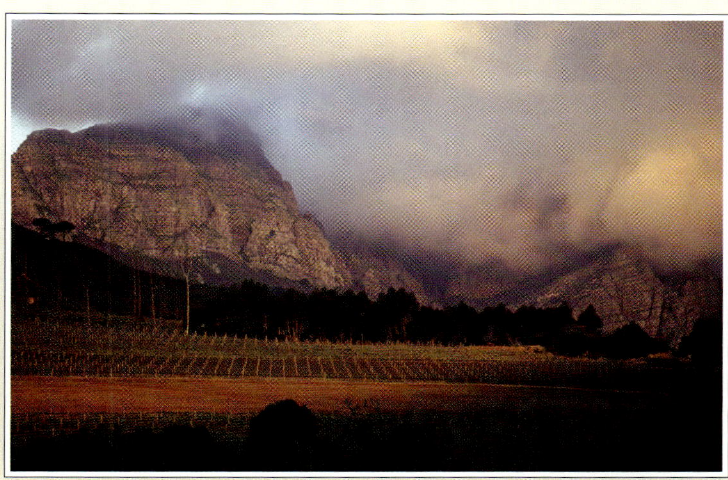

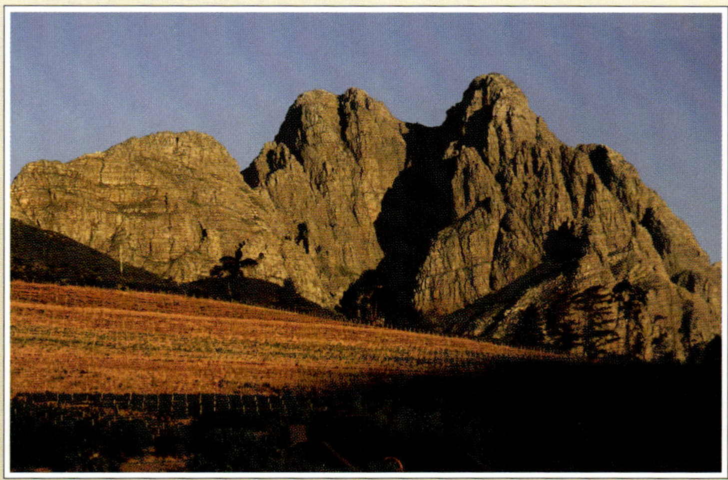

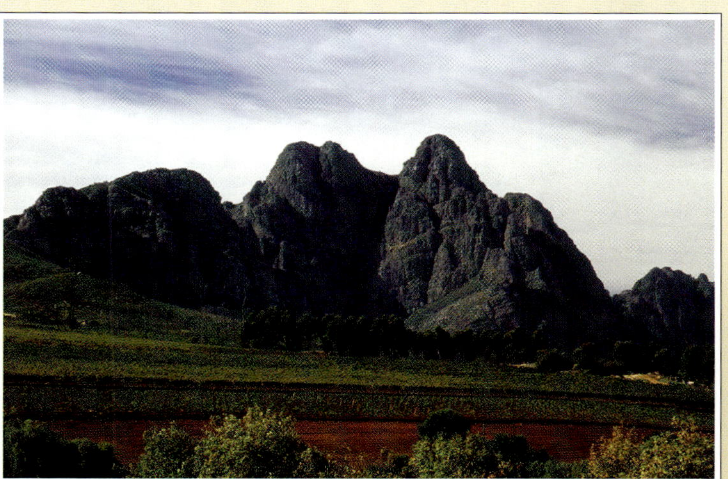

The majestic Jonkershoek Mountains tower above a picturesque valley to the southeast of Stellenbosch. In the haze and mist of early morning only the outlines of the main peaks are visible, but by late afternoon they stand revealed in all their rugged glory.

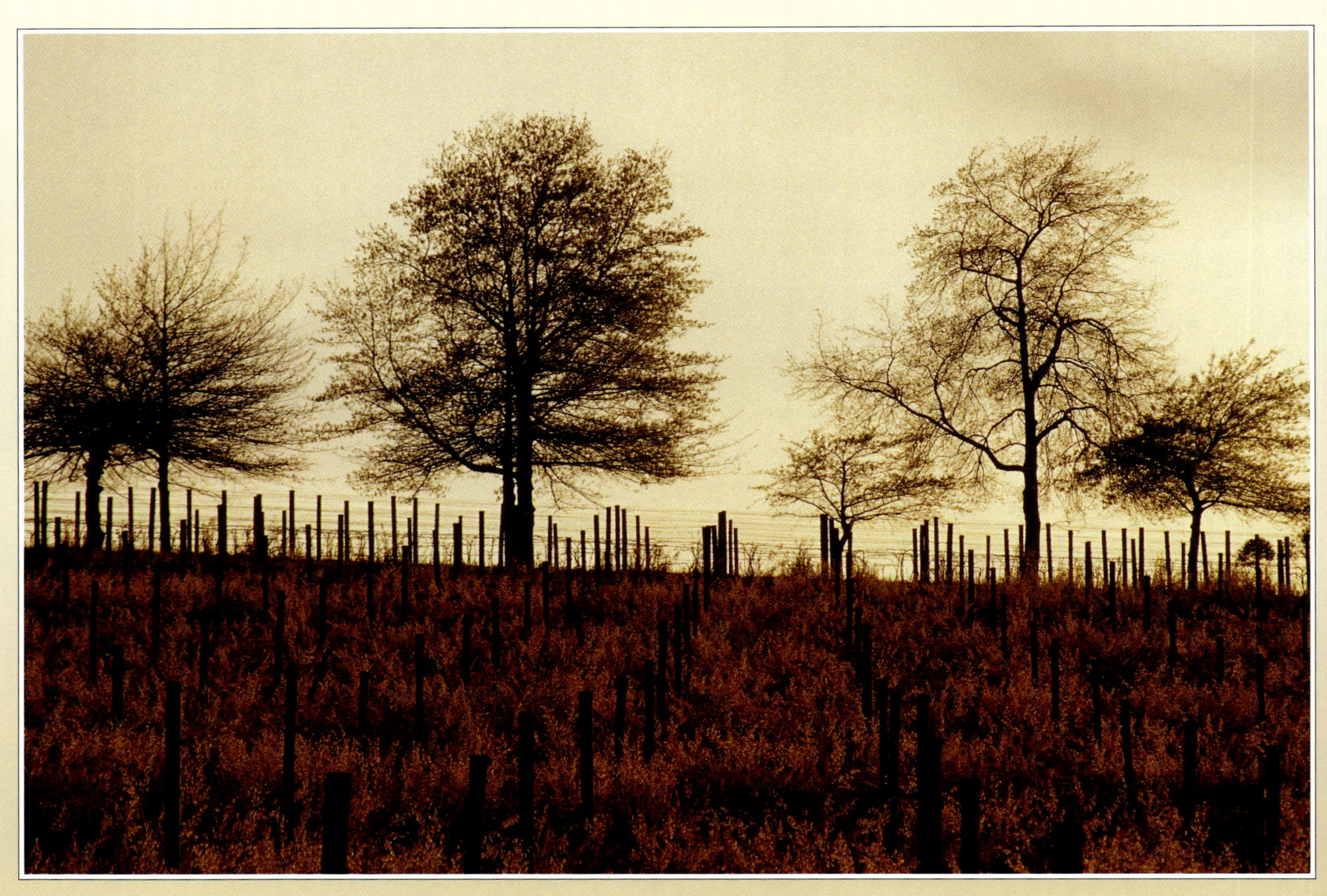

Bare trees and vine trellises on a farm near the top of Helshoogte Pass between Stellenbosch and Franschhoek.

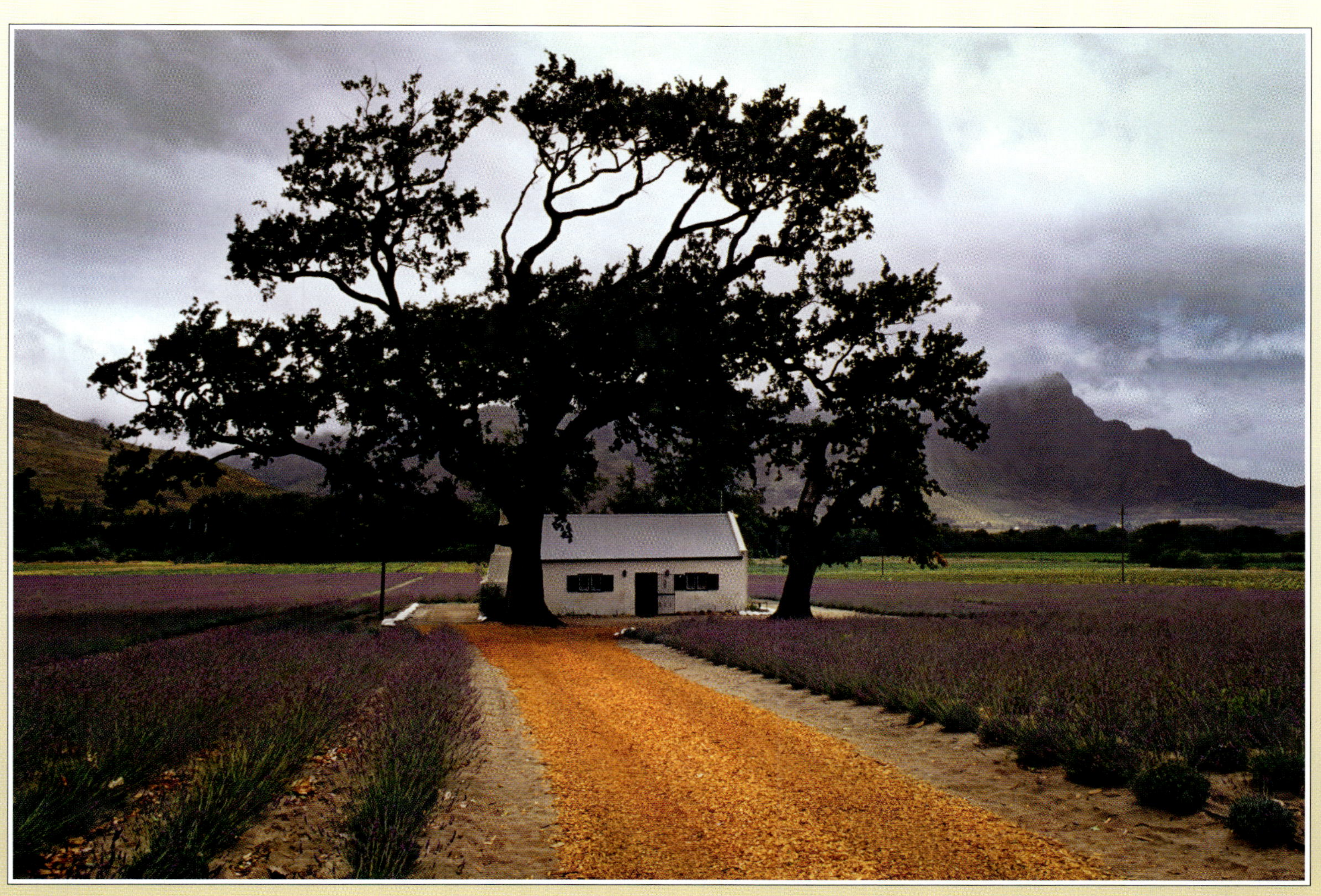

Lavender fields and olive groves now vie with the ubiquitous vineyards to complete the French image of the Franschhoek district.

DAY 6

Kogelberg Coast

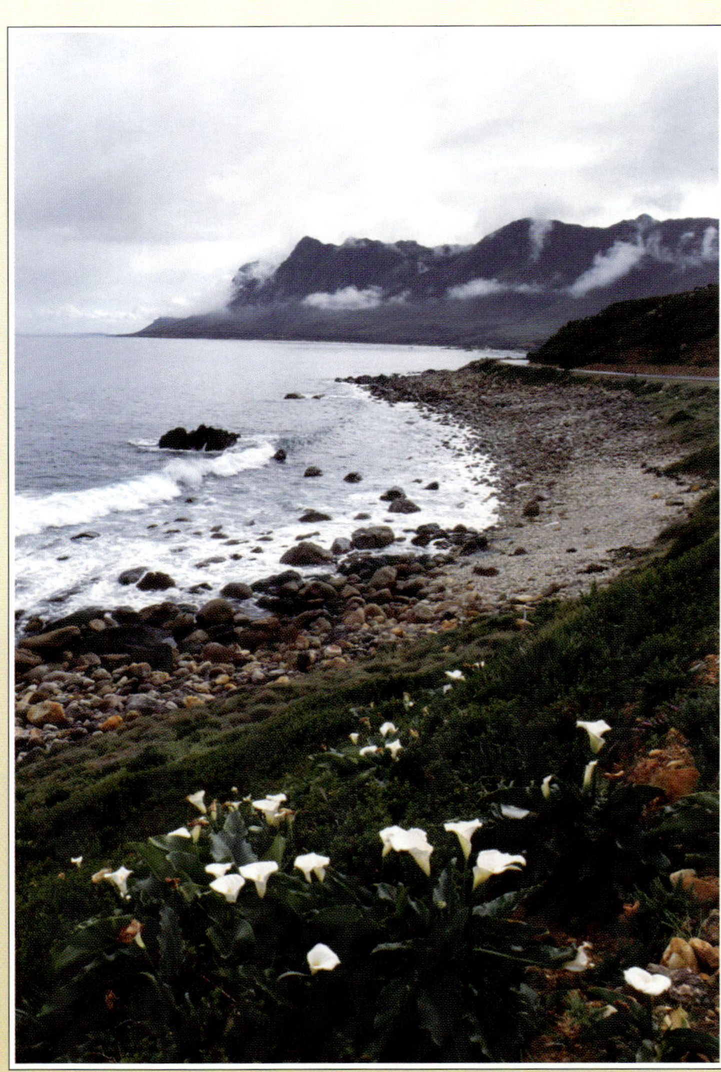

The southern tip of the Hottentots Holland Mountains juts into the sea along the northern end of Kogel Bay.

The coastal road between Somerset West and Hermanus is scenically comparable to that which follows the western side of the Cape Peninsula. Sea and mountains meet at Gordon's Bay with its small harbour used mainly by pleasure craft; from here the road winds southward along the foot of the Hottentots Holland, Koeëlberg and Blousteenberg mountain ranges, often with a sheer drop to the ocean below. After reaching the seaside village of Rooi Els, the road no longer sticks rigidly to the coastline and follows an easterly course through the towns of Pringle Bay, Betty's Bay and Kleinmond, which have all been built on the narrow stretch of land separating the mountains and the sea. Continuing in an easterly direction, the road skirts the wide expanse of water forming the Bot River estuary, heading southward to Hawston and then eastward again to Hermanus.

The whole mountainous terrain between the Gordon's Bay–Pringle Bay coastline and the Bot River constitutes the Kogelberg Biosphere Reserve, of which the Kogelberg Nature Reserve forms the core. Both state and privately owned land have been incorporated in this major conservation project. The Harold Porter Nature Reserve at Betty's Bay is a fynbos conservancy falling under the jurisdiction of the National Parks Board. The sea, the (generally rocky) shore, the mountains and the fynbos vegetation between them provide an endless variety of photographic opportunities, with the lake-like waters of the Bot River estuary contrasting with the massive waves for which the southern coast is particularly famous.

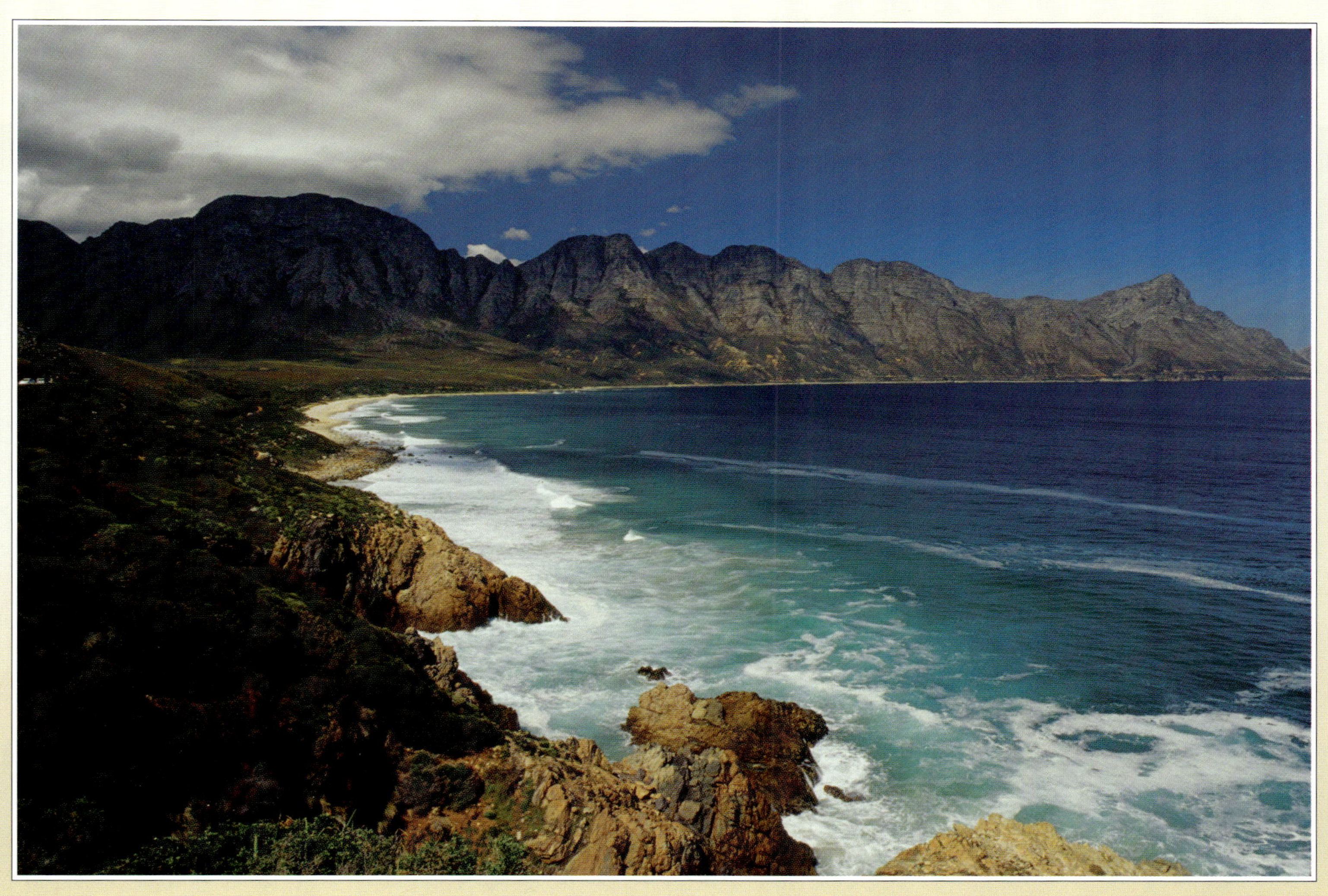

This classic Kogel Bay panorama, with the Blousteenberg mountains in the background, epitomises the Western Cape's scenic beauty.

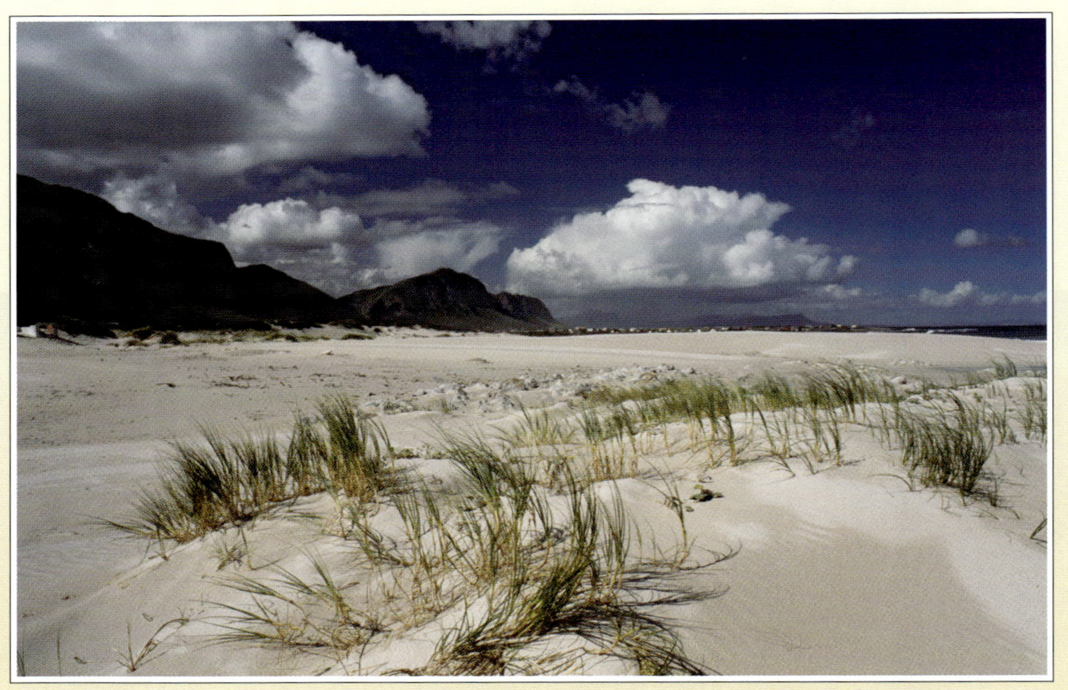

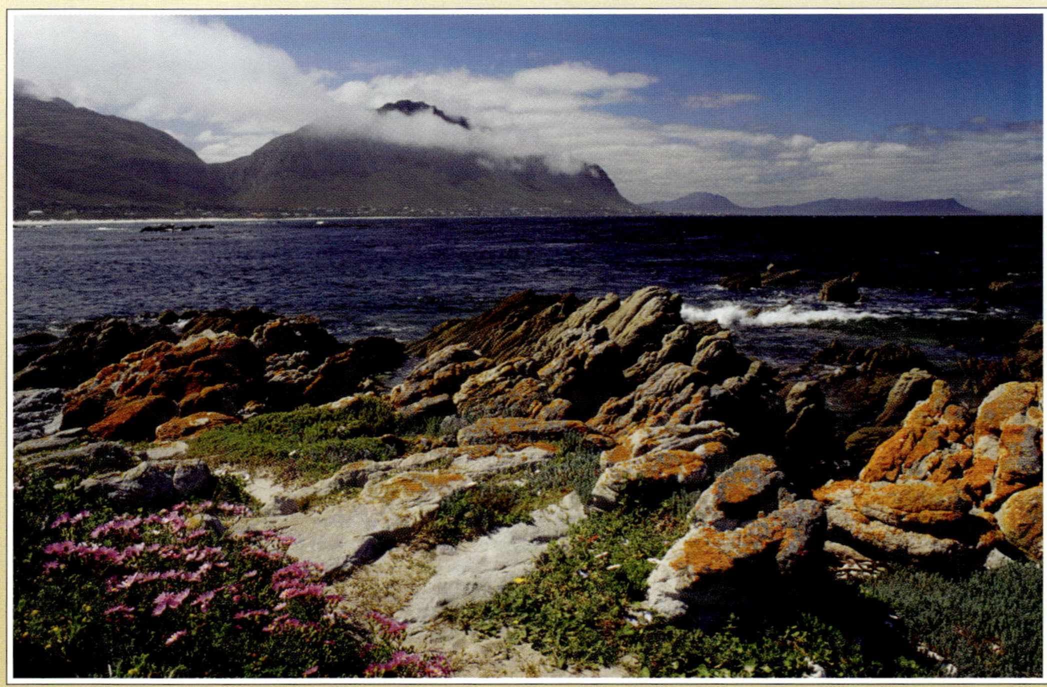

Top:
Clumps of grass cling precariously to life among the sand dunes; the western end of Betty's Bay is just visible in the distance.

Bottom:
With the sea on one side and the mountains on the other, Betty's Bay residents have the best of both worlds.

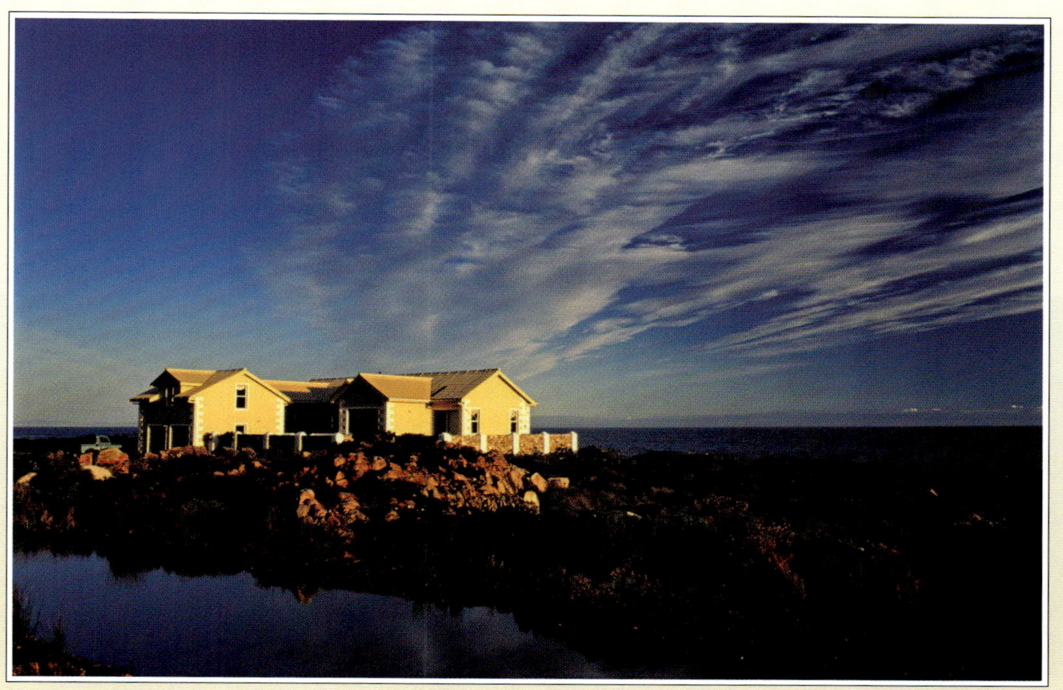

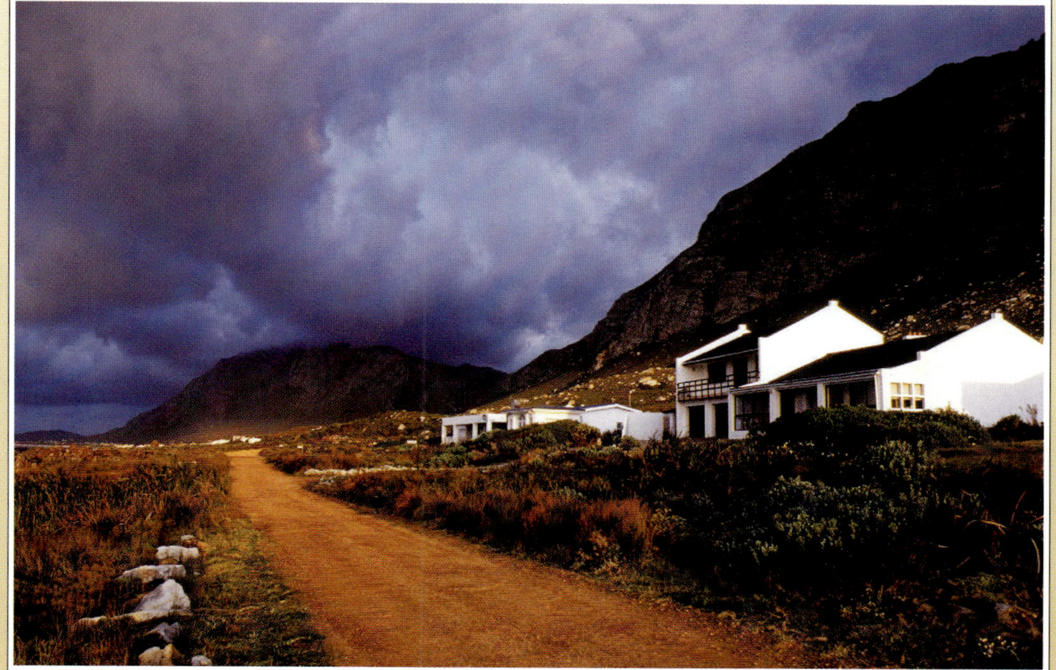

The constantly changing weather makes the planning of outdoor activities difficult for those living or holidaying along this part of the Cape coast. Calm seas, clear skies, moonlit nights and gentle breezes can rapidly give way to gale-force winds, wild waves, scudding clouds and unexpected showers.

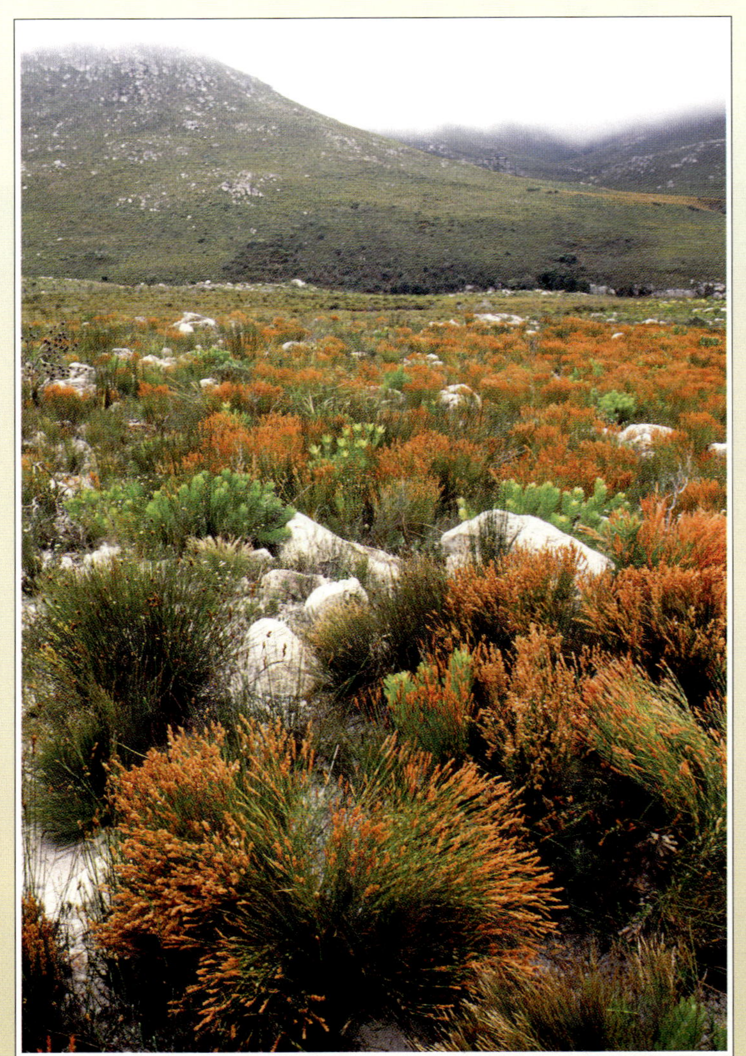

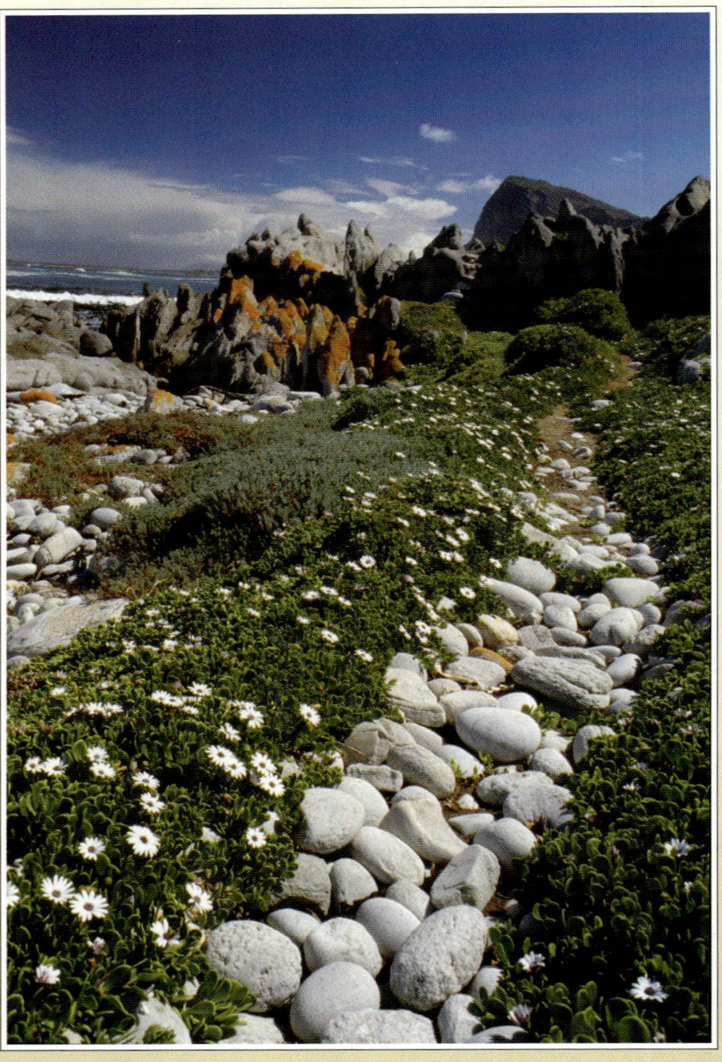

Hardy restios are a typical part of the fynbos vegetation flanking the Palmiet River in the Kogelberg Nature Reserve.

White daisies hug a pebbly path as it winds its way along the water's edge in the Sea Farm Nature Reserve near Betty's Bay.

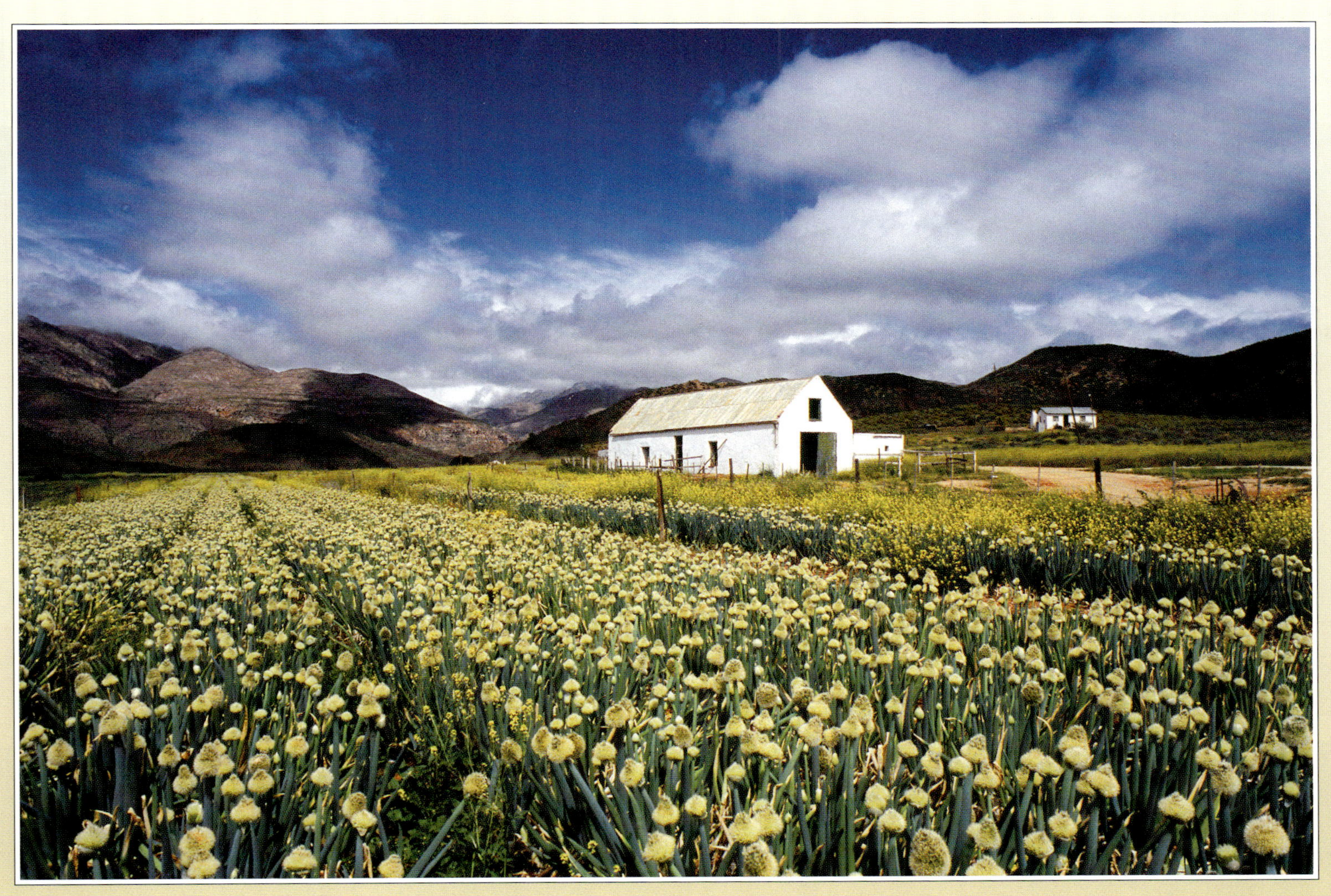

A bumper onion harvest would no doubt have been reaped on this farm between De Rust and Uniondale.

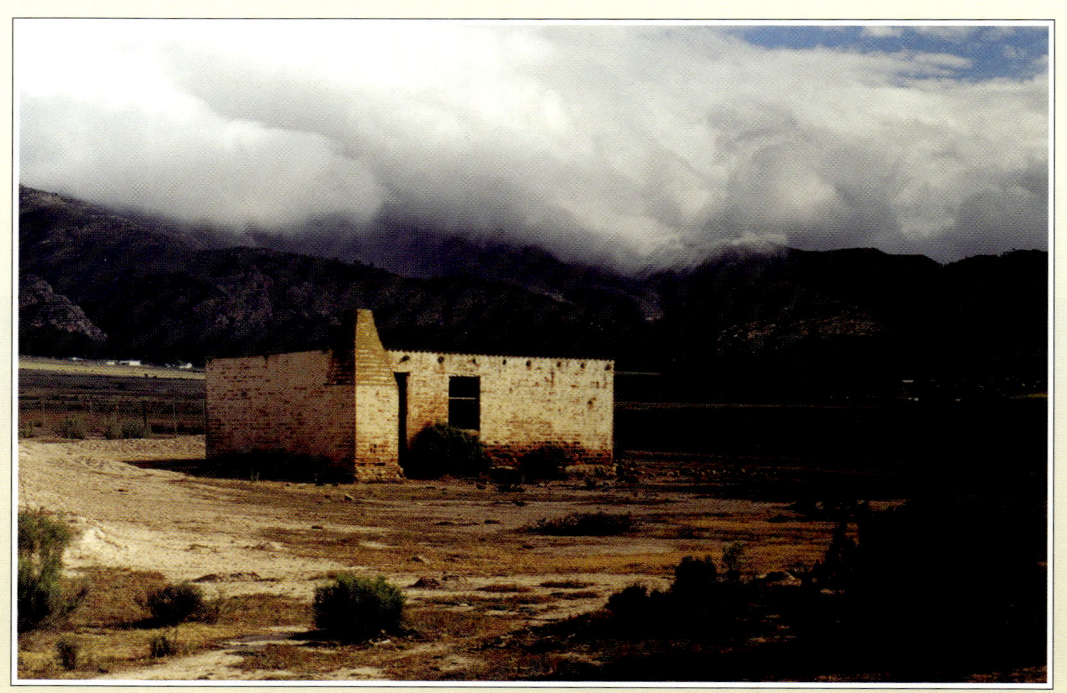

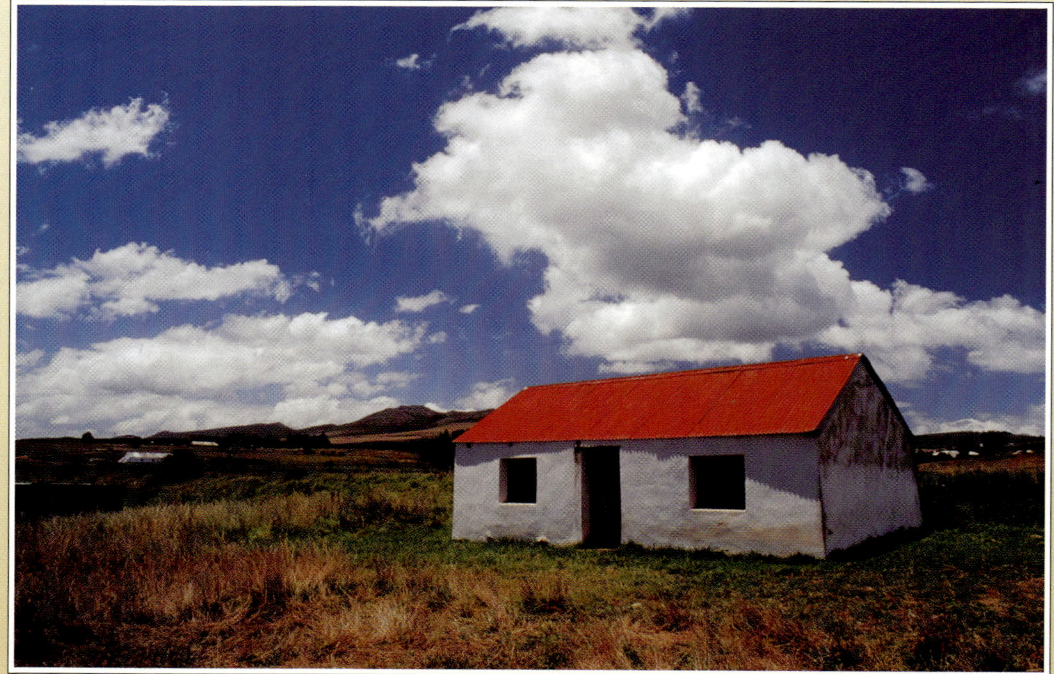

Farm workers have for generations lived in simple cottages like these in the western Langkloof where southeasters often bring low cloud and mist tumbling over the mountains that separate the valley from the coastal area to the south.

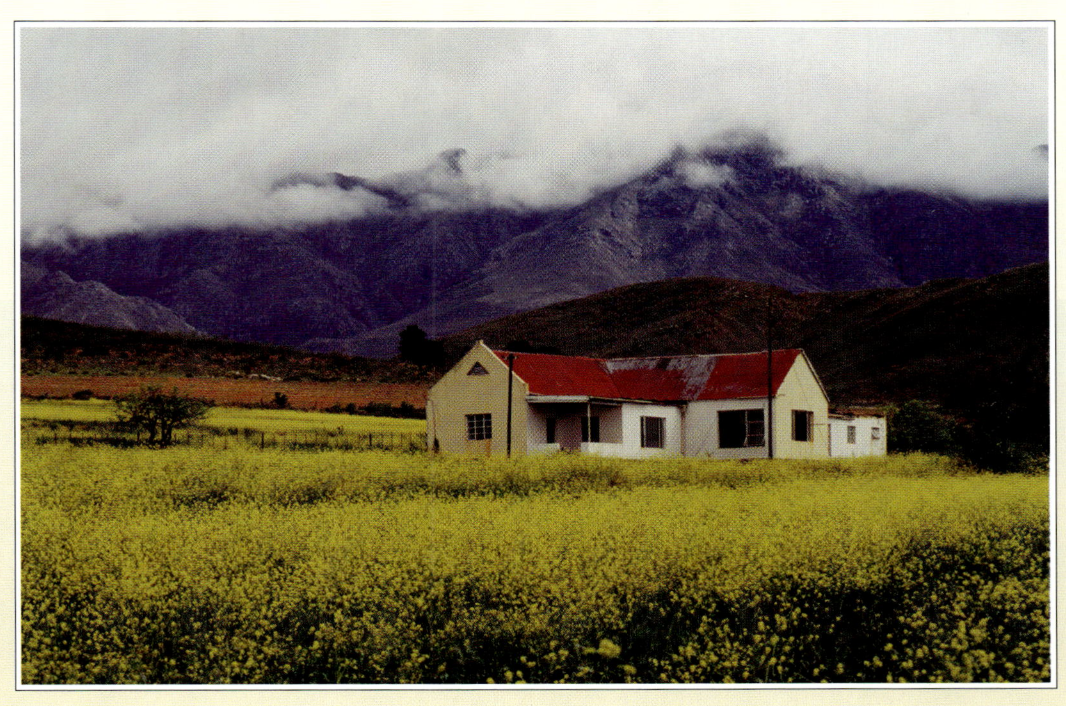

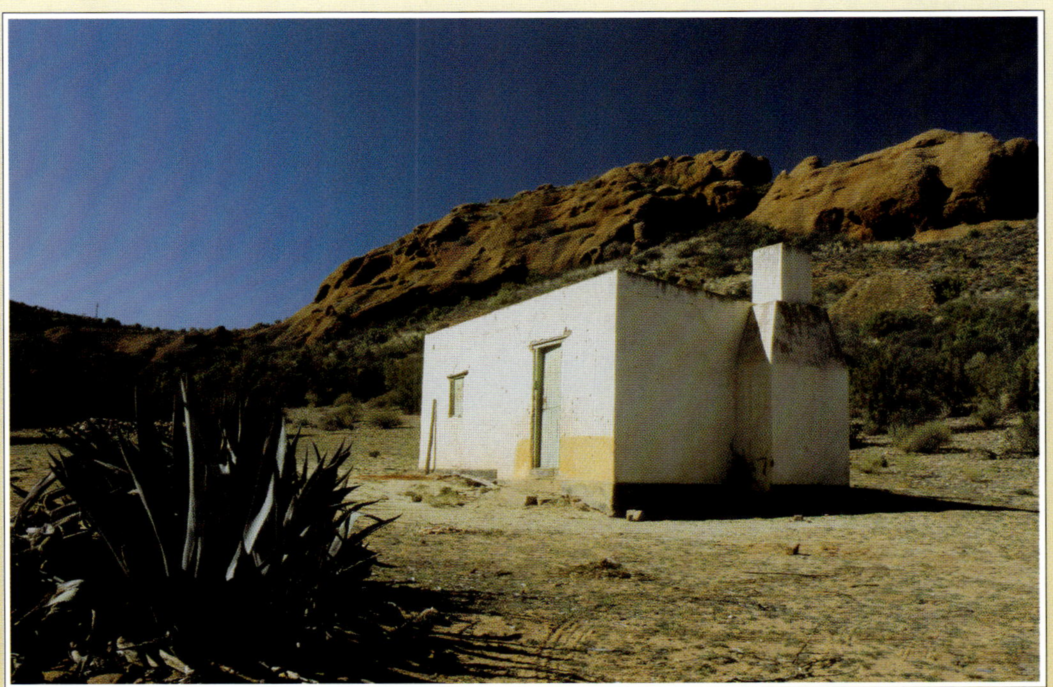

Top:
A deserted farmhouse near Matjiesrivier, surrounded by canola fields, has the Swartberg mountains as a backdrop.

Bottom:
Spiny agaves are the only surviving evidence of gardening activity around this solitary dwelling near the Calitzdorp–Kruisrivier road.

DAY 9

Garden Route

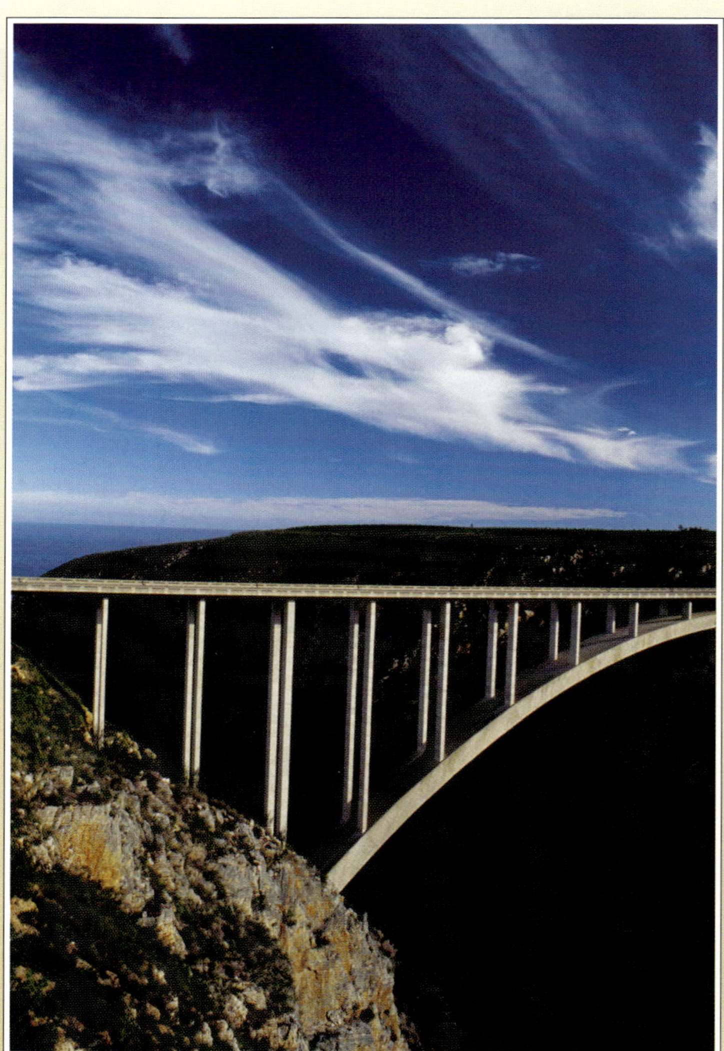

The bridge over the Bloukrans River, with its classic arched design, is the site of one of the world's highest bungee jumps.

The strip of coast between Mossel Bay in the west and the Storms River in the east, flanked to the north by the majestic Outeniqua and Tsitsikamma Mountains, is commonly known as the "Garden Route". The origin of the name is somewhat obscure since "garden" is perhaps not the most appropriate epithet for an area where long stretches of rugged, rocky coastline contrast with magnificent white beaches, where tracts of indigenous forest and fynbos vegetation alternate with pine and eucalyptus plantations, and where steep-sided river gorges open out into calm natural lakes. But from the point of view of scenic beauty it is indeed a veritable Garden of Eden. Mossel Bay, George, Knysna and Plettenberg Bay are the main towns, but Victoria Bay, Herold's Bay, Wilderness, Sedgefield, Keurboomstrand and Nature's Valley are attractive coastal towns catering mainly for holidaymakers. The Wilderness and Tsitsikamma National Parks (which both offer accommodation for visitors) as well as a number of other nature reserves serve to protect the most ecologically sensitive areas. The Otter and Tsitsikamma hiking trails, along the coast and mountains respectively, offer tough but highly rewarding encounters with the natural environment.

The close juxtaposition of a scenic coast, unspoilt natural vegetation, lakes, rivers and mountains provide a wealth of photographic opportunities. The distinct reddish-brown colour of the river water, produced by decaying fynbos vegetation, is a unique feature of the area. Proteas, ericas and watsonias put on colourful displays at certain times of the year. Interesting historical buildings, particularly churches, in the older towns are also worth photographing.

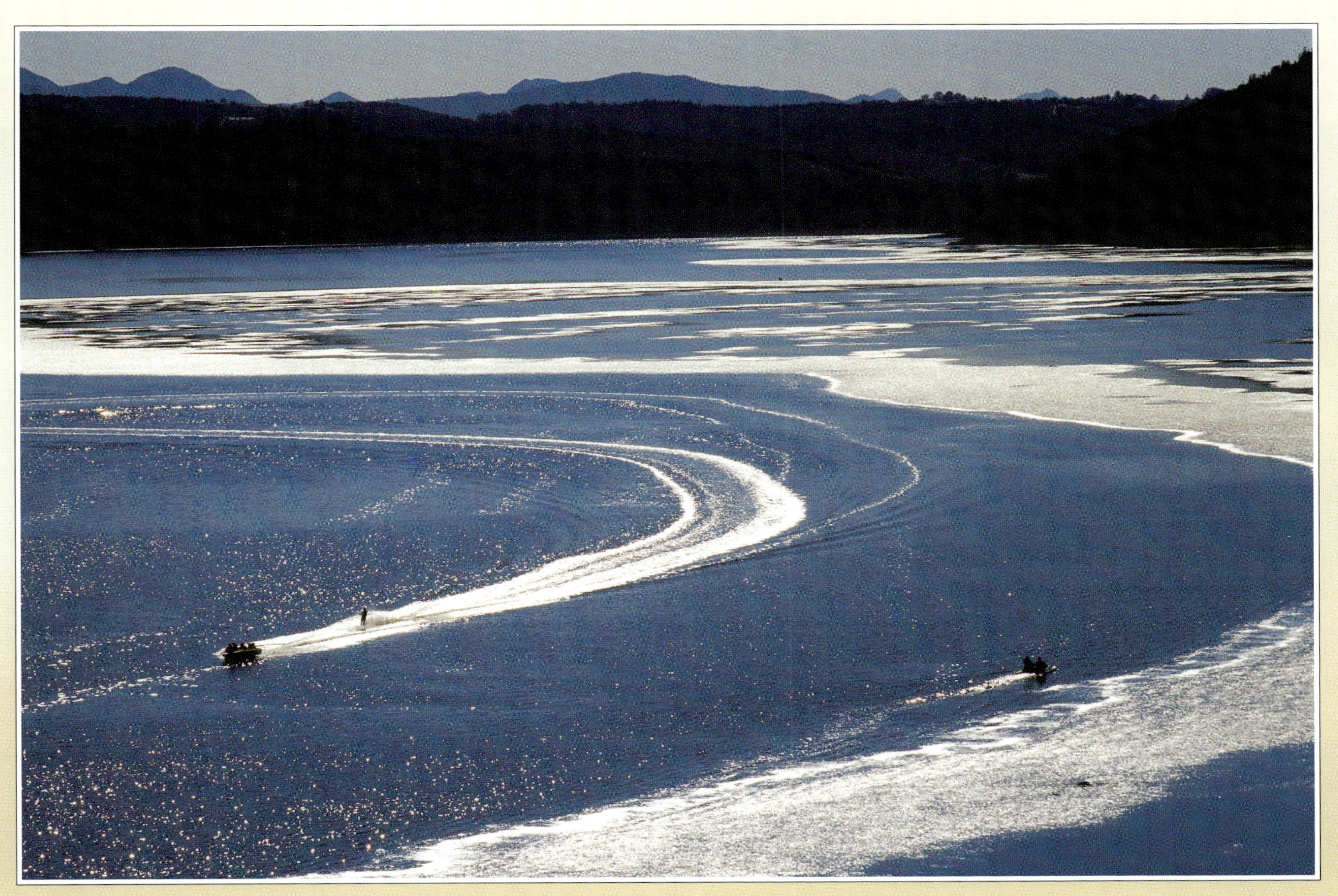

The wake of a lone water skier forms a graceful arc on Swartvlei west of Sedgefield in South Africa's "Lake District".

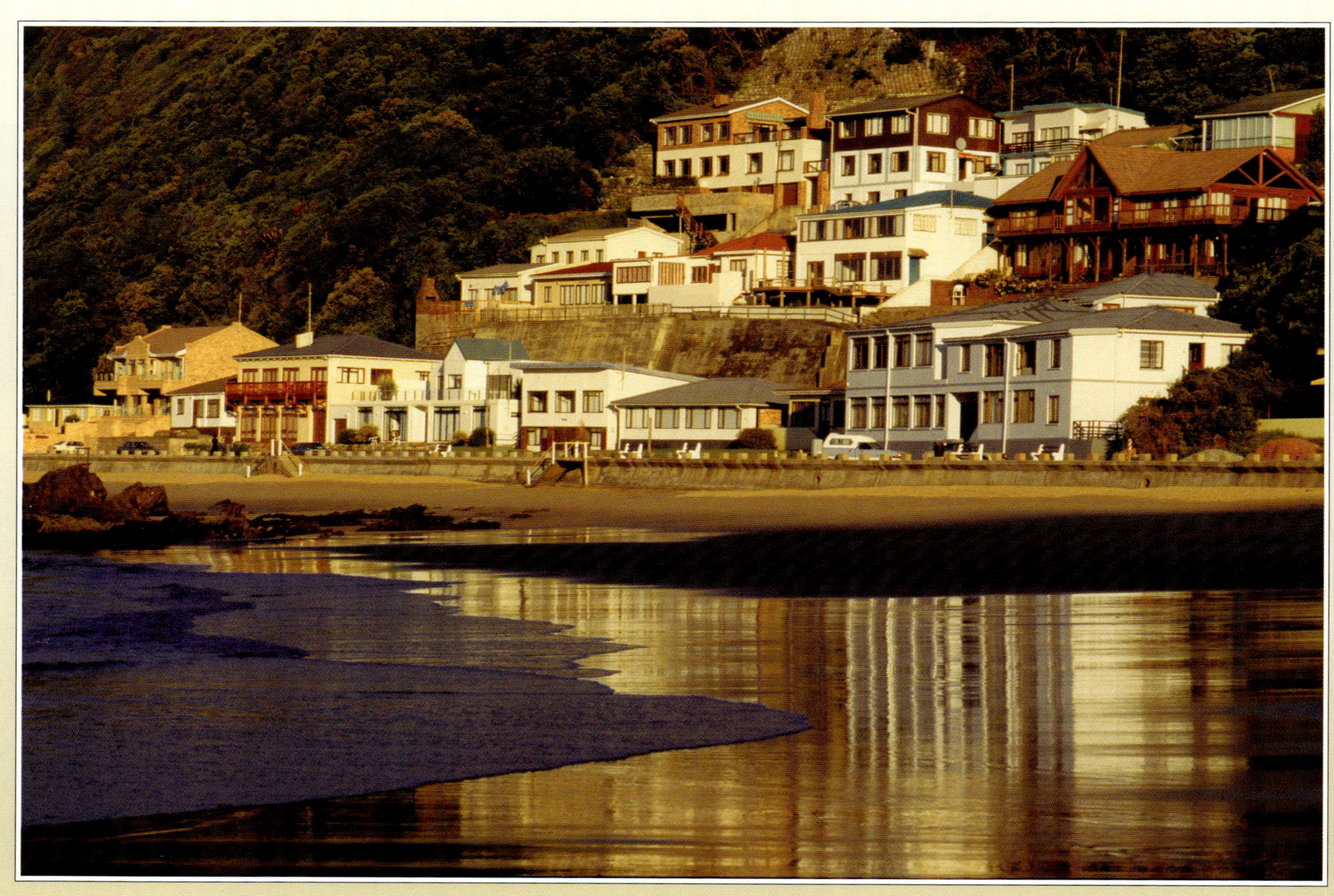

These seaside "cottages" at Herold's Bay (and those added since the photo was taken) command spectacular views of the bay below them.

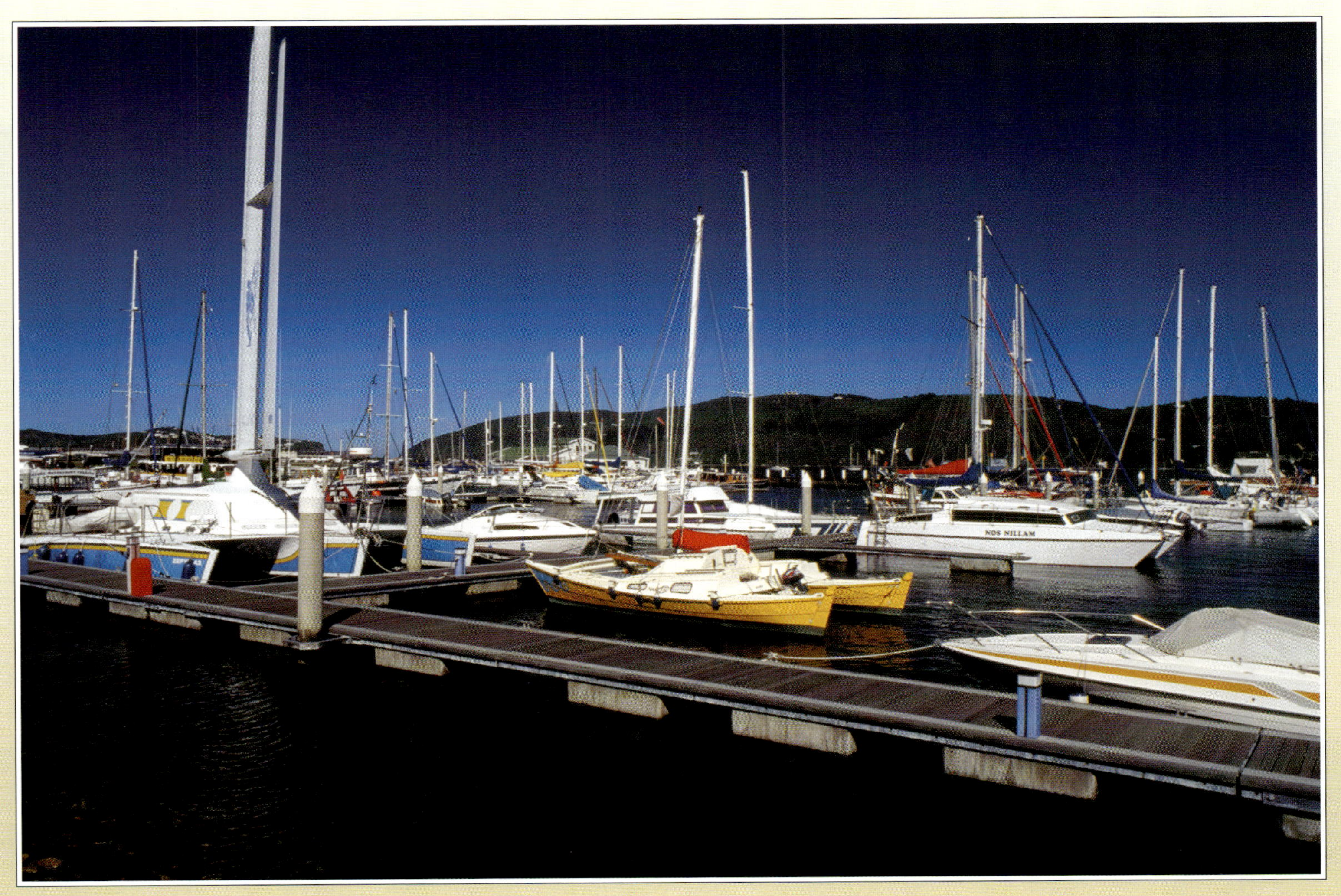

The busy yacht harbour at Knysna contains a wide variety of craft, each reflecting the aspirations (and bank balance) of its owner.

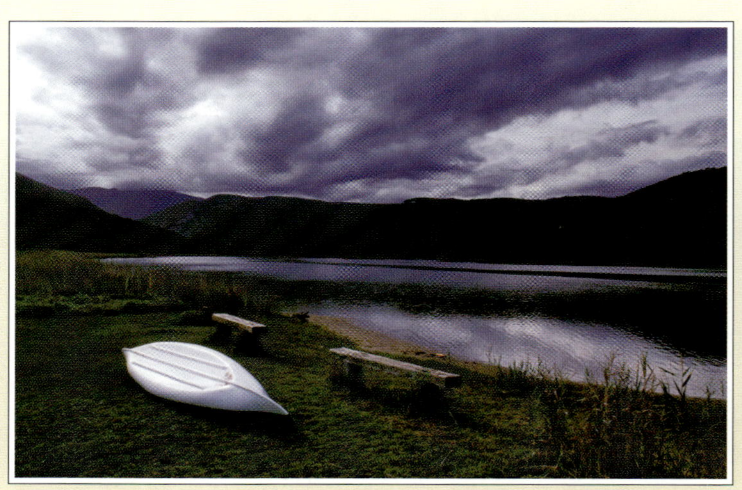
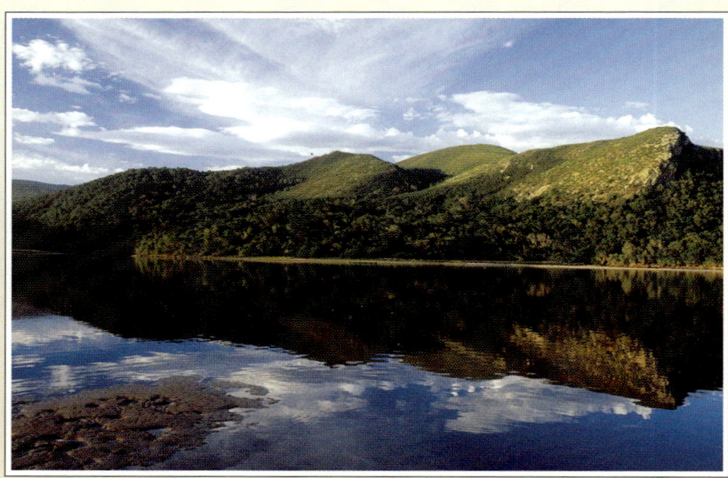
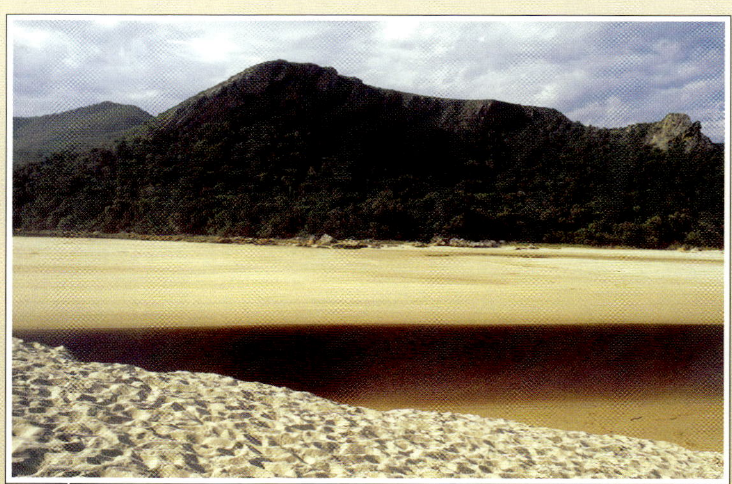
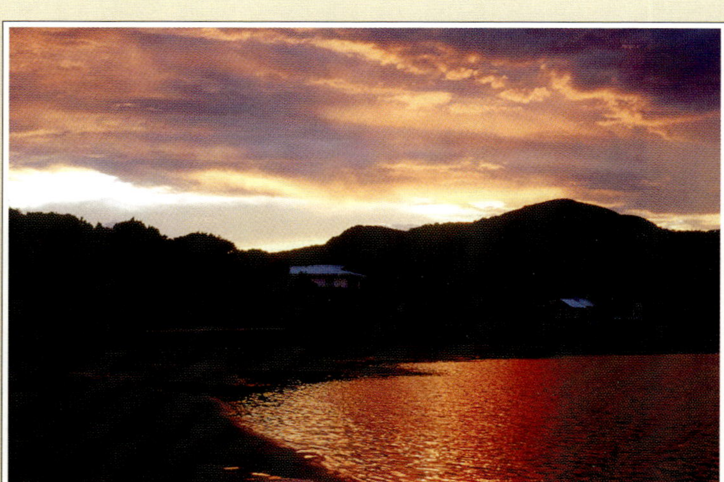

The estuary of the Groot River at Nature's Valley is a quiet holiday destination for those staying in the houses that nestle among the indigenous trees. The time of day and the weather determine the many different moods that this tranquil lagoon and the surrounding hills and forests display.

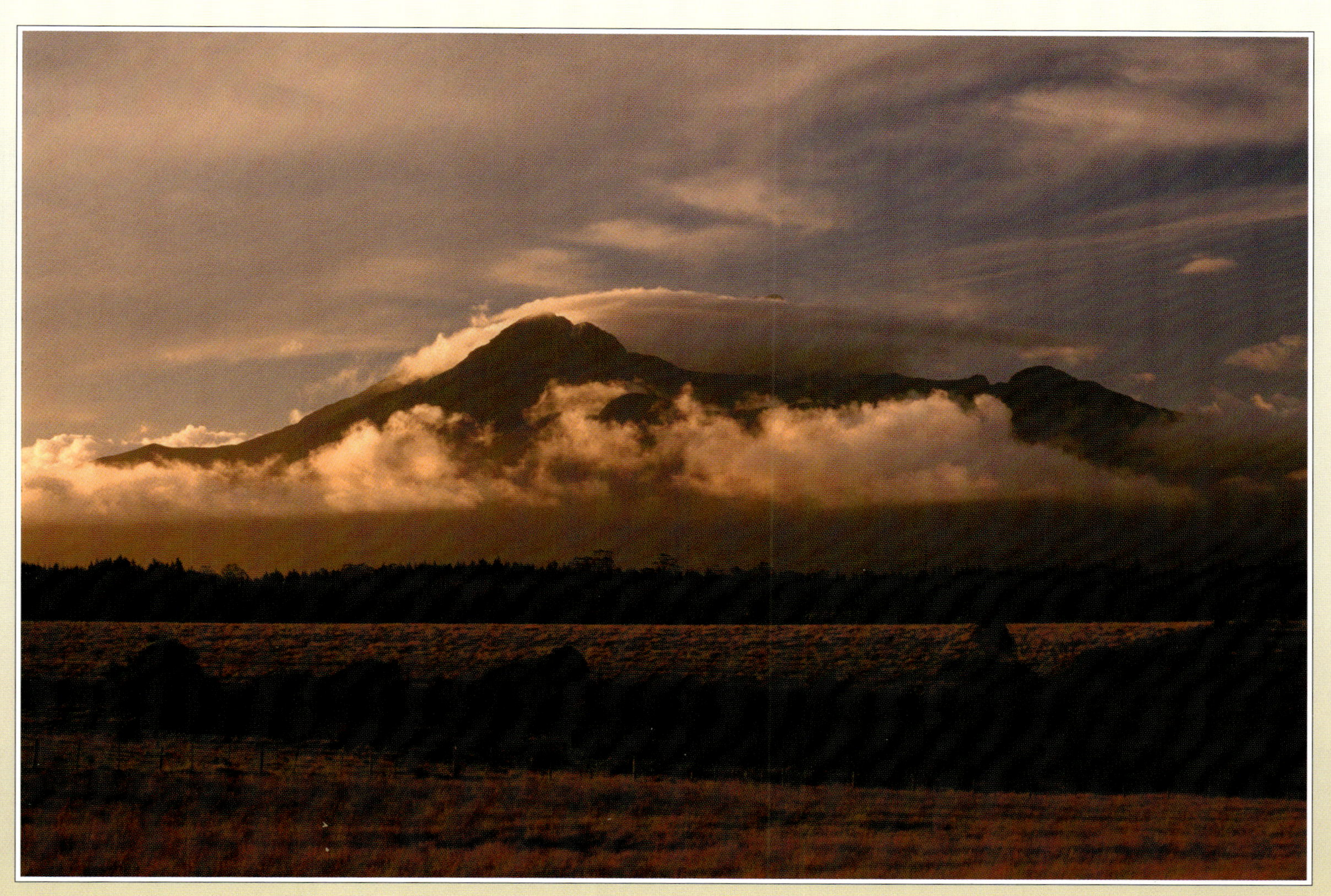

The various levels of cloud surrounding these mountain peaks east of George seem to defy meteorological explanation.

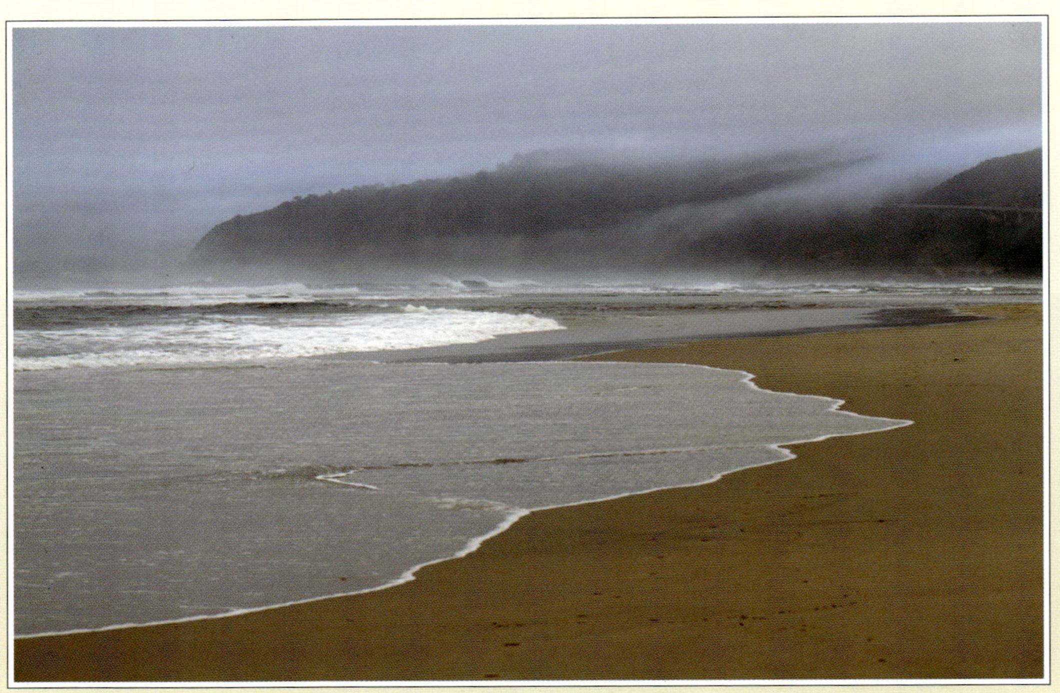

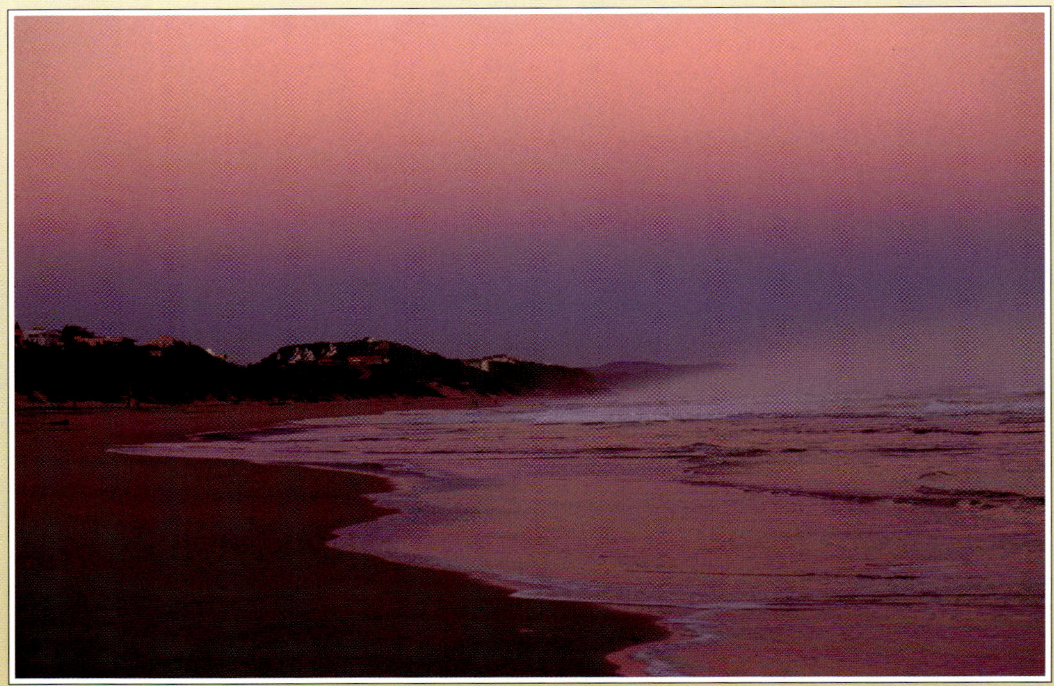

Beautiful sandy beaches are a feature of the Wilderness National Park coast between Wilderness and Sedgefield. The greys of a misty morning contrast with the bright pinks of a colourful sunset that provides a fitting end to an invigorating walk along the Indian Ocean or a peaceful day of seaside relaxation.

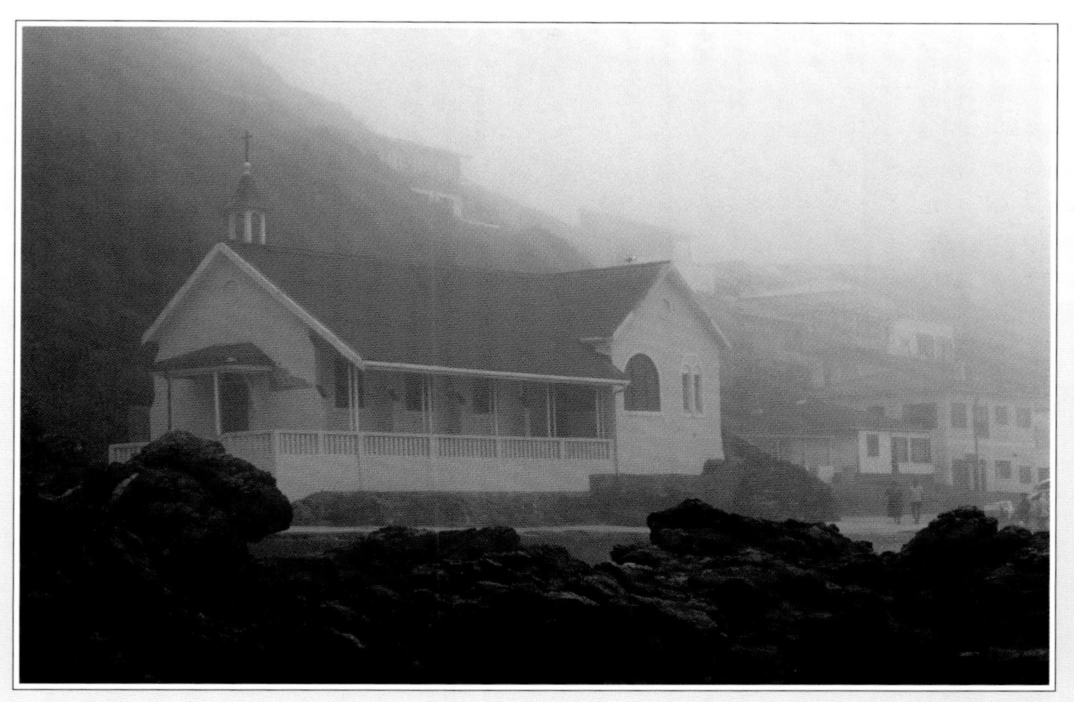

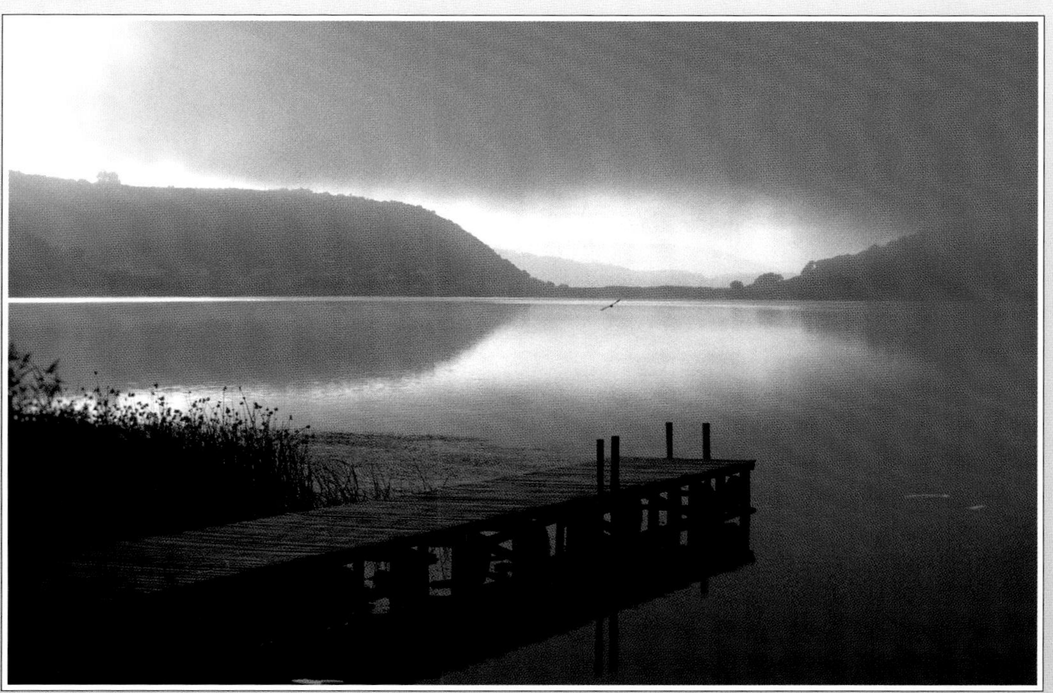

Top:
Built in 1932 on the narrow strip of level ground at the foot of the hill, this small Catholic church in Herold's Bay is still in use.

Bottom:
A peaceful Eilandvlei ("island lake") at the western end of the Wilderness lake system greets the dawn.

DAY 10

Port Elizabeth

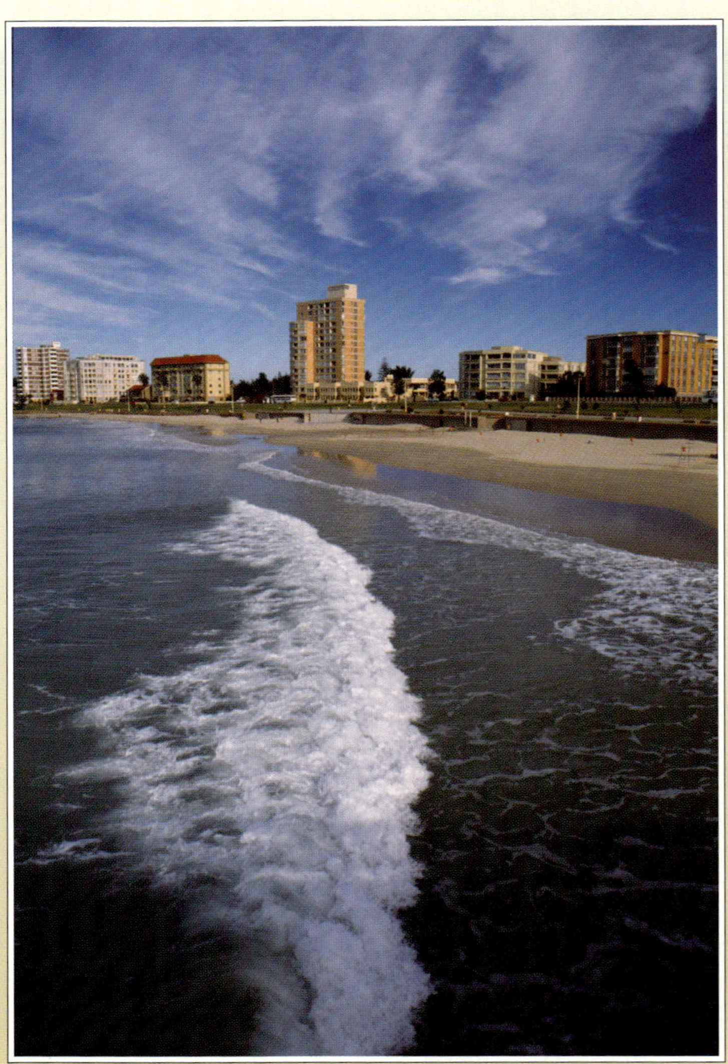

It is obviously not vacation time as holiday apartments look onto a deserted Hoby Beach.

Despite being an essentially industrial city, Port Elizabeth has its fair share of scenic attractions. With a history going back to the early part of the nineteenth century, there are a number of buildings that qualify as national monuments. These include the picturesque row of tenement houses lining the steep Donkin Street, the beautiful library building and various stone churches. The main photographic attractions, however, are along the coastline. In the harbour itself ships and boats of various types and sizes all form suitable subject matter. South of the harbour, beaches such as King's Beach, Humewood Beach and Hoby Beach are separated by outcrops that take the full brunt of the storms that sometimes lash the bay. Shark Rock Pier juts into the sea from one of these outcrops; its seaward end affords a panoramic view of the hotels, holiday apartments and other buildings that make up the city's skyline.

At Cape Recife, with its attractive lighthouse surrounded by sand dunes, the beaches fringing Algoa Bay come to an end and the coastline swings sharply to follow an east-west trend. Here the waves continuously pound long stretches of rocky shore that extend past the small seaside villages of Skoenmakerskop, Sardinia Bay and Seaview as far as the Maitland River mouth, where photographs taken into the setting sun can produce dramatic results. In spring, patches of white daisies and other flowers brighten the grassy slopes above the lichen-covered rocks along the shore-hugging Sacramento hiking trail which extends from Skoenmakerskop to Sardinia Bay.

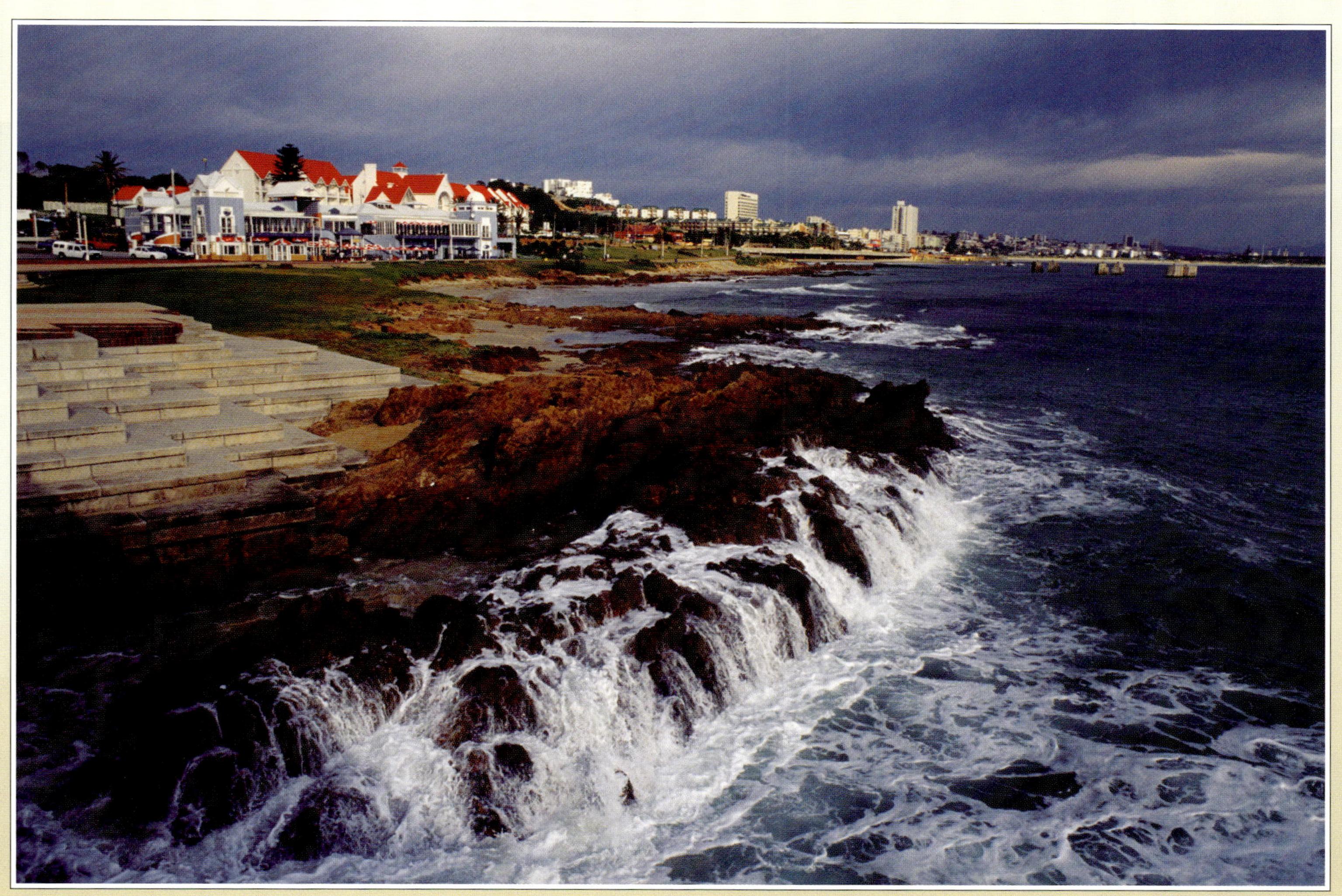

Taking a breather during an early morning walk along the Summerstrand beachfront, one can watch the waves break over the rocks from the safety of Shark Rock pier.

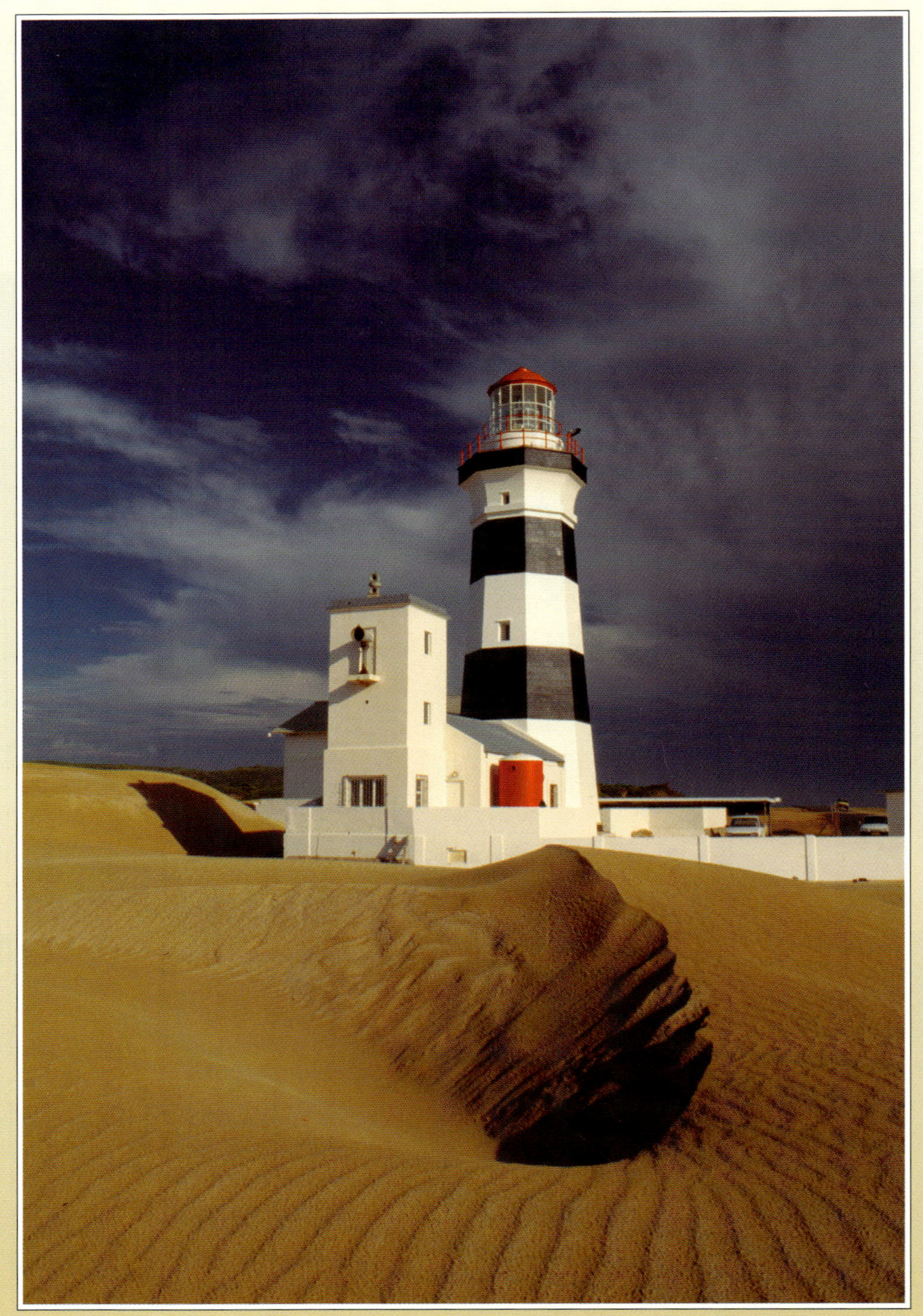

Dark storm clouds gather behind the lighthouse at Cape Recife, south of Port Elizabeth.

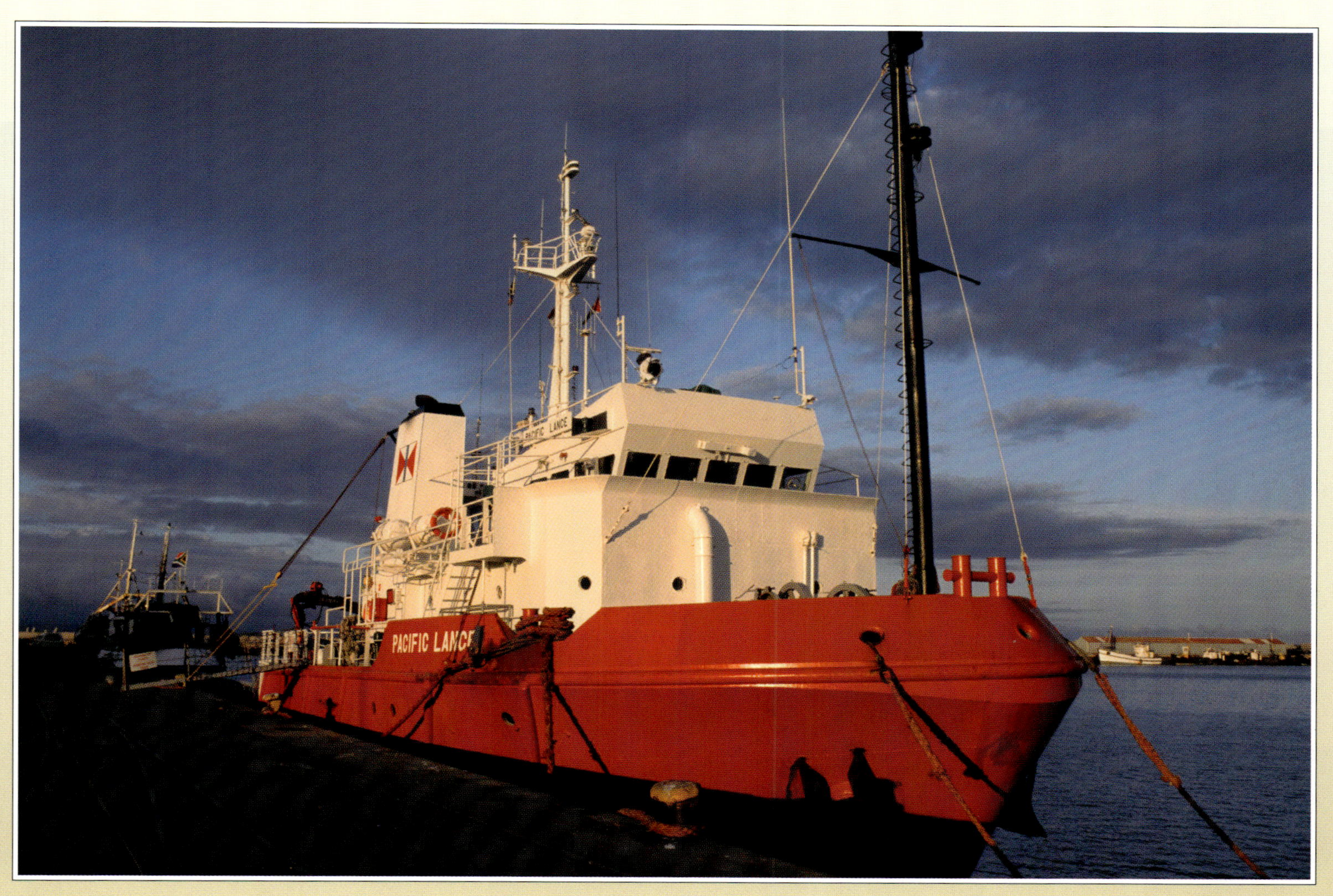

Resplendent in its red and cream colour scheme, the Pacific Lance lies moored in Port Elizabeth's harbour.

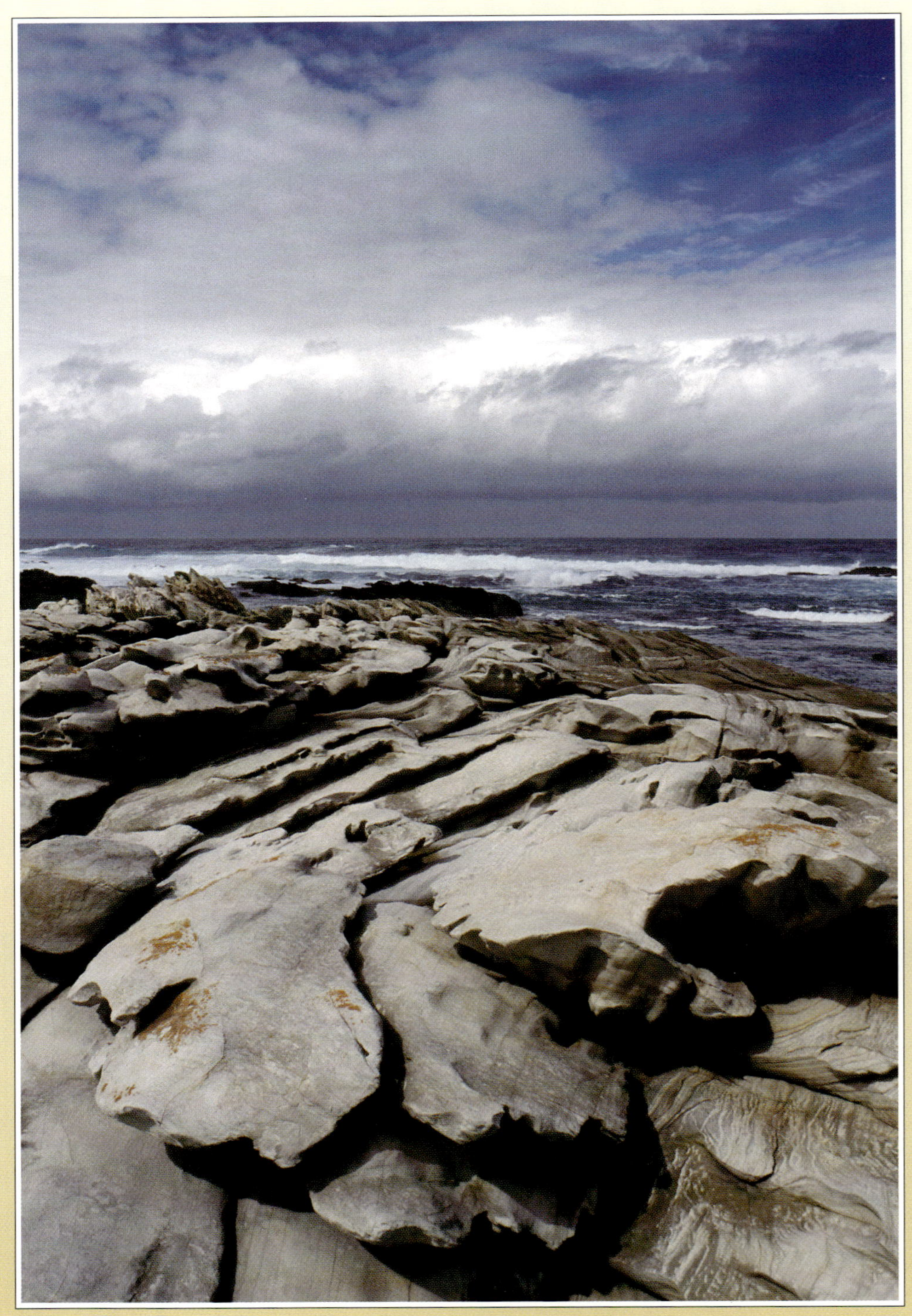

Curved layers of grey rock harmonise with the approaching clouds along the coast near Skoenmakerskop west of Port Elizabeth.

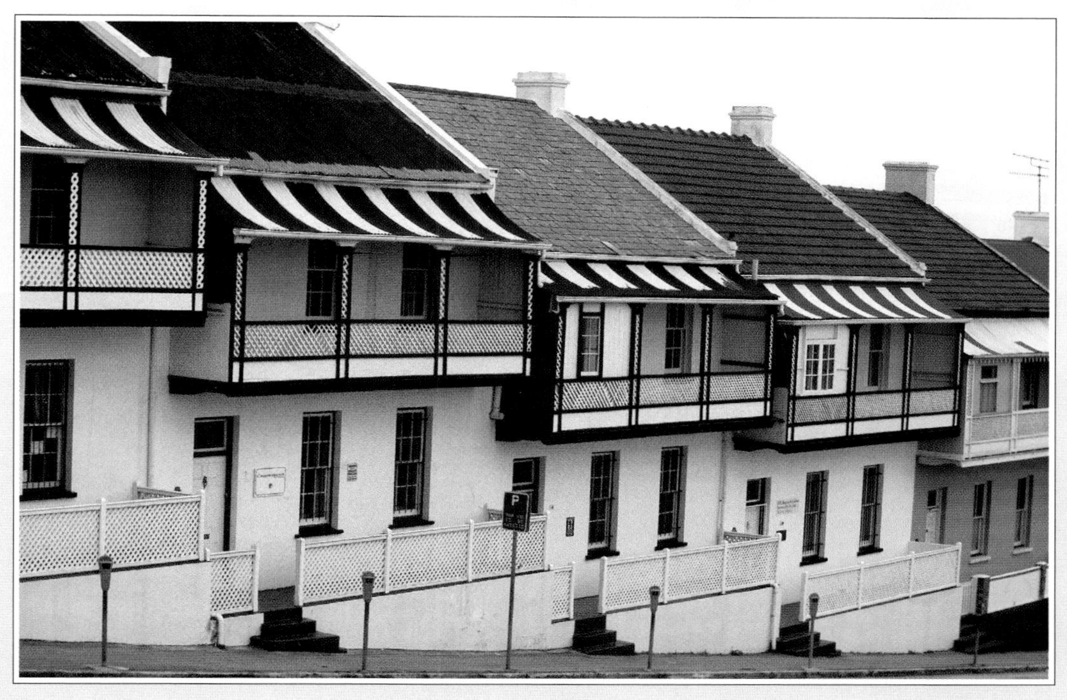

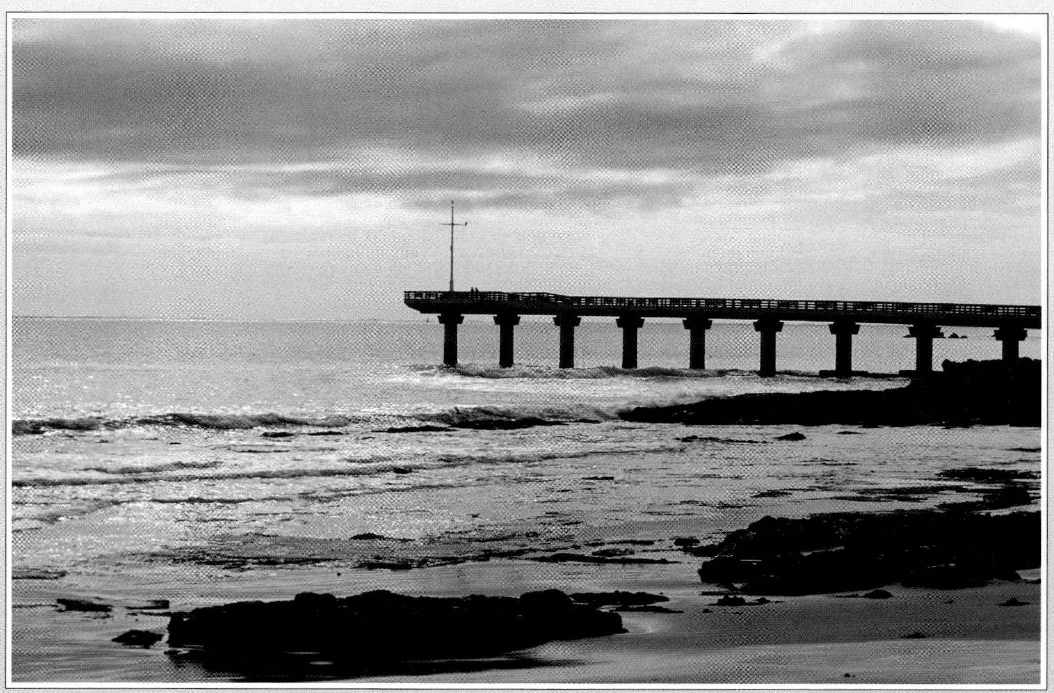

Top:
A row of restored nineteenth century houses in Donkin Street overlooks the harbour and the wide expanse of Algoa Bay.

Bottom:
Shark Rock pier is silhouetted against a lightly overcast morning sky in this monochrome scene.

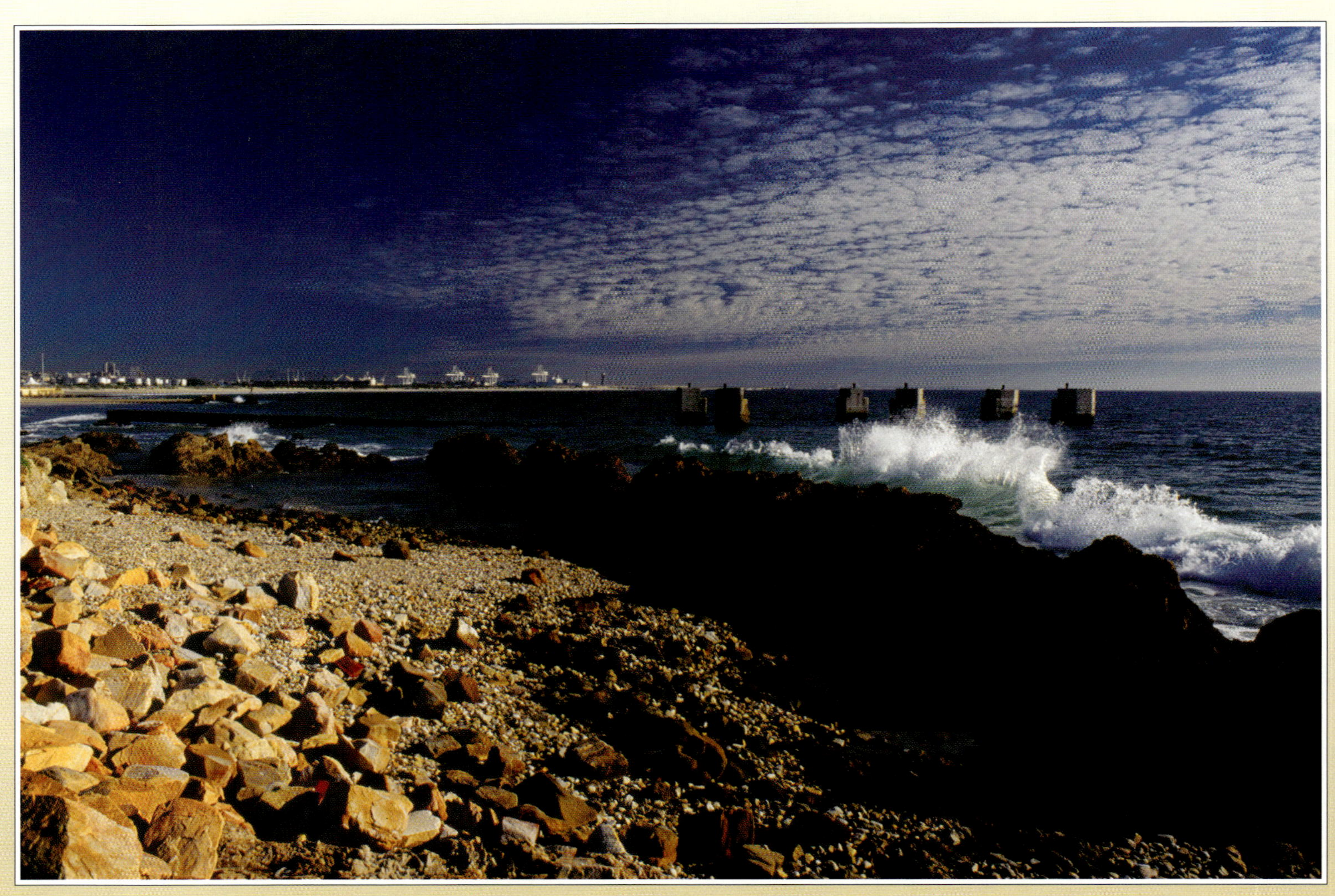

A breaking wave turns translucent for a brief moment behind a dark rock barrier close to Humewood Beach, with the harbour cranes gracing the horizon.

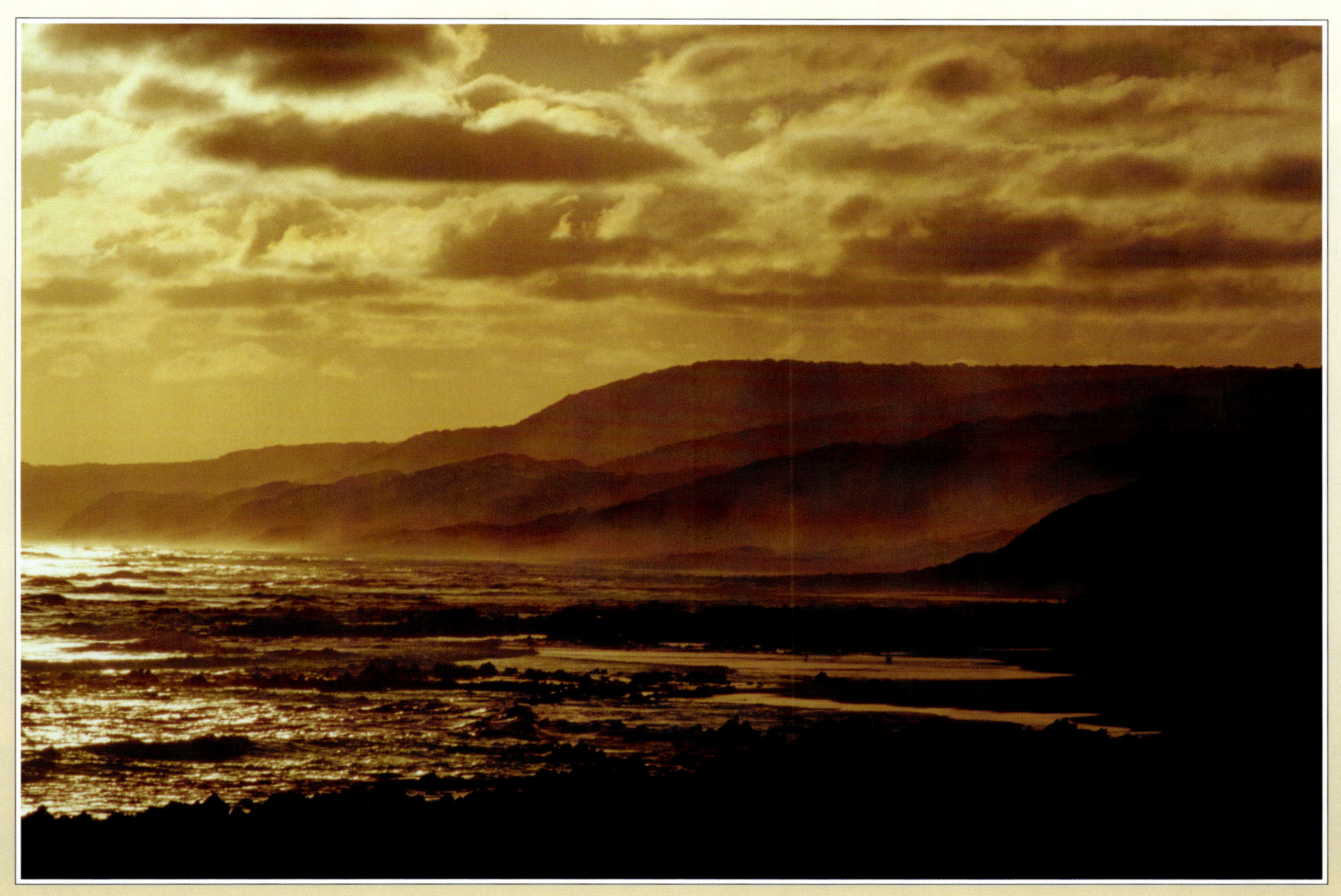

A low sun casts an orange spell over sky, land and sea in the vicinity of the Maitland River mouth, west of Port Elizabeth.

DAY 11

East London

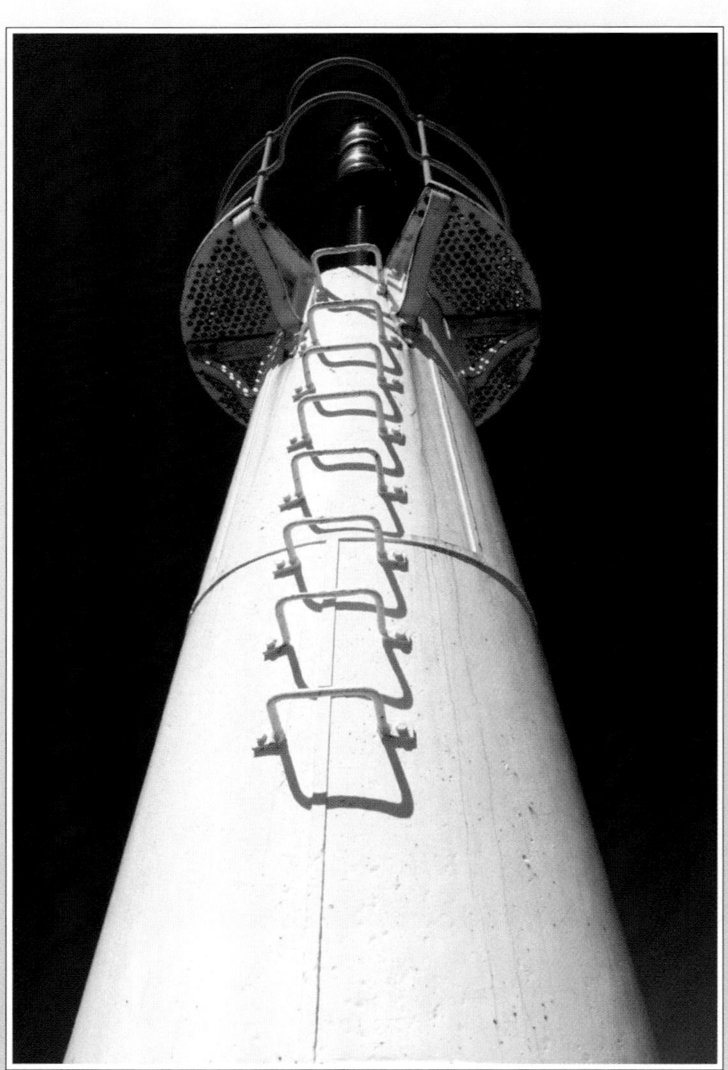

Unauthorised access to the top of the Orient Pier lighthouse at the entrance to East London's harbour is clearly discouraged!

East London straddles the Buffalo River, and the deep-water harbour built at its mouth is the city's main asset and the original reason for its establishment. Both young and old can watch the big and not-so-big vessels that enter and leave the harbour from the easily accessible pier that separates it from the adjacent Orient Beach. The city's ever-popular beaches attract many visitors to its hotels, holiday flats and caravan parks. East London is in fact located in the middle of a string of holiday resorts, stretching from Hamburg in the southwest to Cintsa in the northeast, which have capitalised on the many safe, sandy beaches that abound along this stretch of coast. Fishing from the rocky areas that separate these beaches is a favourite pastime for both local residents and visitors. The estuaries of many of the smaller rivers in the area, such as the Nahoon, Igoda and Gqunube, are navigable for some distance inland and are ideal for various boating activities.

For the photographer, it is the sea in its many moods, the beaches, the sand dunes, the rock pools, the quiet river estuaries and the harbour that provide the main scenic attractions. Sand ripples caused by wind or waves, interesting reflections in tidal pools or on wet sand, and close-up details of various kinds are all challenges to creativity. The rich colours of a magnificent sunrise or sunset will always be an added bonus, but one needs to plan ahead to be in the right place at the right time. And if a change from the sea is needed, a visit to one of East London's parks or the Queen's Park Zoo as well as East London's museum (of Coelacanth fame) are alternative possibilities.

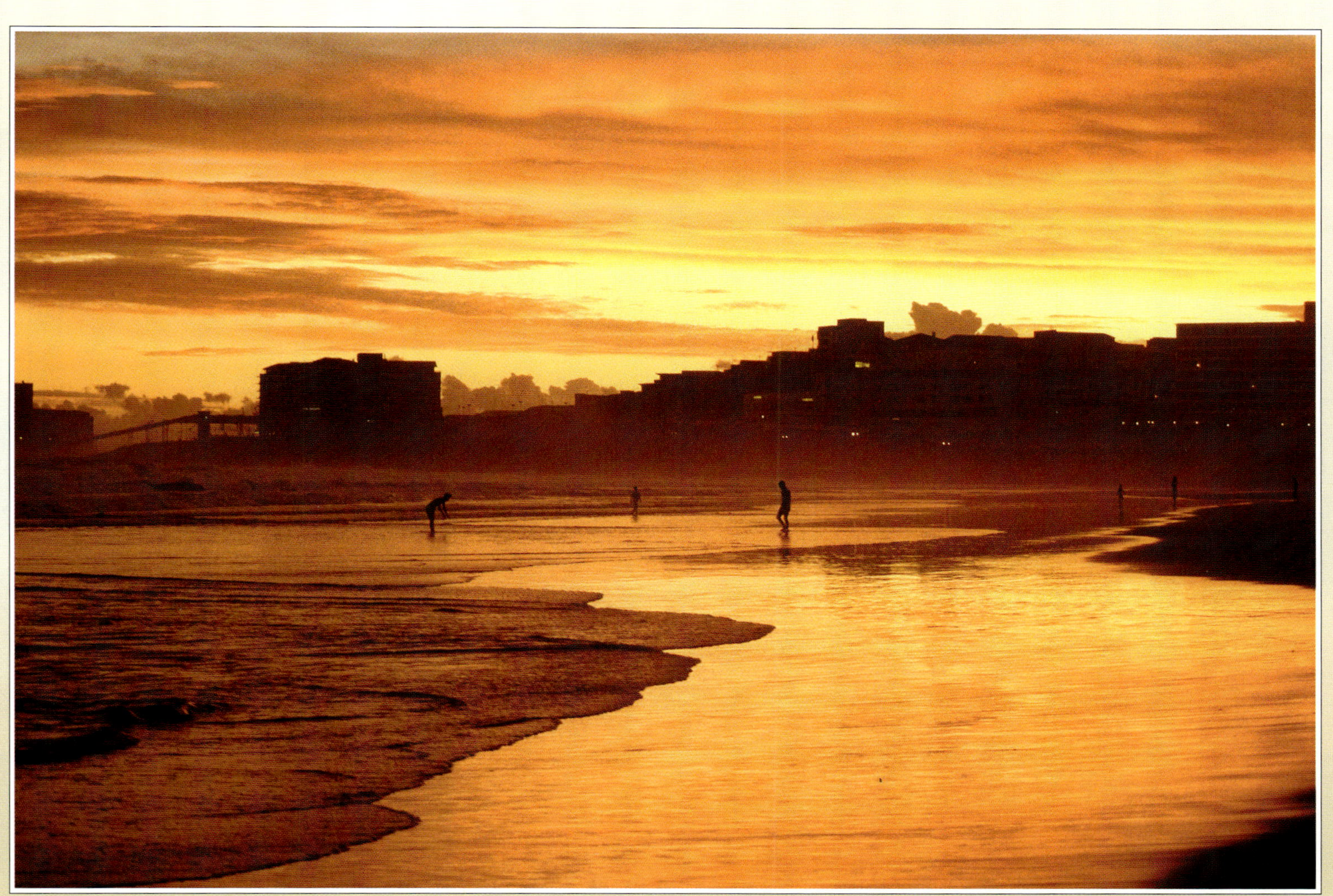

A dramatic sunset is mirrored in the wet sand along East London's Eastern Beach.

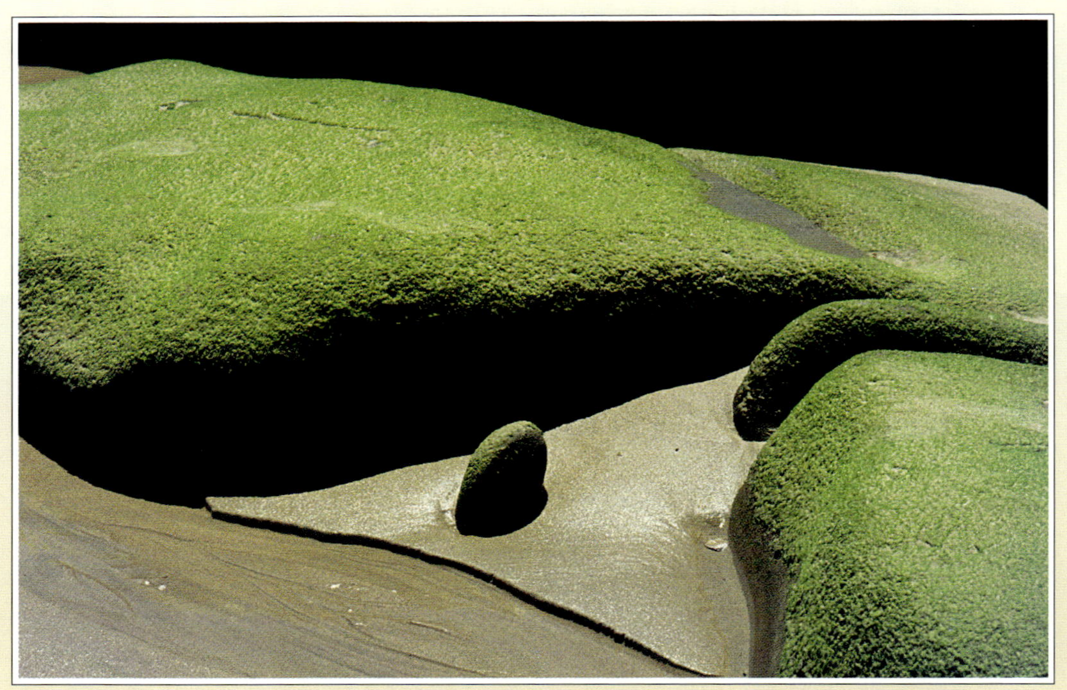

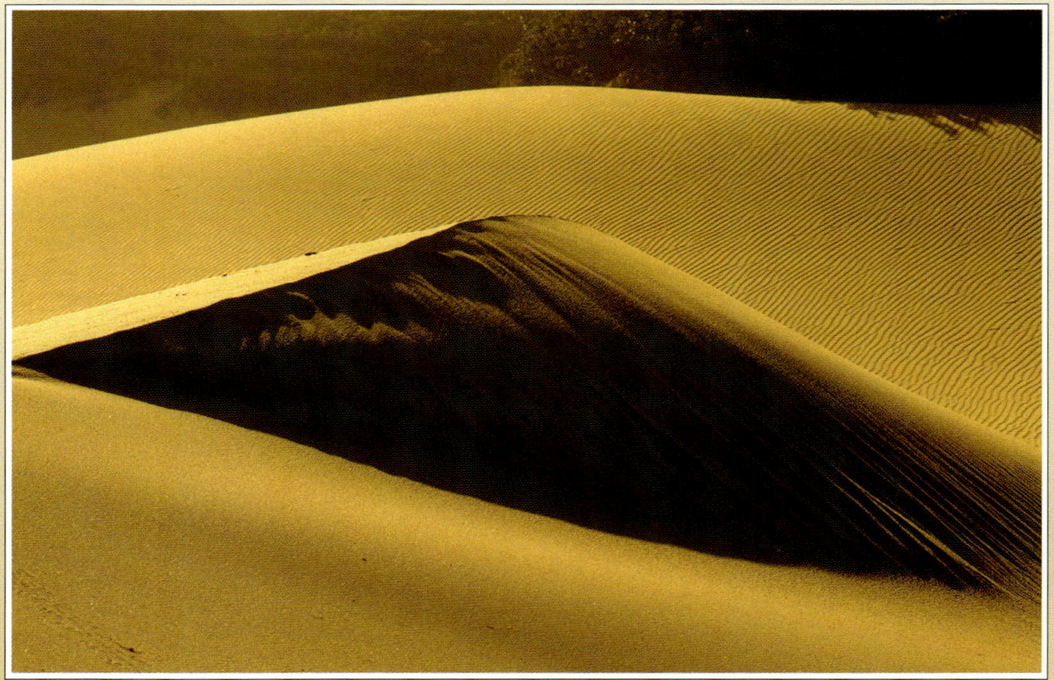

Top:
These green, seaweed-covered rocks could be mistaken for an aerial view of grassy hills flanking a sandy riverbed.

Bottom:
Although uncommon in the East London area, bare sand dunes have interesting shapes that are always worth exploring.

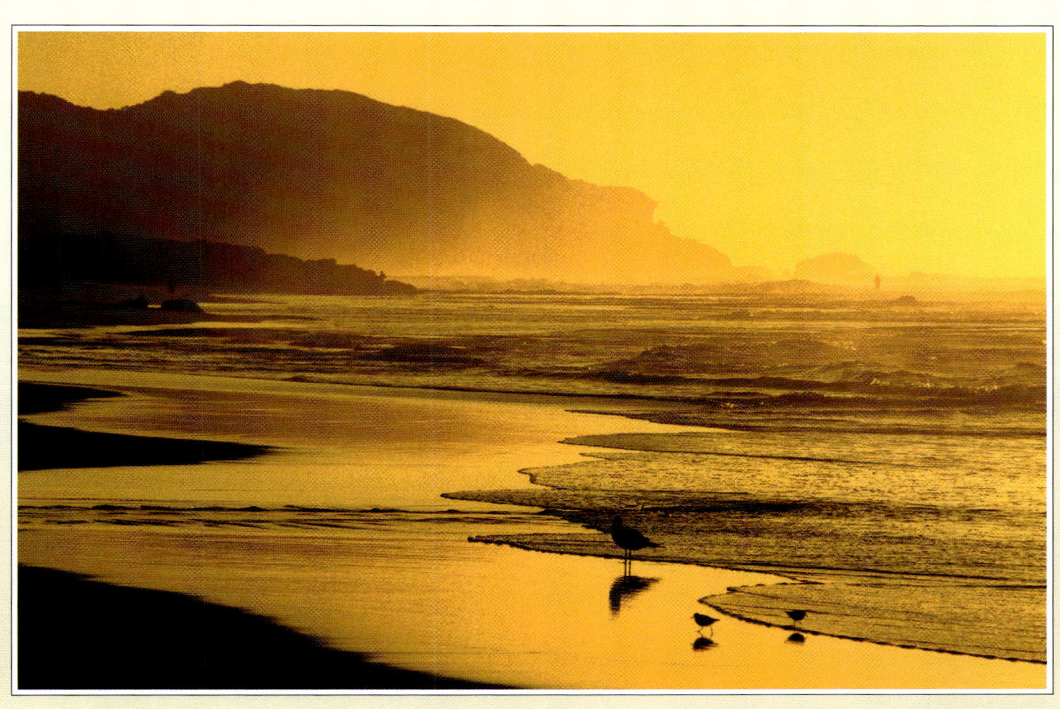

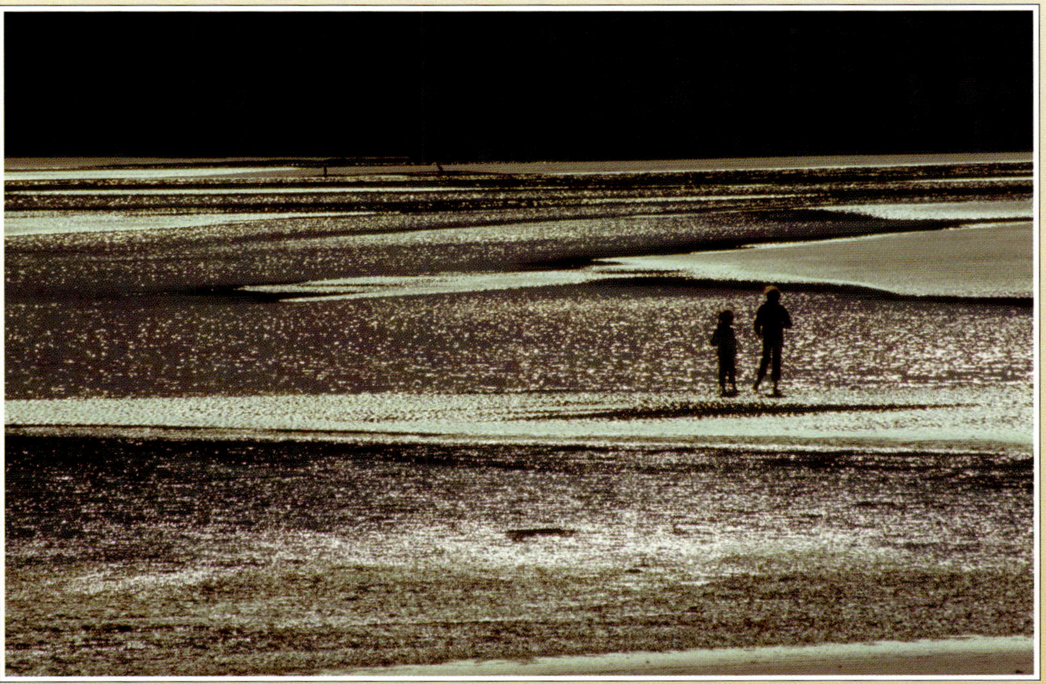

Top:
Late afternoon and early morning are undoubtedly the best times for strolling along the beach with a camera.

Bottom:
Stretches of shimmering water separate wet sand bars exposed at low tide in the Nahoon River estuary.

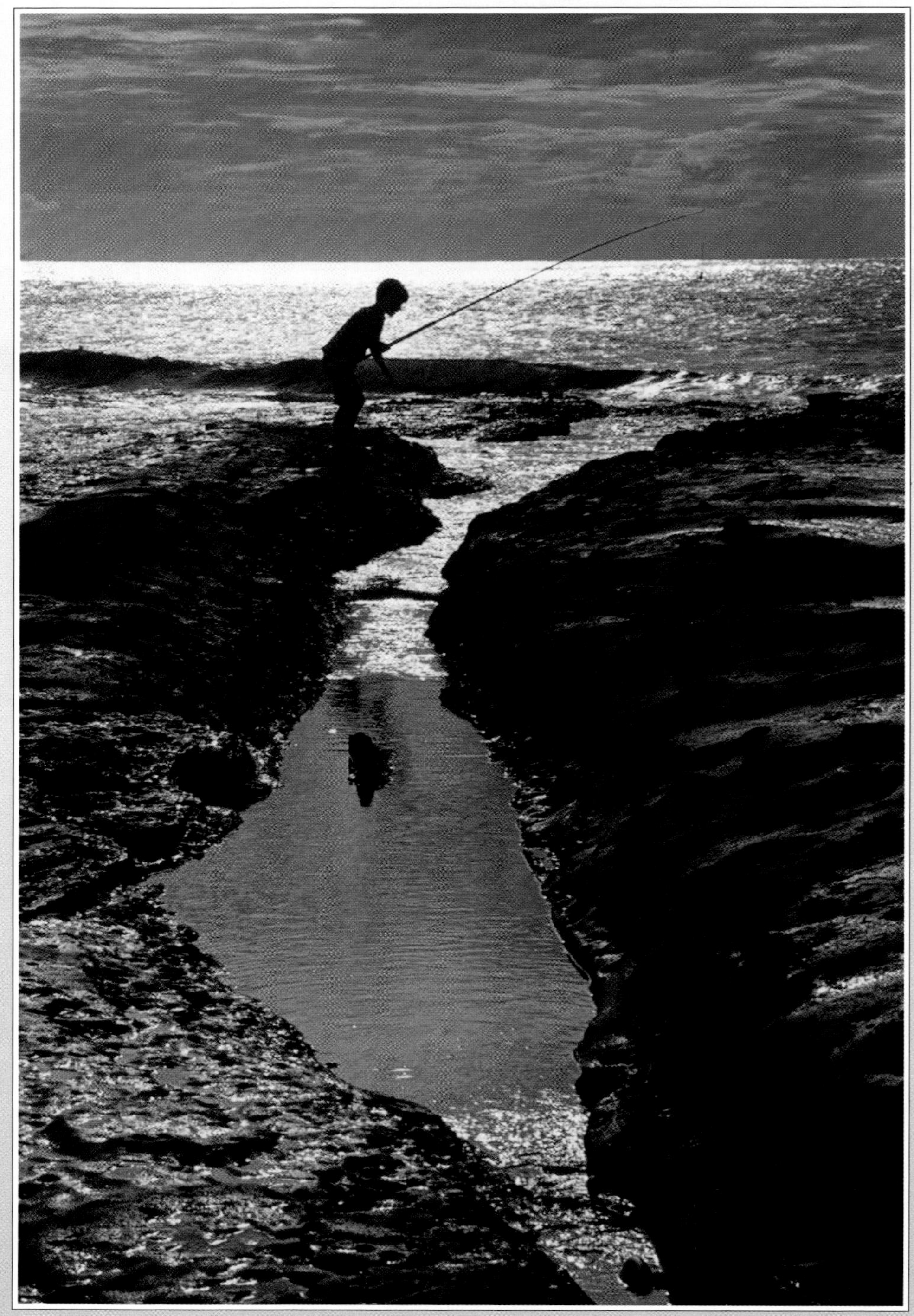

A young fisherman looks for a suitable spot from which to try his luck along the rocks at Cintsa, northeast of East London.

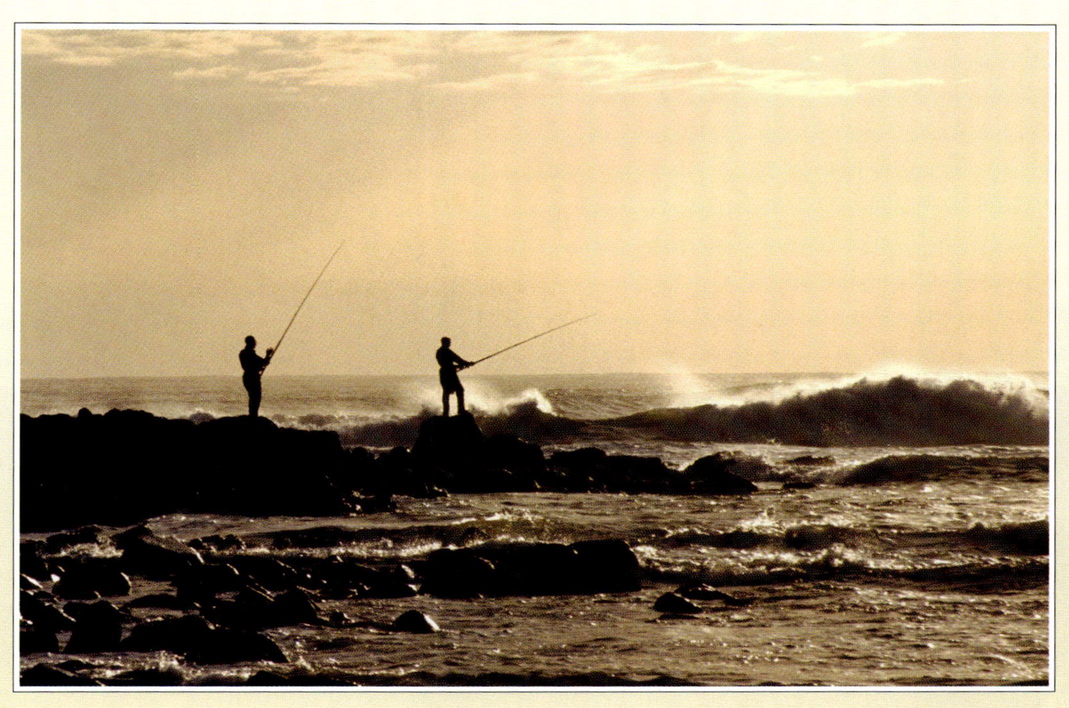

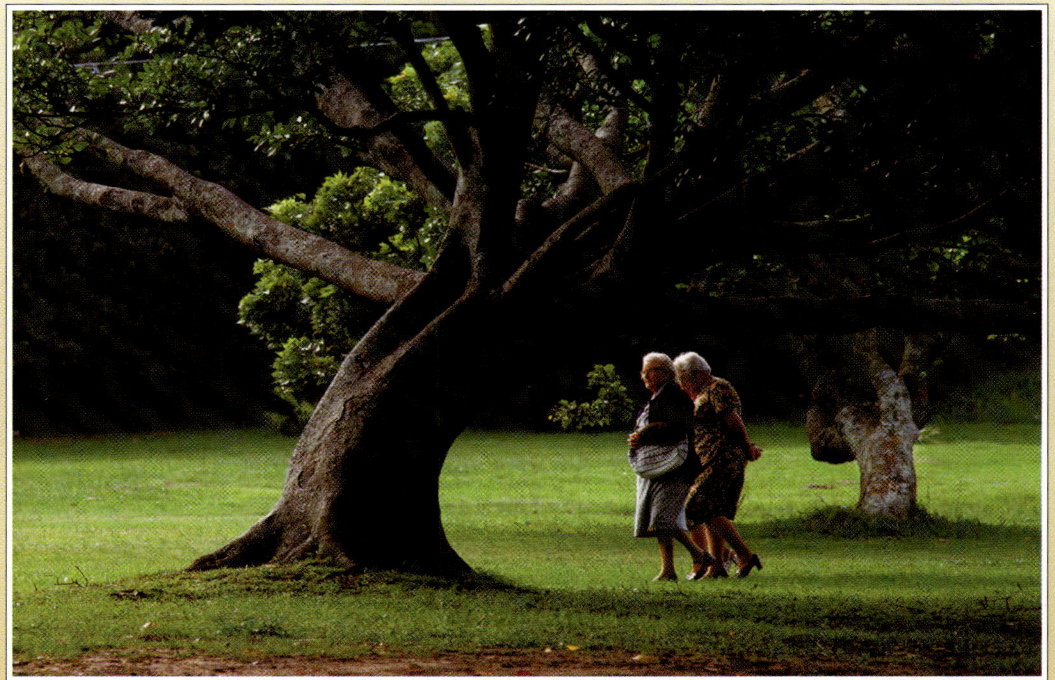

Top:
Two anglers on a wave-swept ledge south of East London are silhouetted against the western sky.

Bottom:
Two (or is it three?) senior citizens take a leisurely stroll through one of East London's many parks.

DAY 12

Hogsback

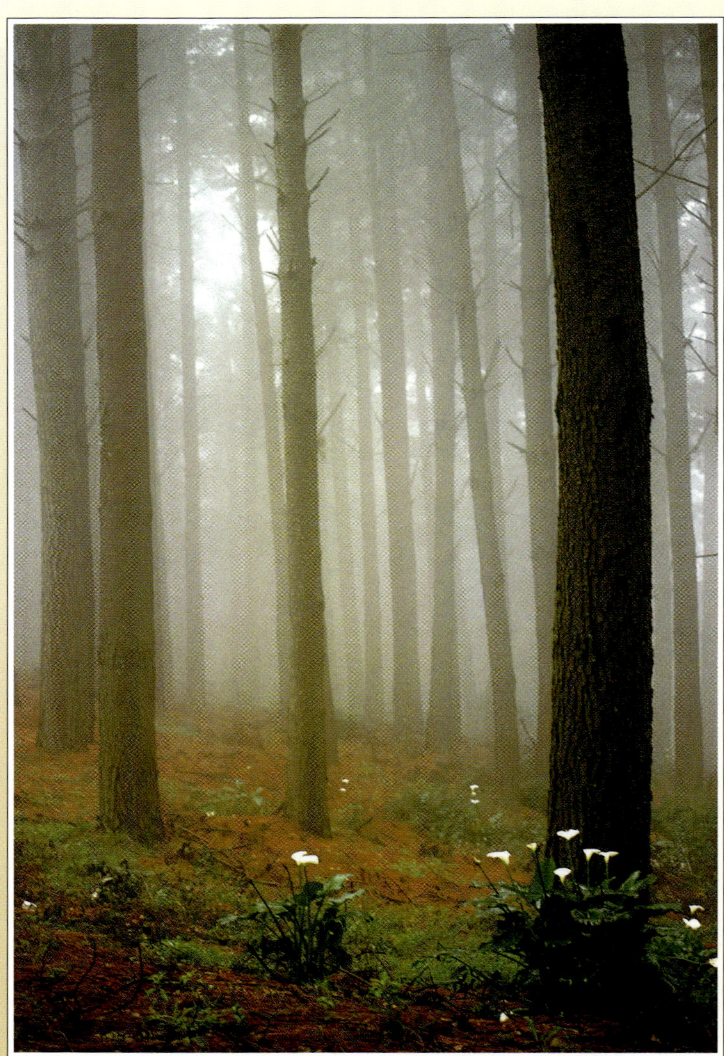

A group of arum lilies nestles at the base of a tall pine tree in a Hogsback plantation.

Nestling in the Amatola Mountains to the north of Alice, the picturesque village of Hogsback has been a long-time favourite with those wanting a total escape from the stress and strain of city life. It offers numerous walks through indigenous forests and past waterfalls with romantic names like "The Thirty-nine Steps", "Bridal Veil Falls" and "Madonna and Child". Scenic drives wind through pine and eucalyptus plantations, while the tough Amatola hiking trail has Hogsback as its western terminus. The scattered houses comprise mainly holiday homes and the permanent residences of retired folk; two country hotels, a few shops and the quaint little stone-and-thatch church of St. Patrick-on-the-Hill are strung out along the main road through the village.

The moss-covered rocks and tree trunks, the lush ferns carpeting the ground under the tree canopy and the mushrooms thriving on the forest floor reflect the fact that Hogsback enjoys more than its fair share of rainy and misty weather. The climate suits the azaleas, rhododendrons and other flowering trees and shrubs which put on a glorious display every spring. In winter snowfalls are not uncommon and cosy log fires are an indispensable feature of village life in the cold winter months. The mountains, the trees, the waterfalls, the lush undergrowth, the spring flowers and the autumn colours between them guarantee that there will be no lack of suitable subject matter for the photographer. To the north of Hogsback the road leads through an attractive farming landscape with neat fields and stands of poplars and willows that form bright yellow patches along the river courses in autumn.

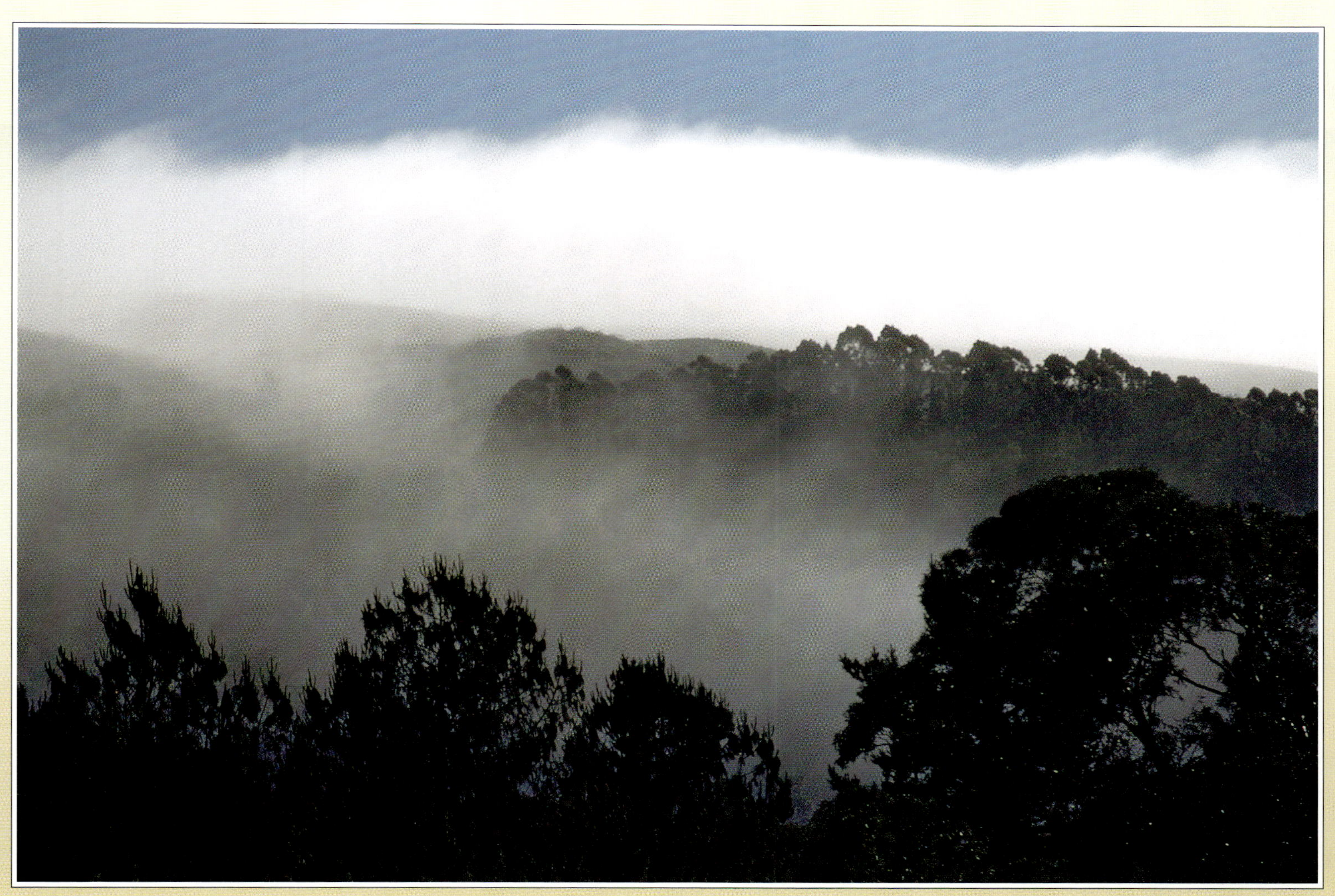

Forest-covered hills start emerging as the early morning mist yields to the increasingly warm rays of the sun.

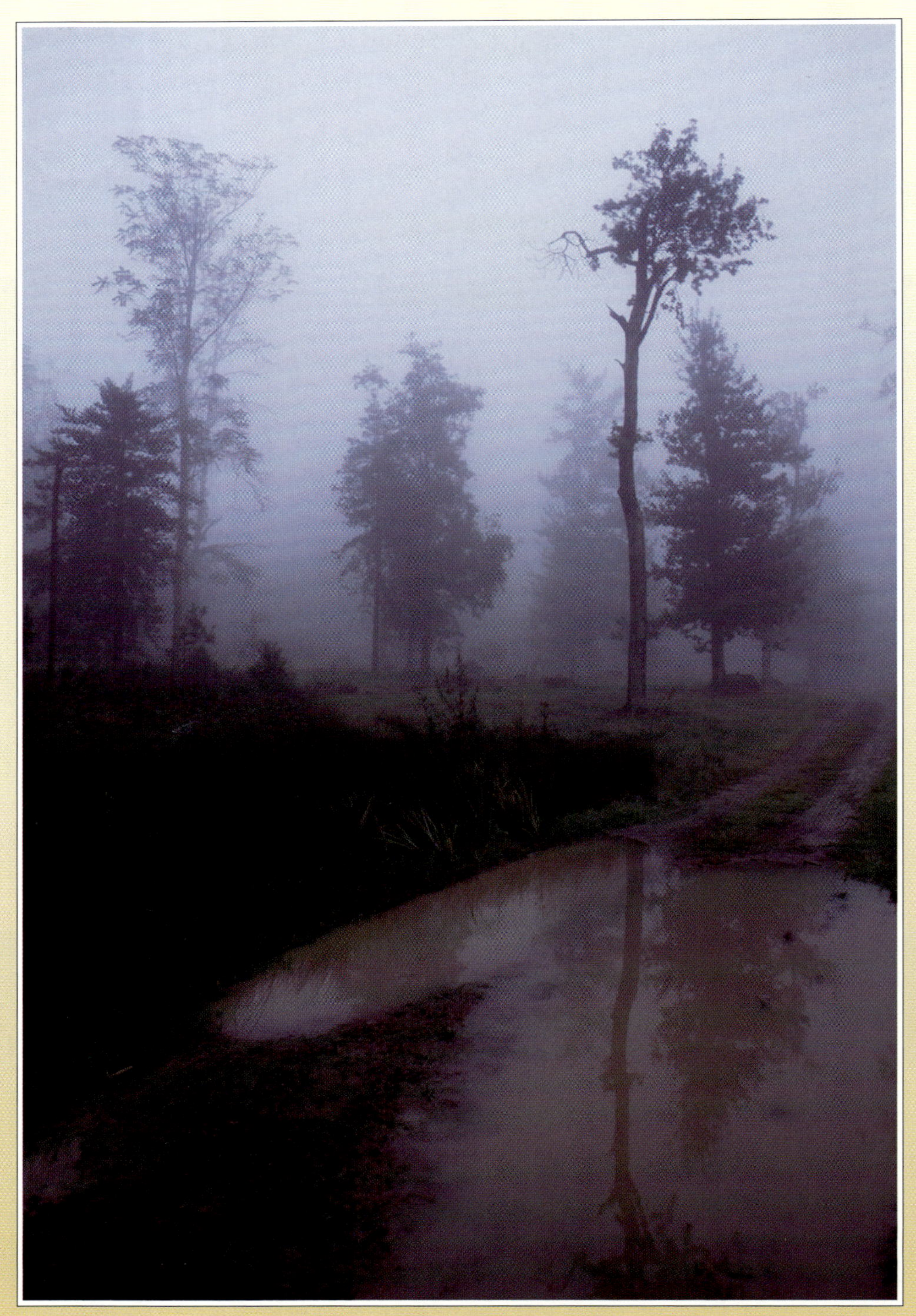

A water-logged road with trees disappearing into the rain and mist is a common Hogsback sight.

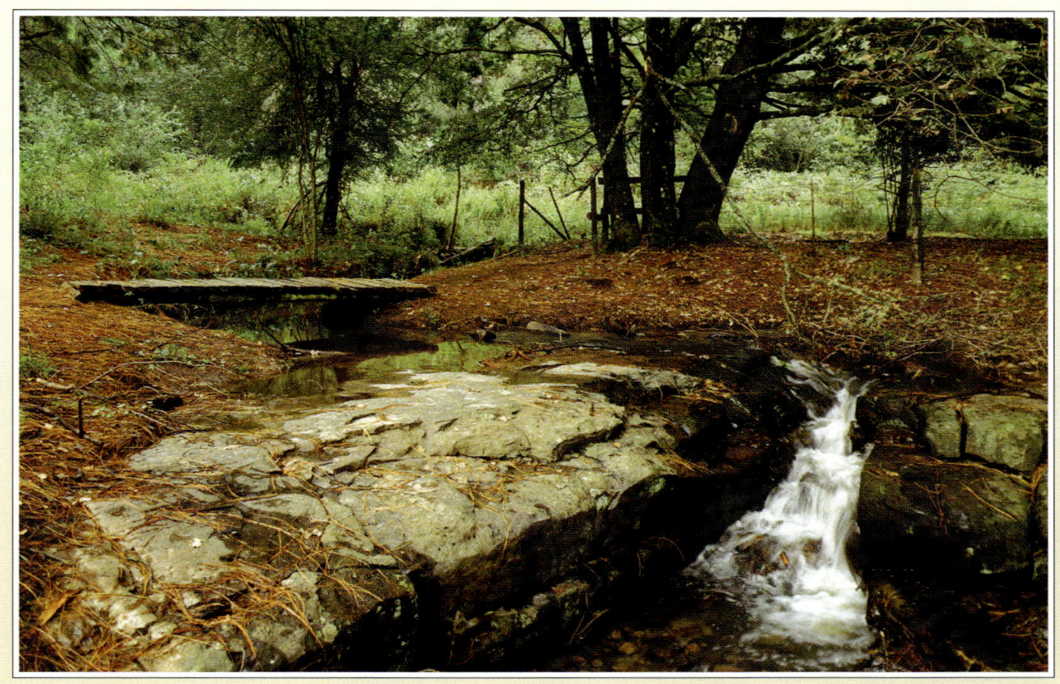

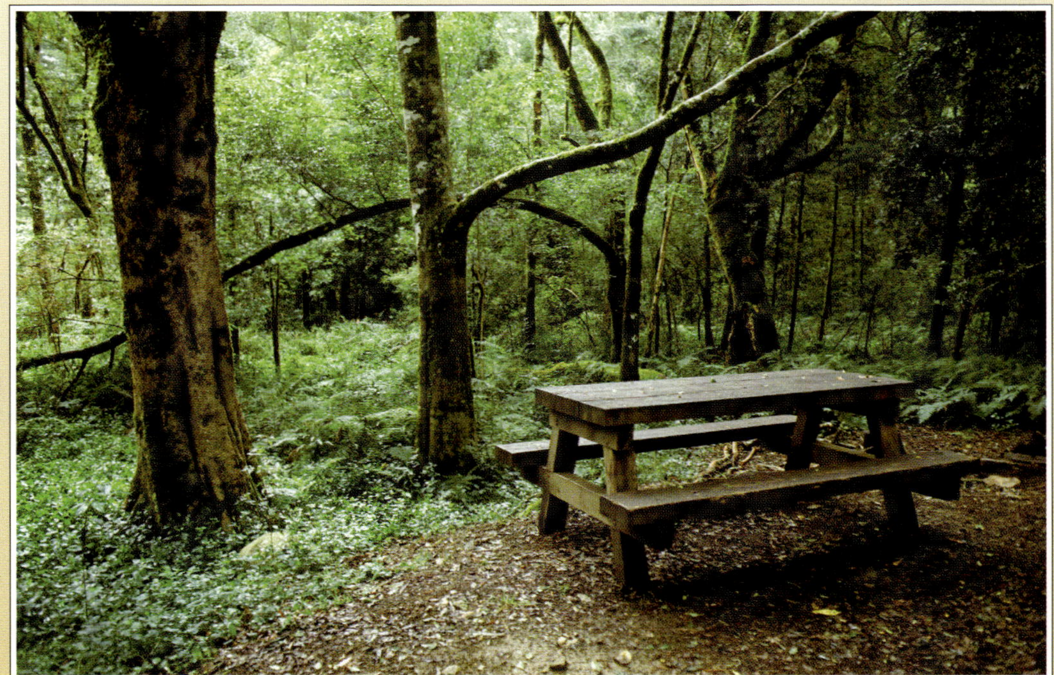

Hogsback's many overcast, cool, damp days seem to emphasise the greens of the forests and provide ideal conditions for an exhilarating hike. On the other hand, just to stand around listening to water gently dripping from the saturated canopy overhead is also a therapeutic experience.

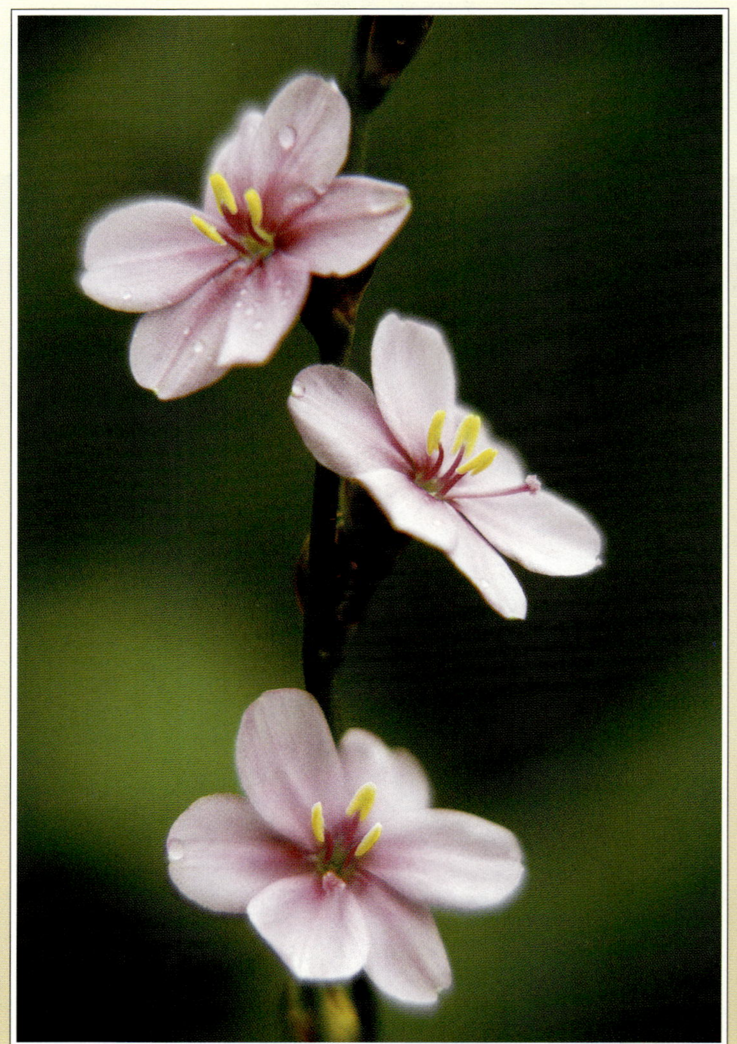
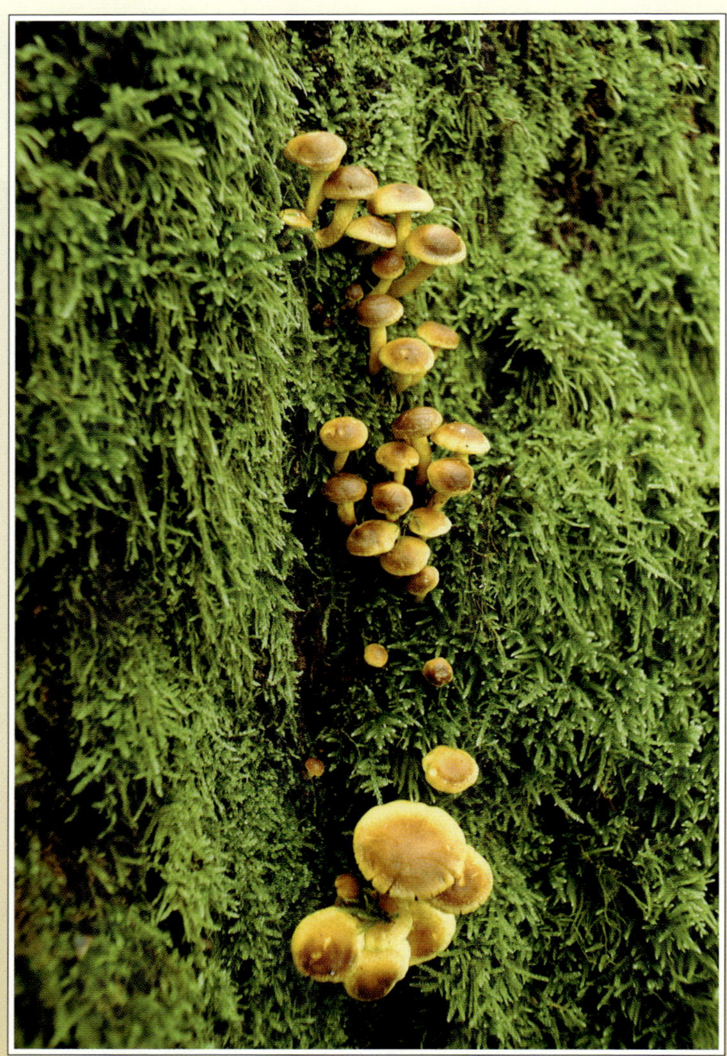

The area's obvious attractions, such as its forests, mountains and waterfalls, or the azaleas and rhododendrons in spring, should not blind one to the beauty that exists everywhere on a smaller scale. A simple flower spike or bright orange fungi are the kind of things the hasty visitor can easily overlook.

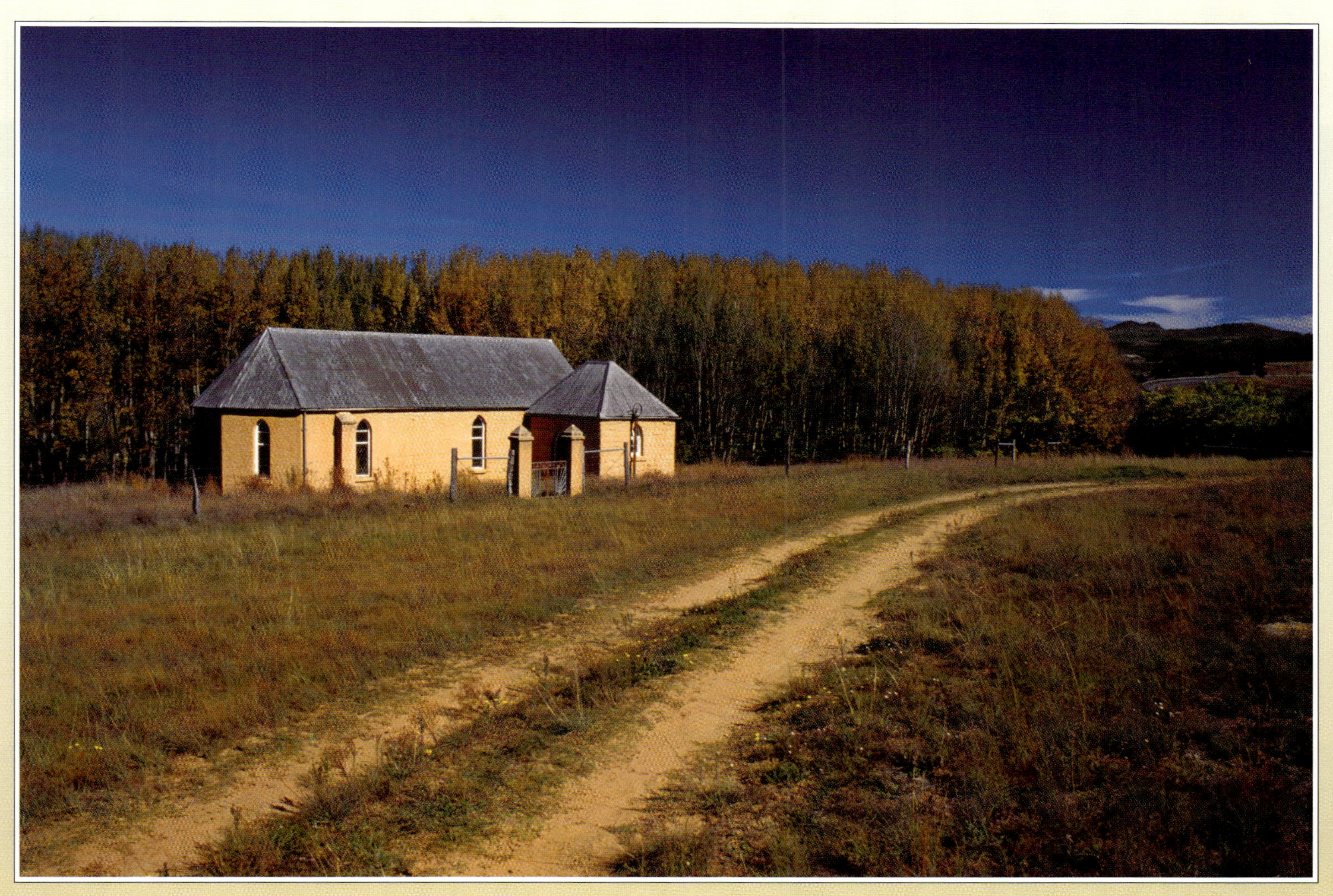

This small church—and the graveyard behind it—stands all alone in the bare veld between Hogsback and Cathcart.

DAY 13

Cape Drakensberg

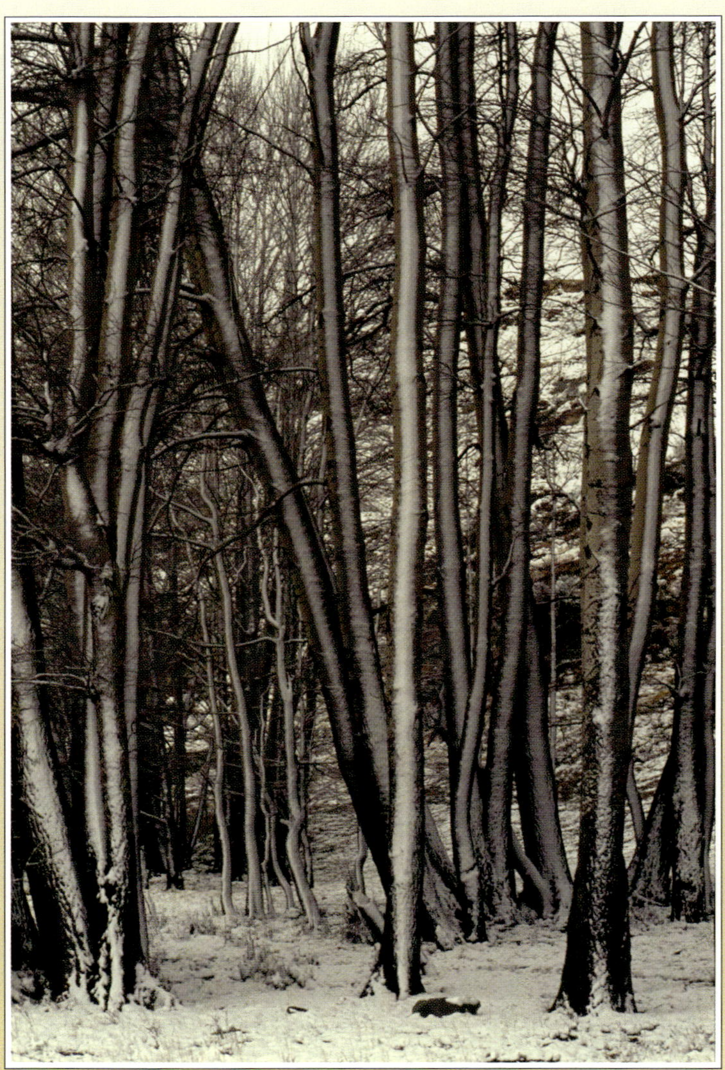

The coating of snow on these trees alongside the Elliot–Barkly East road clearly shows which way the wind was blowing.

This leg of the journey is devoted to the scenic attractions of the so-called Cape Drakensberg—the southern end of a mountain range that extends for a further 900 km northwards. This part of the Drakensberg is probably at its most impressive in the area north of Elliot, where the mountains are capped by sculptured sandstone cliffs and make a majestic backdrop to the Thompson Dam, which can itself be remarkably photogenic under the right conditions. Pleasant rural scenes also abound along both the main and farm roads that radiate from Elliot in all directions; time permitting, the first section of the gravel road to Barkly East via the Otto du Plessis Pass is particularly worth exploring.

To experience the mountains at close range we have to head northwards up the Barkly Pass. Beyond the pass, the road heads for Barkly East along the picturesque Langkloofspruit valley, where the poplars put on a brilliant display of yellow and gold every autumn. Travellers with suitable vehicles and a few extra hours in hand should consider driving the scenic gravel road from Barkly East to Maclear via the quaint village of Rhodes and Naude's Nek Pass (at 2500 m the highest public road in South Africa). Those who do so will encounter some breathtaking scenery along the way, but lesser mortals will have to retrace their steps to Elliot and continue their journey from there. In winter there is always a chance that one may strike it lucky and see an unexpected snowfall transform the whole landscape in a few hours. Should this happen, the drive over the Barkly Pass (road conditions permitting) to the farms beyond will provide rich photographic rewards.

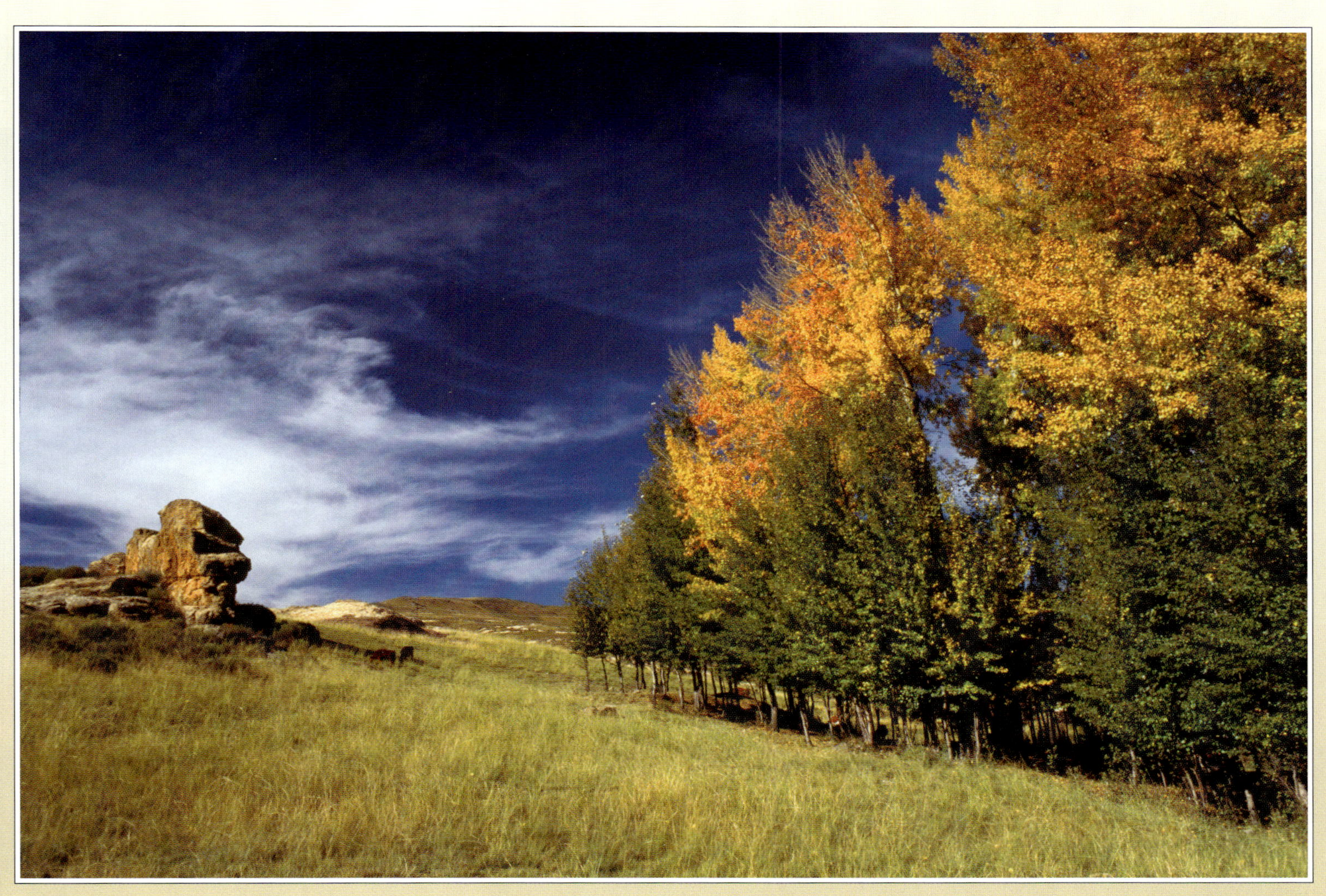

Summer and autumn meet in this stand of poplars near the road from Elliot to Barkly East.

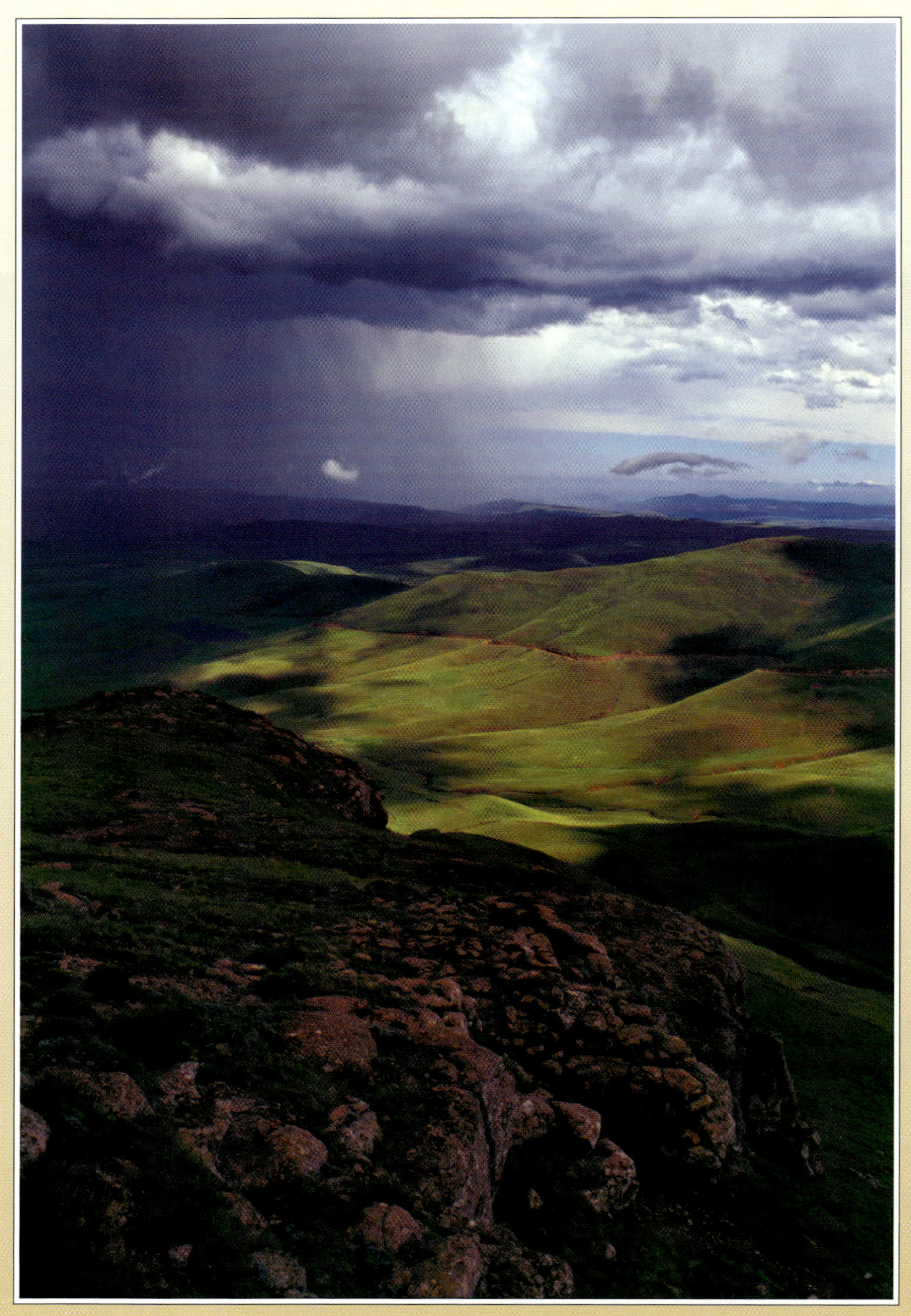

A spectacular view from the top of Naude's Nek Pass rewards those who have braved the slow and arduous road from Rhodes.

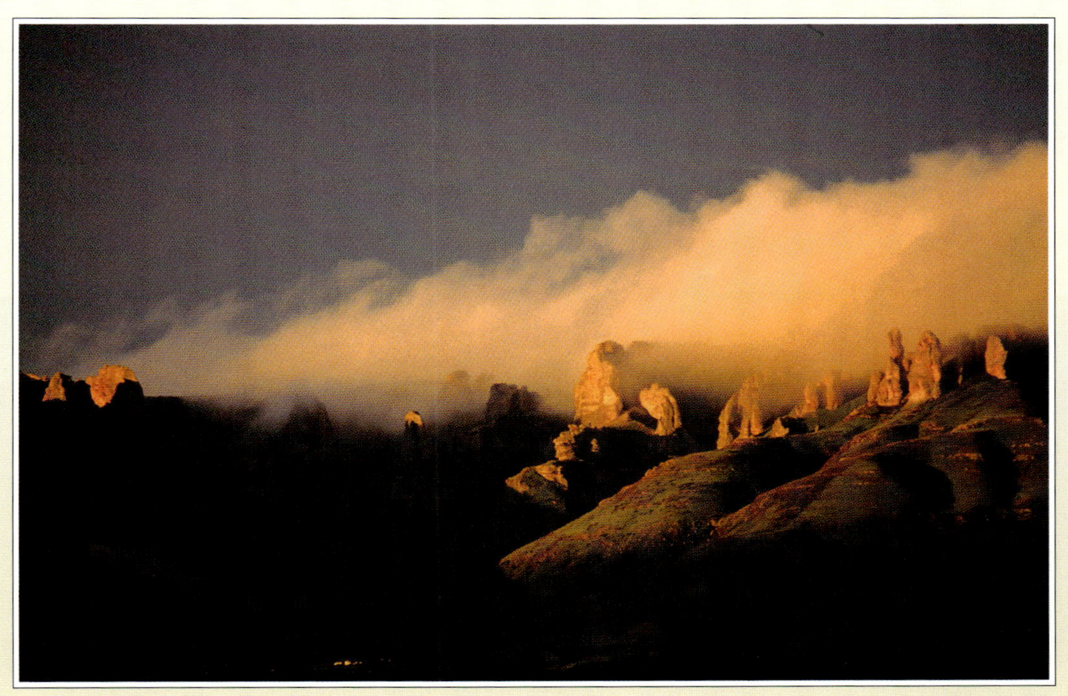

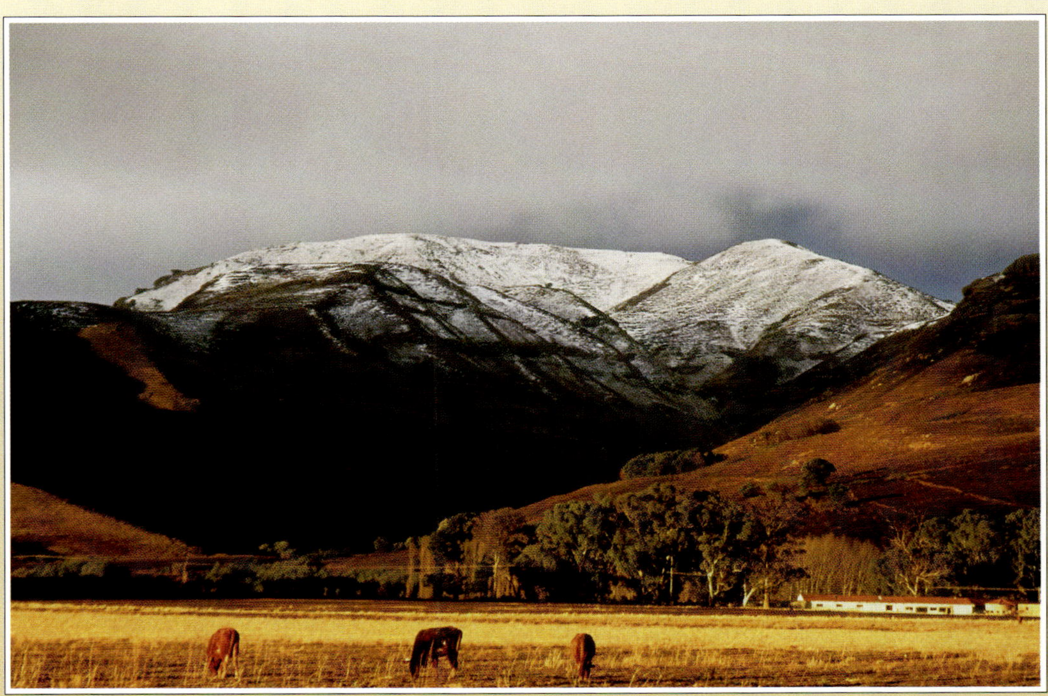

Top:
A thunderstorm has come and gone, and the re-emerging sun just catches the tops of the sandstone cliffs capping the mountains north of Elliot.

Bottom:
The hills behind Elliot's Thompson Dam glow in the late afternoon sunlight in this winter scene.

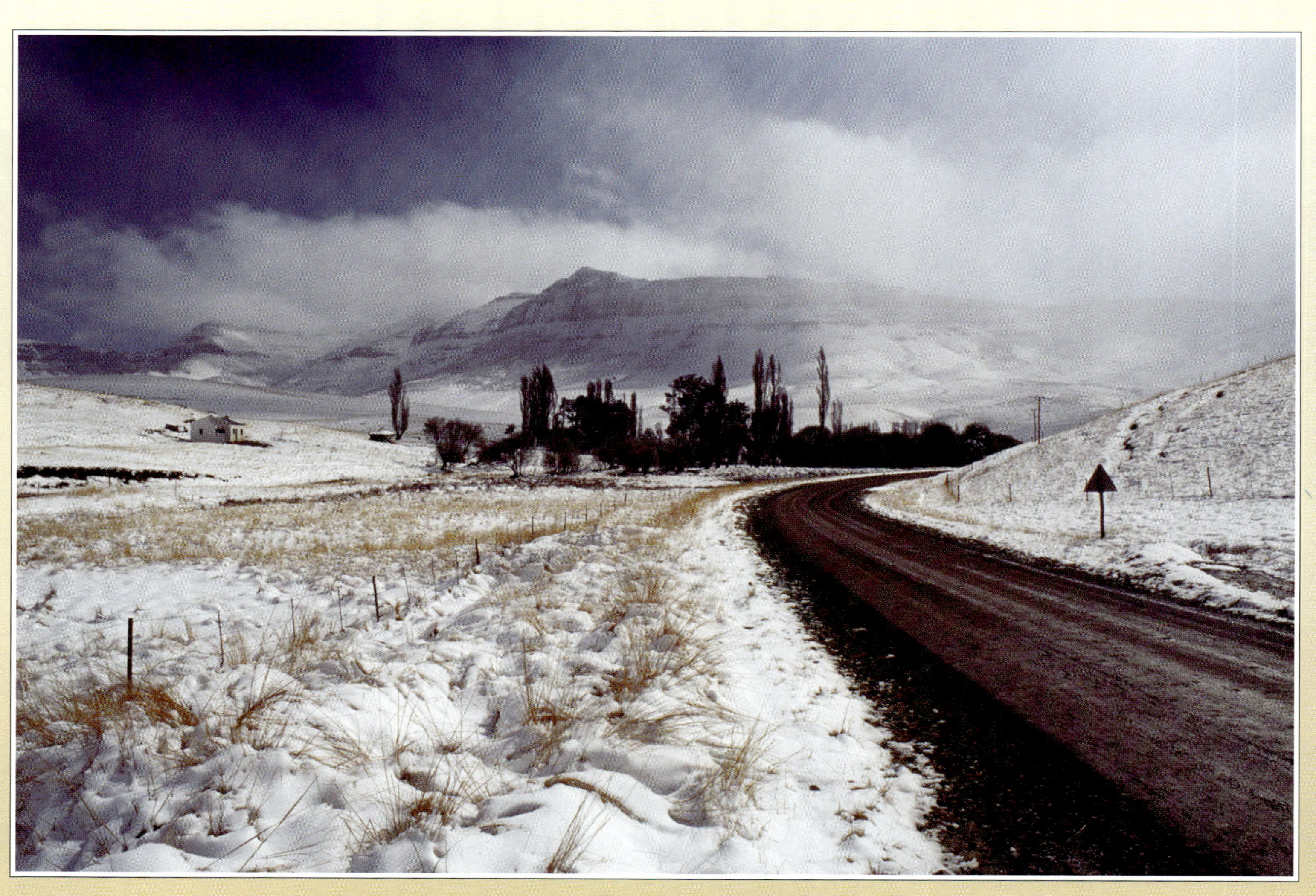

A dark road heads into the snow-covered countryside near the Mountain Shadows Hotel at the top of Barkly Pass.

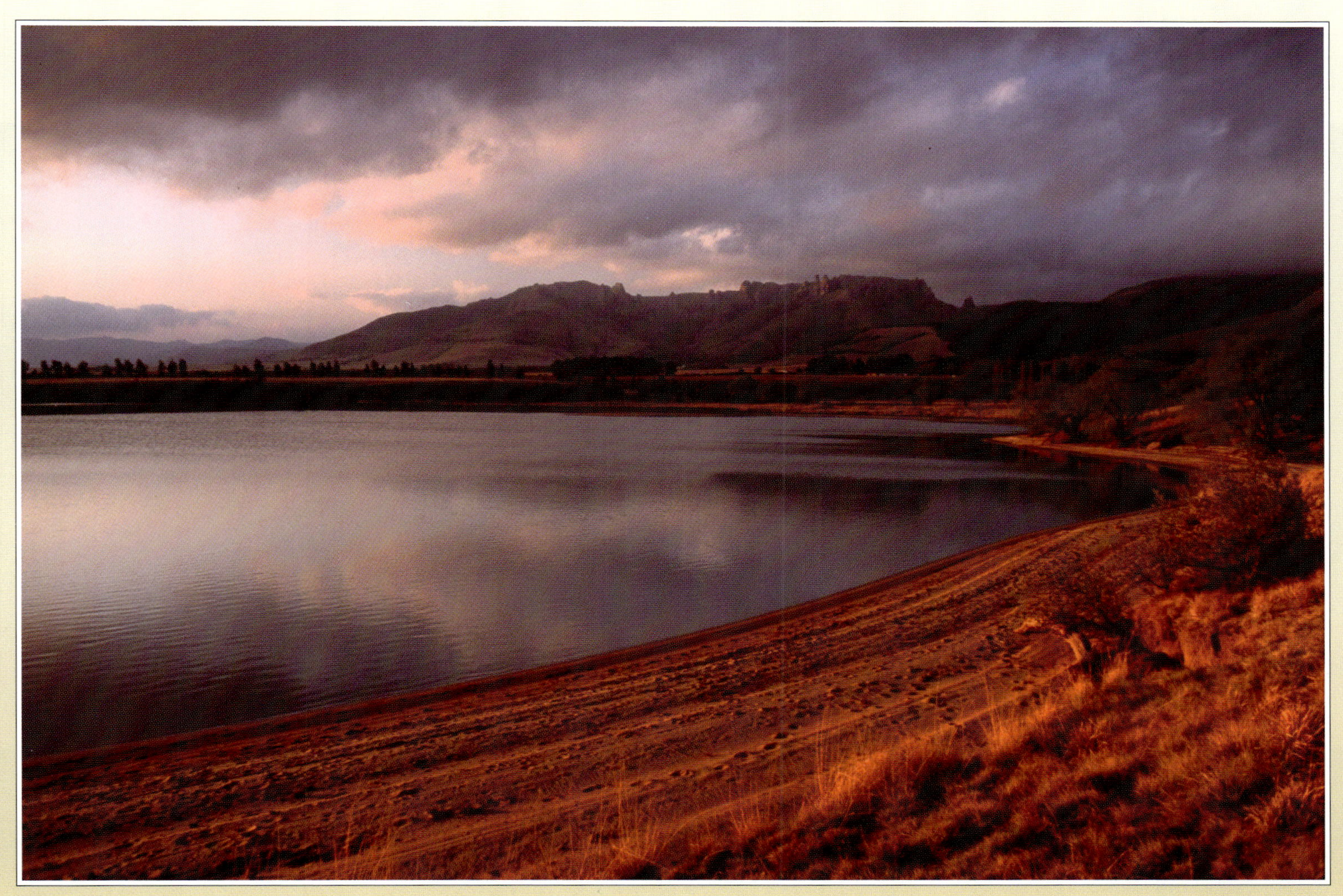

The low water level of the Thompson Dam at Elliot during a drought has created a temporary sandy "beach".

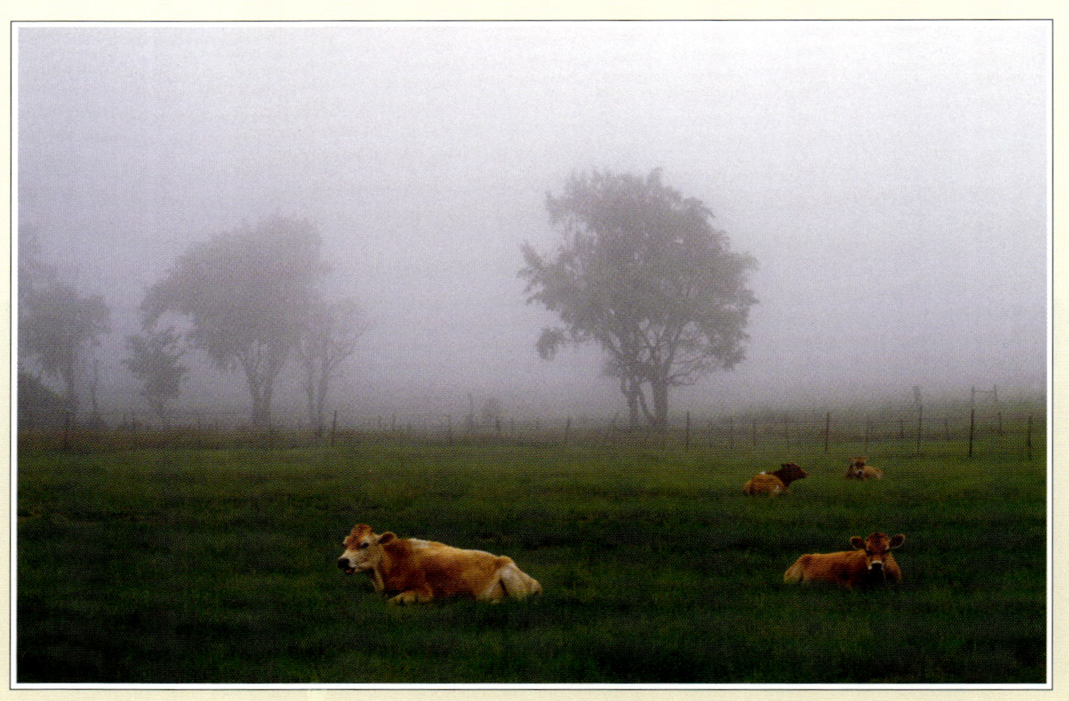

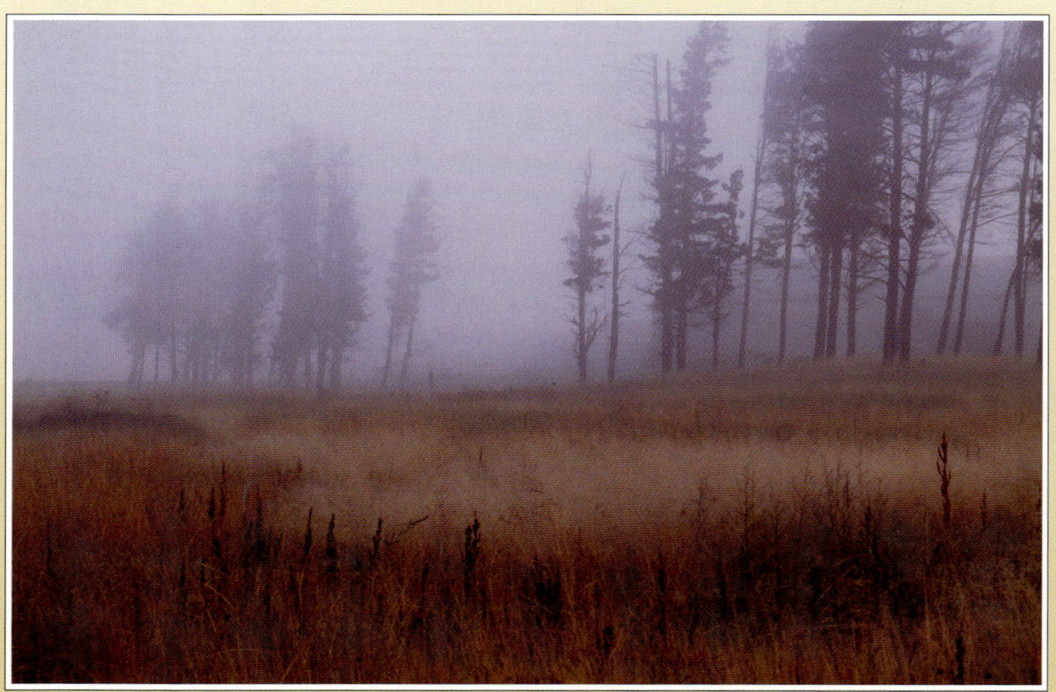

Top:
Cows take life easy in a green field as thick mist blots out the surrounding countryside.

Bottom:
Early morning mist has transformed an otherwise ordinary scene near Elliot station.

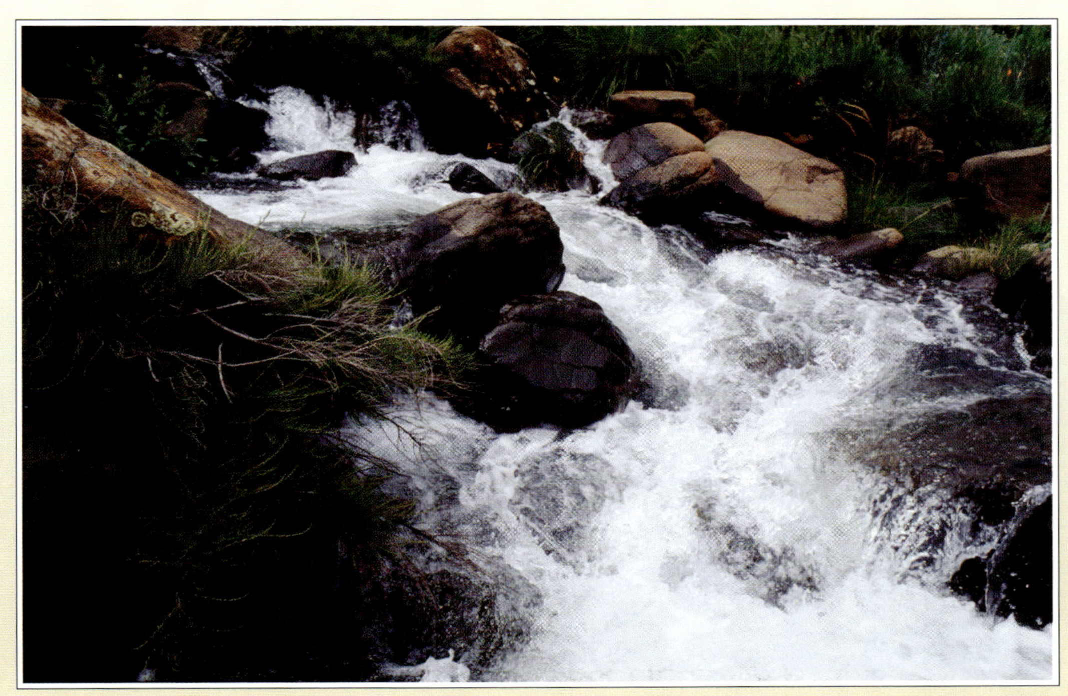

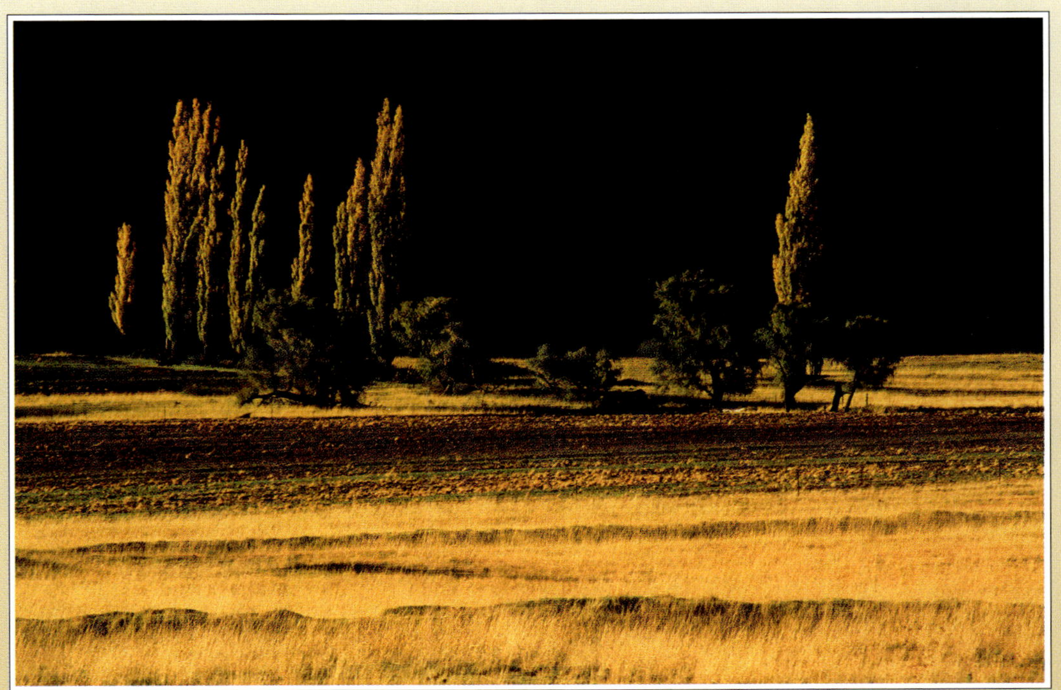

Top:
A cool, clear mountain stream tumbles down a hillside near the "Bastervoetpad", a quaintly named farm track over the mountains north of Elliot.

Bottom:
Yellow fields and a row of golden poplars catch the late afternoon sun on a farm between Indwe and Elliot.

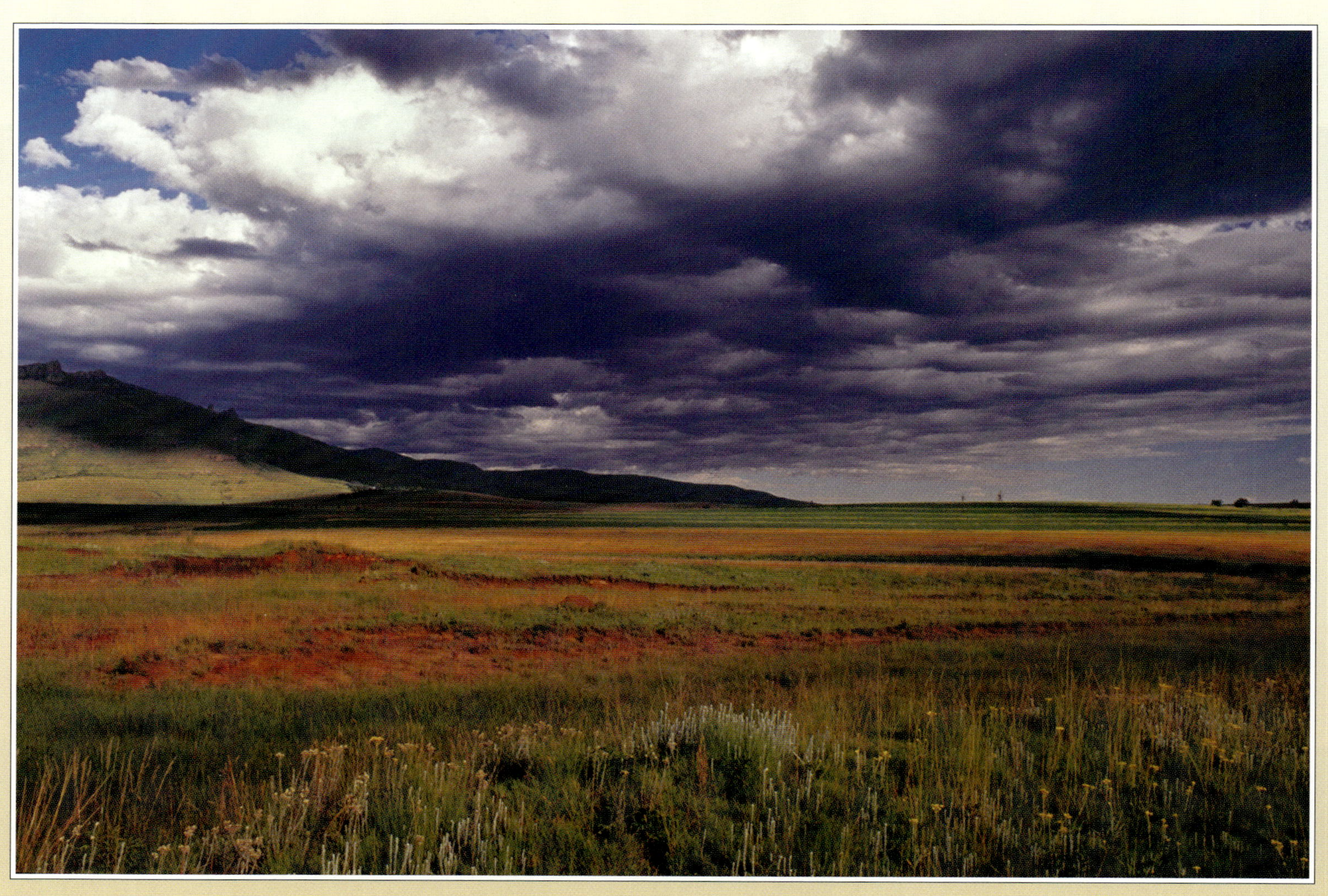

A drive from Elliot towards the Barkly Pass at the right time of day can reward the photographer with dramatic scenes like this.

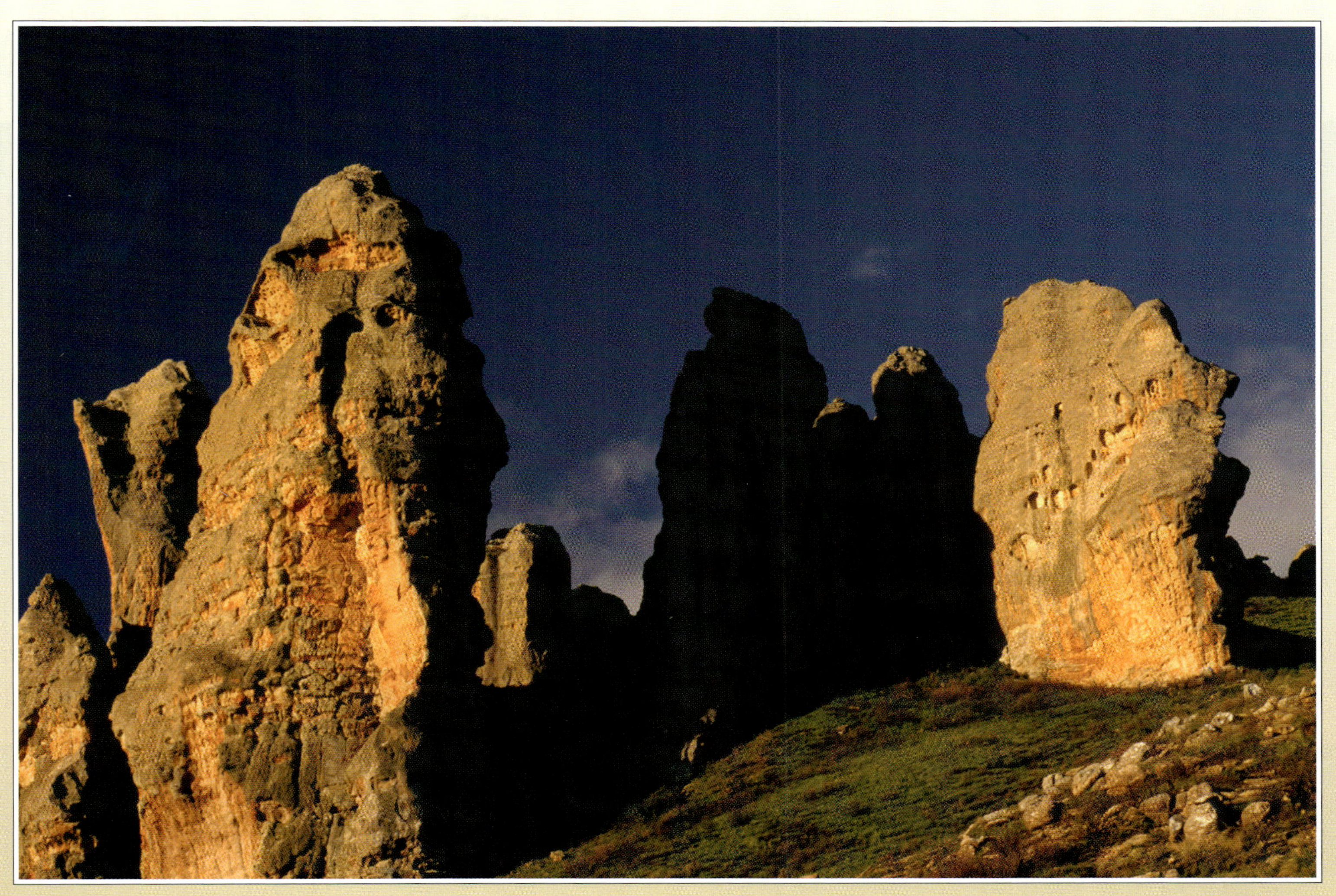

These sandstone pillars, part of a group known as The Guardians, look down on the Thompson Dam and the town of Elliot.

DAY 14

Underberg Area

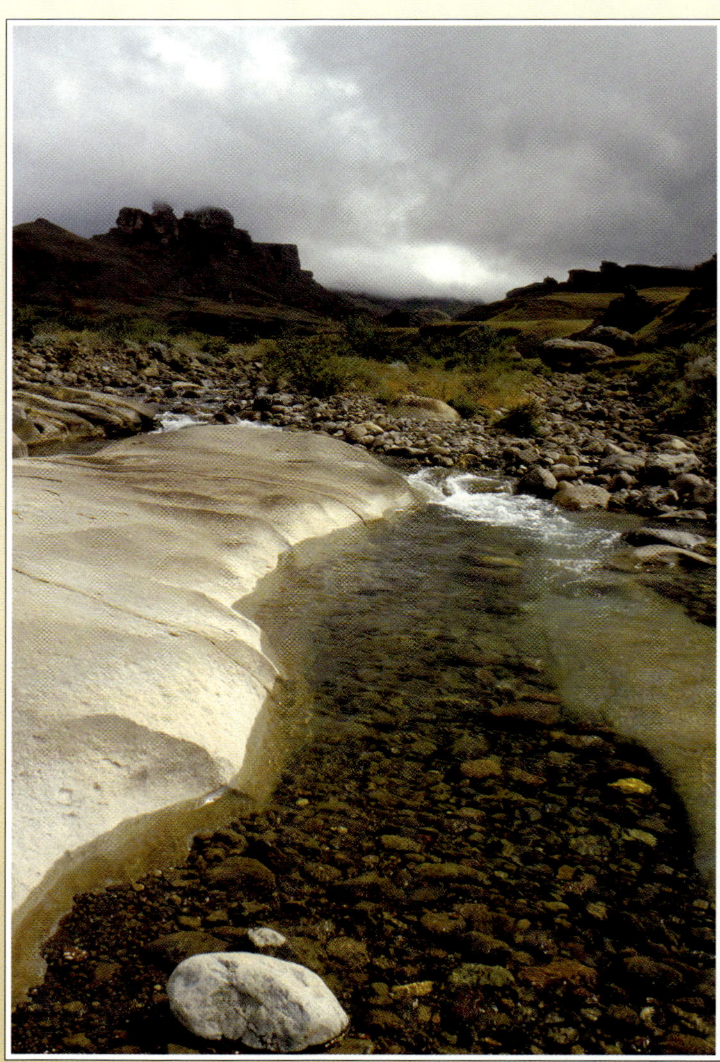

In summer the Hippo Pools in the Mlambonja River at Drakensberg Gardens are an ideal place to cool off after a long hike.

The mountainous area lying to the west, northwest and north of the town of Underberg, extending from the Bushman's Nek area in the south to Kamberg in the north, is commonly known as the Southern Drakensberg (as opposed to the Cape Drakensberg, which lies still further south). It embraces the southern end of the uKhahlamba-Drakensberg Park, proclaimed a World Heritage Site in November 2000 on the strength of both its natural beauty and cultural uniqueness (with the latter reflecting the wealth of San rock art in the area). Many popular holiday resorts are concentrated in the Drakensberg Gardens area due west of the town, although not all of them fall within the park itself. Popular leisure activities include hiking, horse riding and fly-fishing.

The farmlands adjoining the Park have their own attraction, and are mainly devoted to cattle ranching. Dams of all sizes abound in the area, with the headwaters of major rivers such as the Mzimkulu and Mkomazi reinforcing the impression that this is indeed a well-watered area. While these dams and clear streams challenge trout fishermen to try out their skills, they are also a great asset to the photographer looking for interesting foregrounds to redeem what could otherwise be rather boring pictures of distant mountain peaks. Underberg and the village of Himeville some 6 km to the north are both colourful sights in autumn when the rich yellows, oranges and reds of their many maple, liquidamber and pin-oak trees are on display. As in the case of the Elliot area, winter snowfalls can arrive unexpectedly any time between May and September, and provision has to be made for this eventuality in one's travel plans.

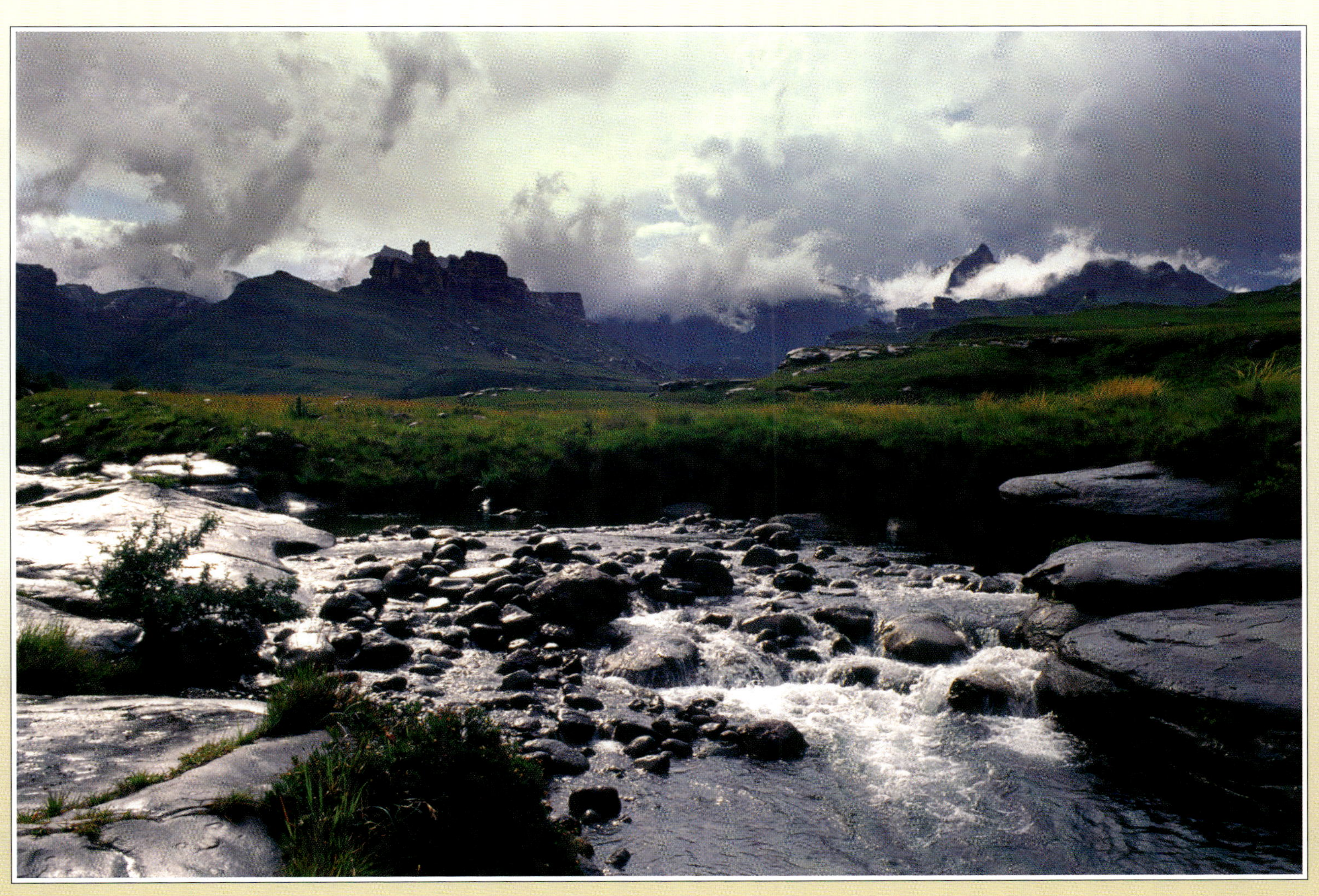

The rain has stopped for now, but clouds swirling around the distant peaks could bring further showers to the Mlambonja River valley.

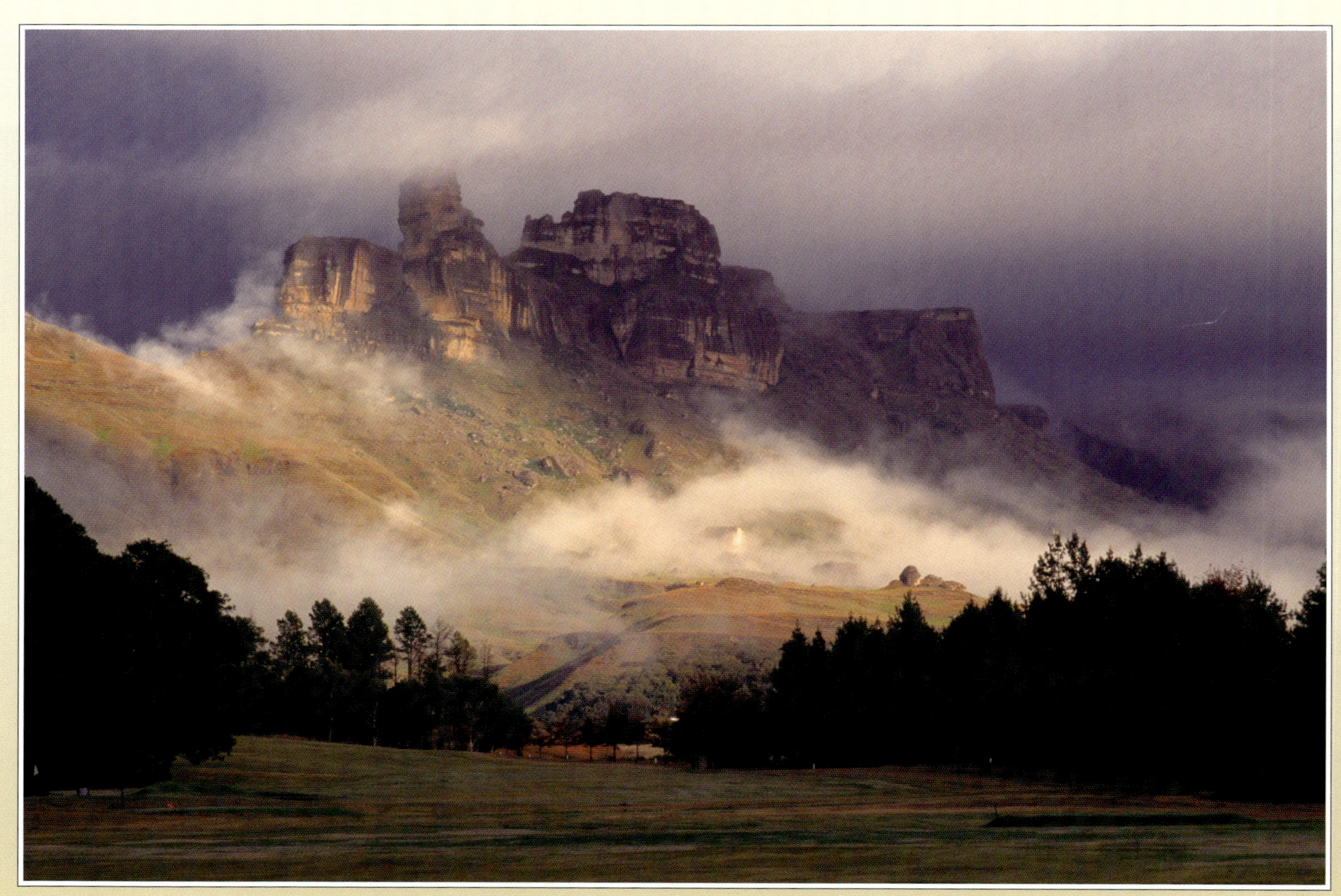

As the morning mist starts clearing, a dramatic backdrop to the Drakensberg Gardens golf course slowly emerges from the shadows.

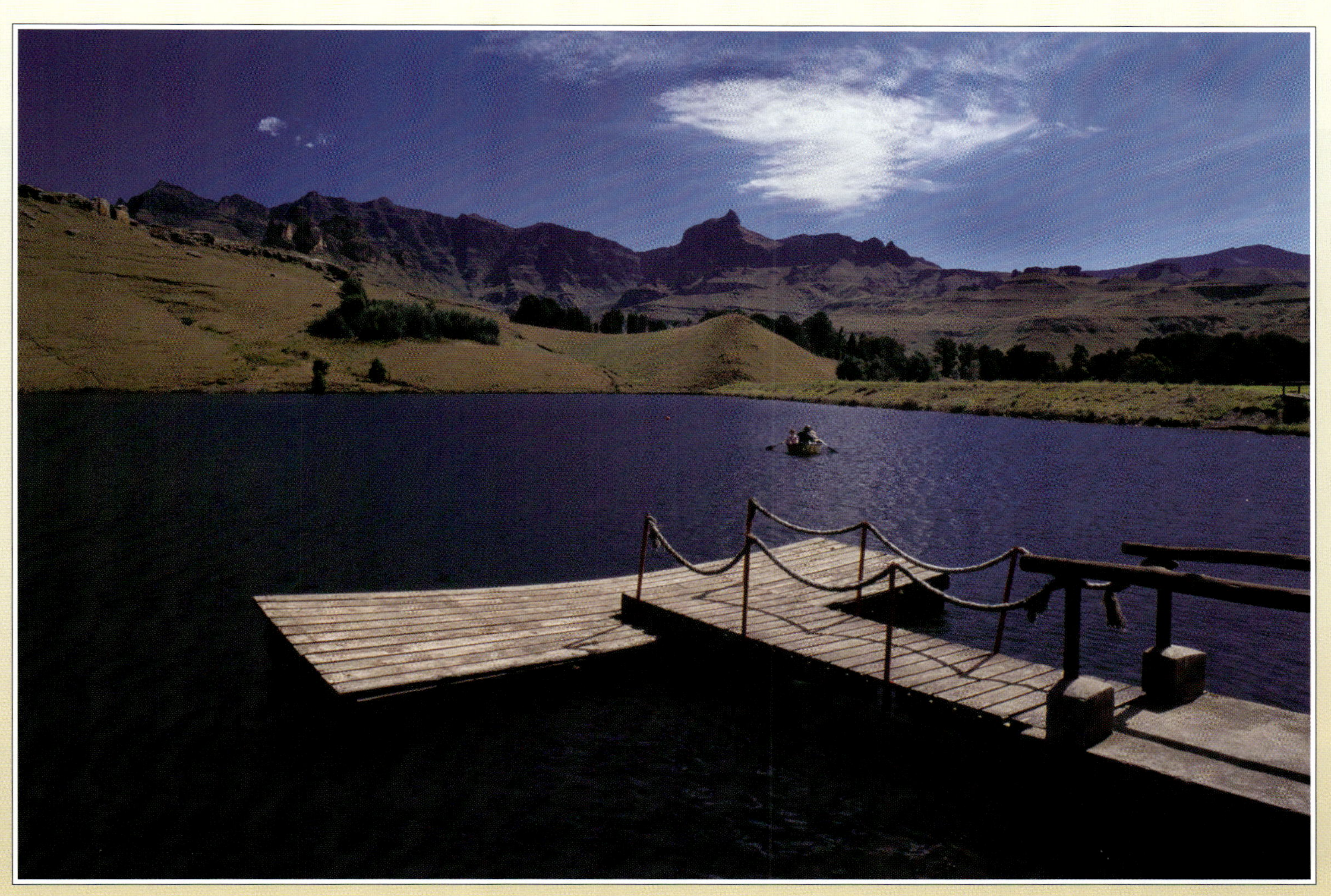

The view from the clubhouse must surely rank as one of the finest among all of South Africa's golf courses!

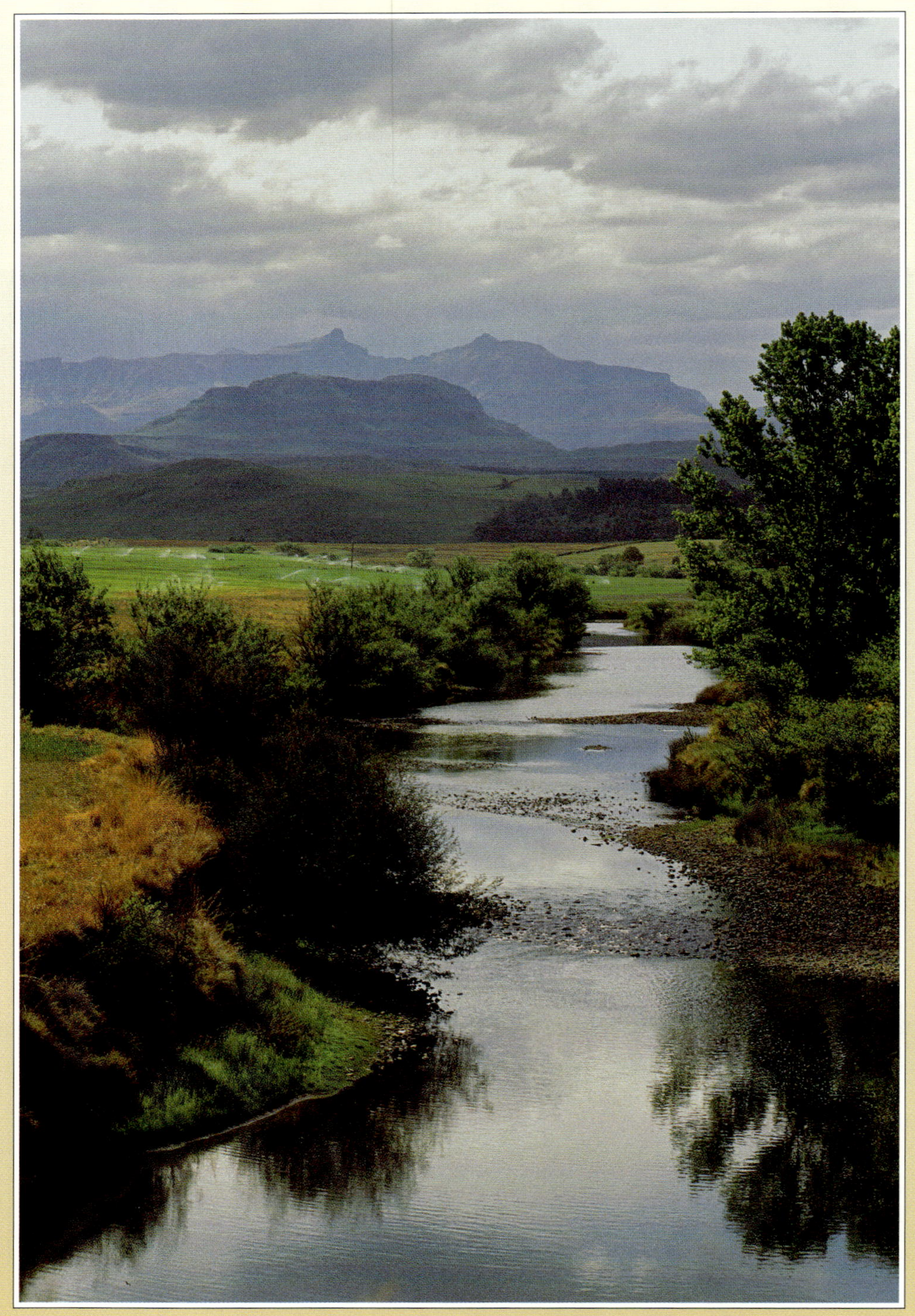

The placid Mzimkulu River, at the turn-off to Drakensberg Gardens from the Underberg–Swartberg road.

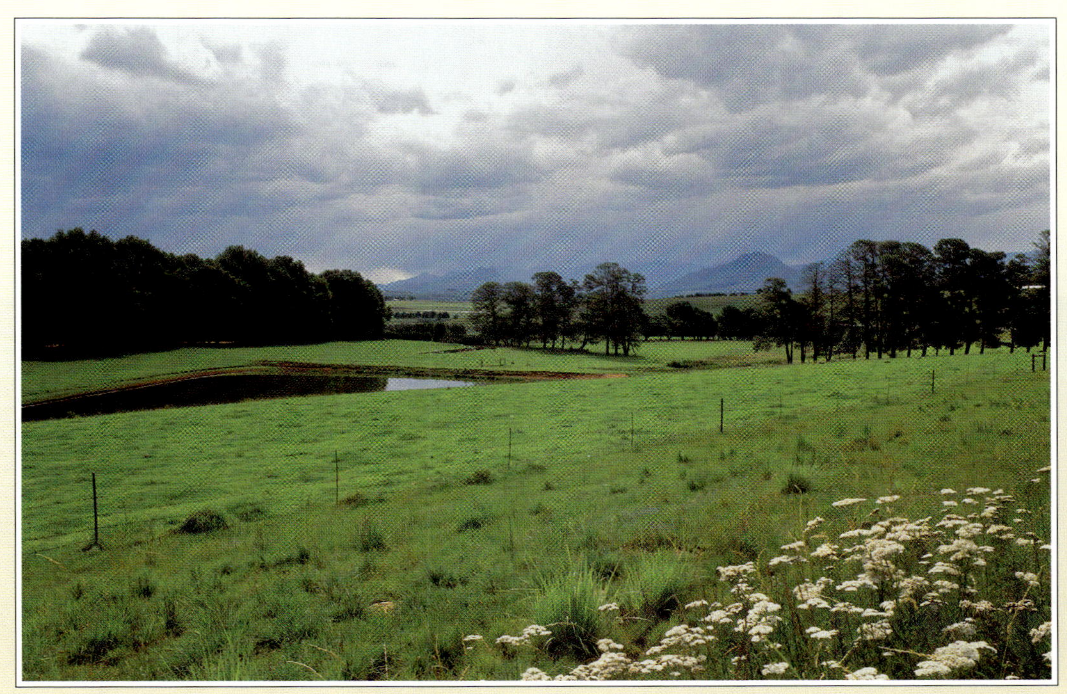

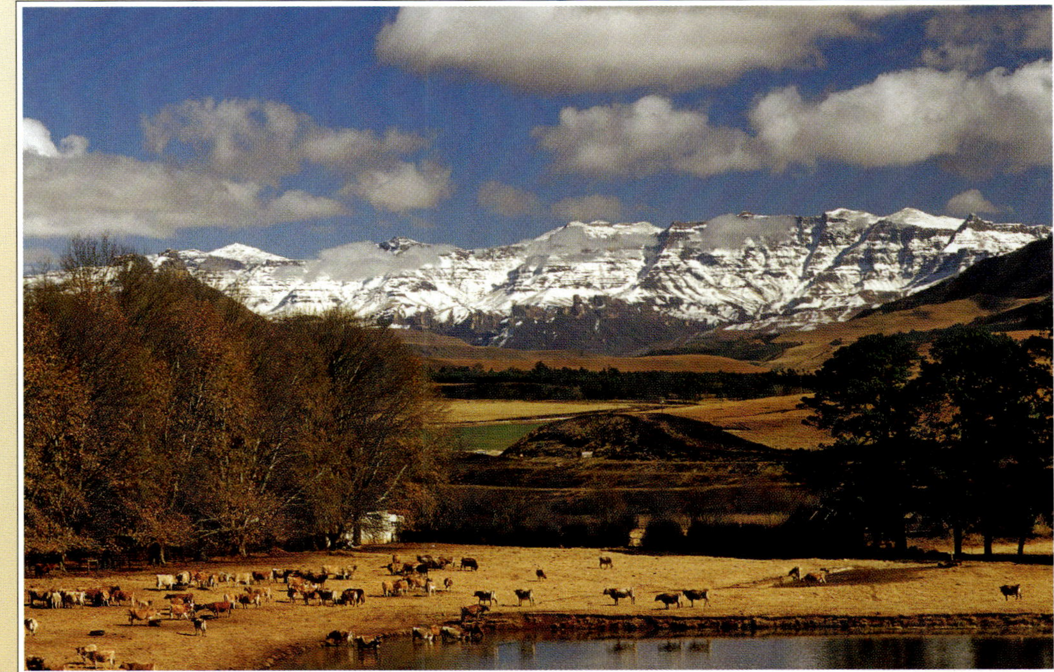

These photos, both taken from the same spot alongside the main road heading west out of Underberg towards Drakensberg Gardens, contrast summer and winter as well as wide-angle and telephoto perspectives.

DAY 15

Midlands Meander

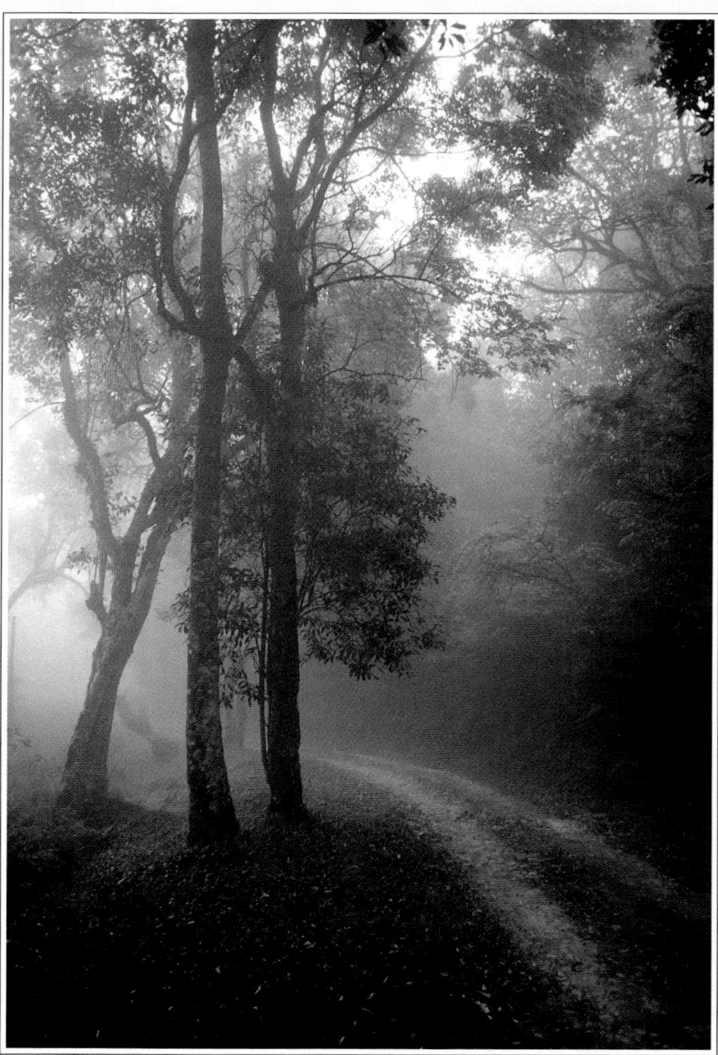

A farm road that winds up the mountains overlooking Byrne village near Richmond passes through remnants of indigenous forest.

On Day 15, the focus of attention falls on the gently rolling hills of the KwaZulu-Natal Midlands, which embrace the area between the warm coastal belt in the east and the rugged Drakensberg range and its foothills in the west. Largely rural in aspect, it nevertheless contains the city of Pietermaritzburg as well as numerous smaller towns and villages. Many of these are located along the so-called Midlands Meander, an arts-and-crafts route that links a host of small shops and "cottage industries" selling a wide variety of locally made products. Refreshments are available from establishments with quaint names like "Mother Goose" and "Granny Mouse's Country House". A number of well-known private schools (Hilton College, Michaelhouse, etc.) are located in the Midlands, which also boasts abundant accommodation for both travellers looking for an overnight stop and families wanting to spend a quiet holiday in the countryside.

The patchwork of farmlands, avenues and groups of oak or plane trees and the rivers and streams which traverse the area all constitute suitable subject matter for the photographer. In places the smooth courses of the rivers are interrupted by breaks ranging from gentle rapids to impressive spectacles like the Howick and Karkloof Falls. Particularly scenic are some of the roads branching off from the main Midlands Meander route, such as the one to the Byrne Valley near Richmond (with a history extending well back into the nineteenth century), the Karkloof Valley road beyond Howick and the road from Rosetta to Kamberg and Highmoor in the Drakensberg. Attractive small country churches serve the villages and surrounding farming communities.

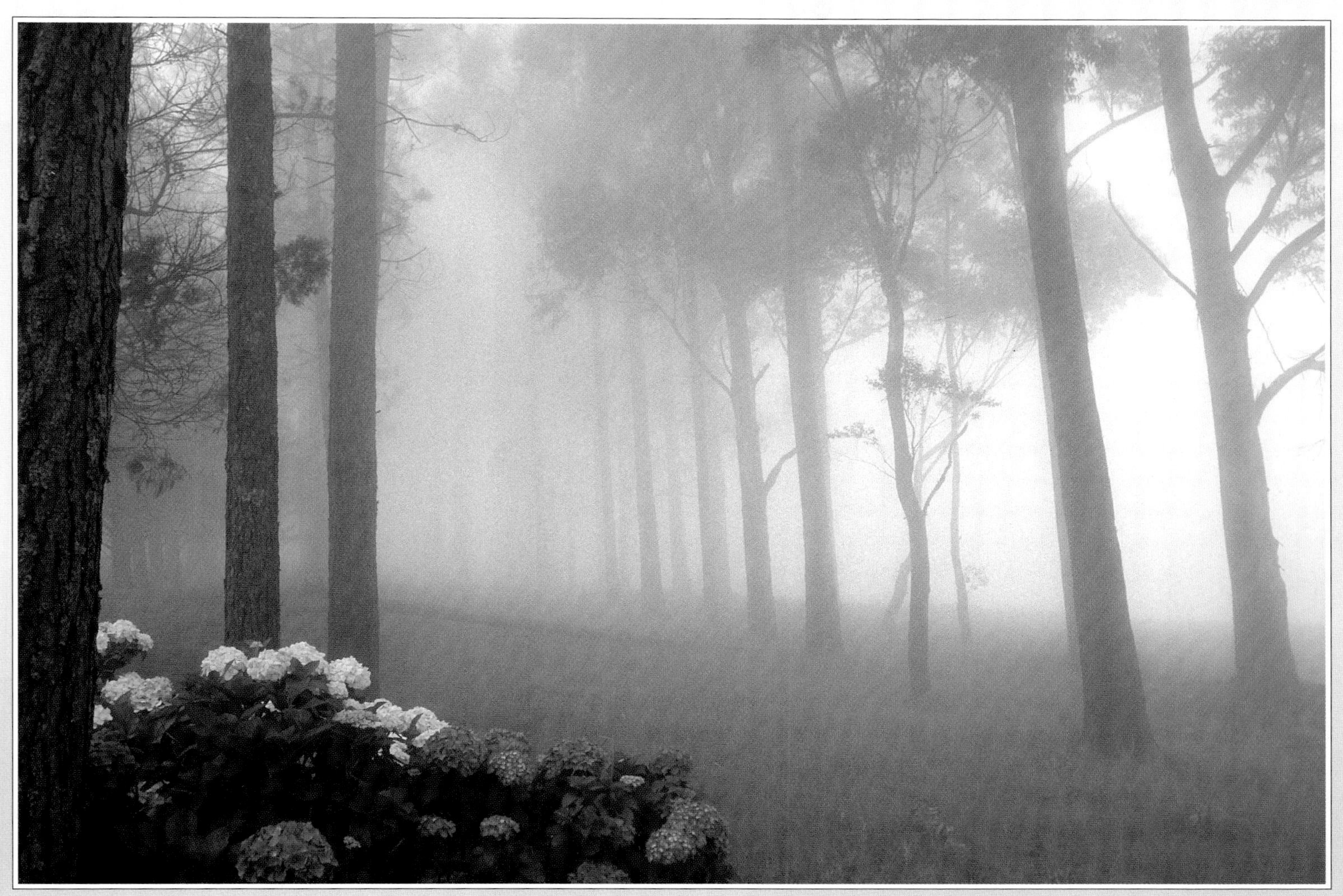

Mist engulfs a stand of eucalyptus trees on a guest farm high up in the mountains above Byrne, with blue hydrangeas adding a touch of colour.

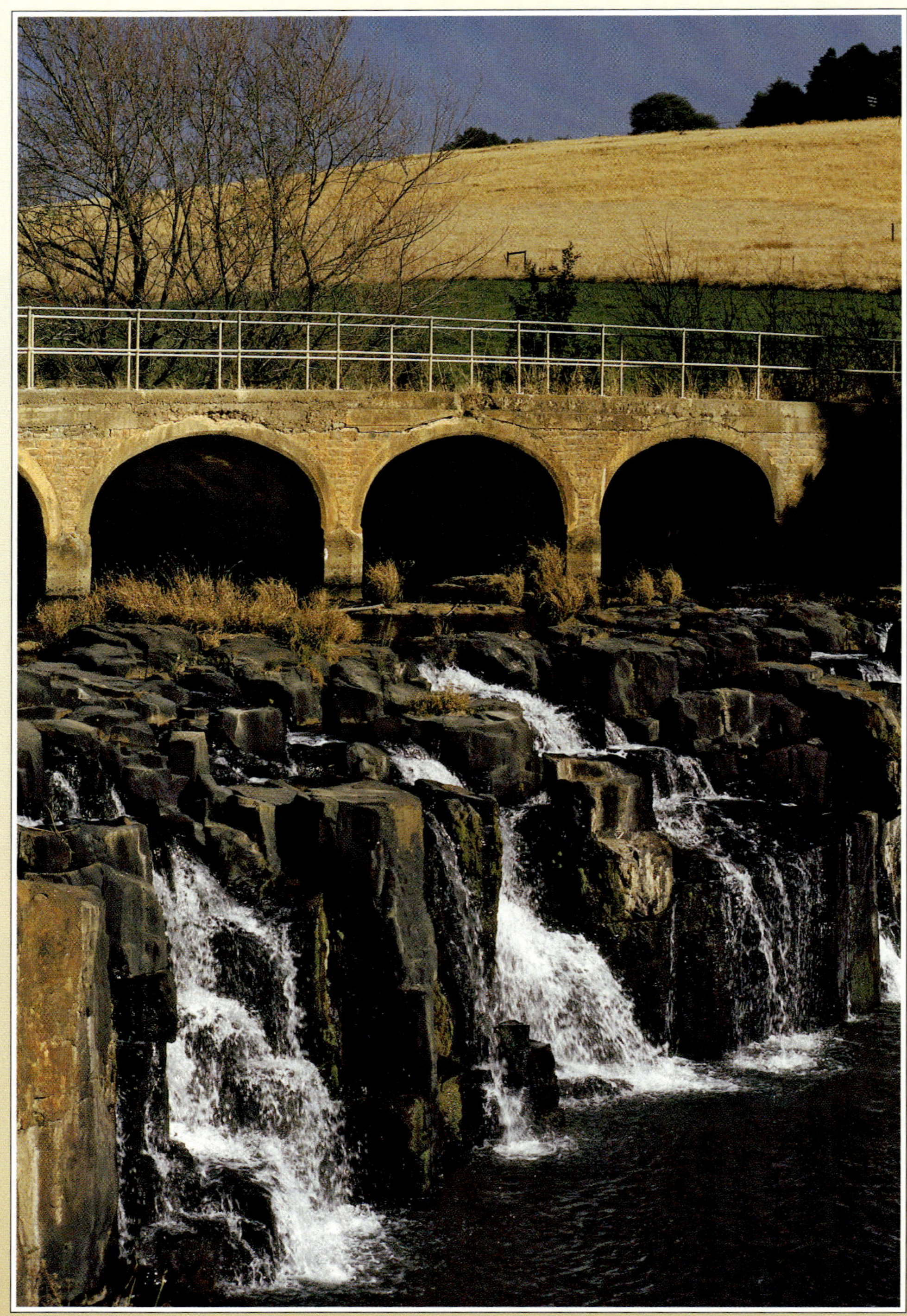

The rustic stone bridge above the waterfall at Caversham Mill near Balgowan probably dates back to around 1855 when the original mill was built.

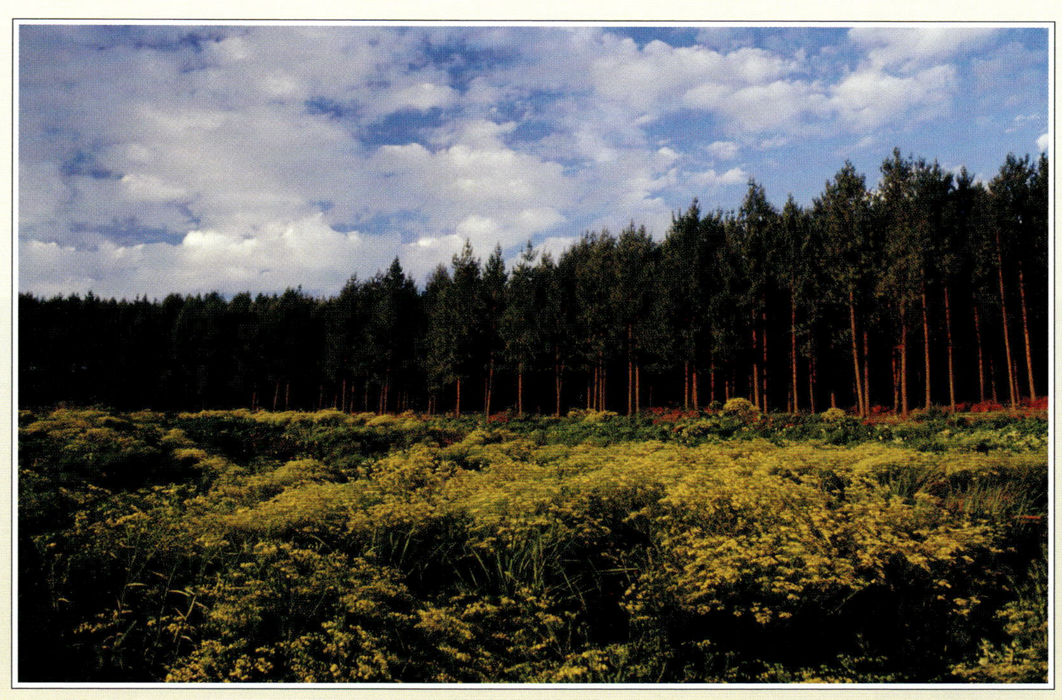

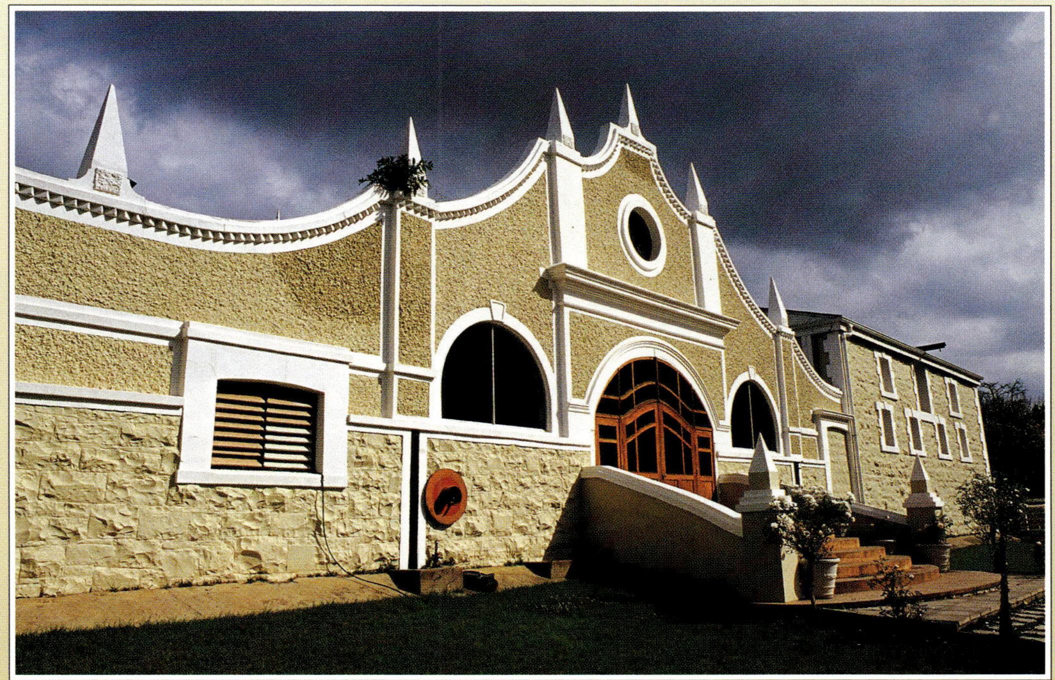

Top:
The late afternoon light has enhanced the appeal of this scene, encountered during a drive along a little-used country road east of Mooi River.

Bottom:
Greenfields Manor House, between Mooi River and Rosetta, is one of many stately country homes in the Midlands area; it now houses shops and a restaurant.

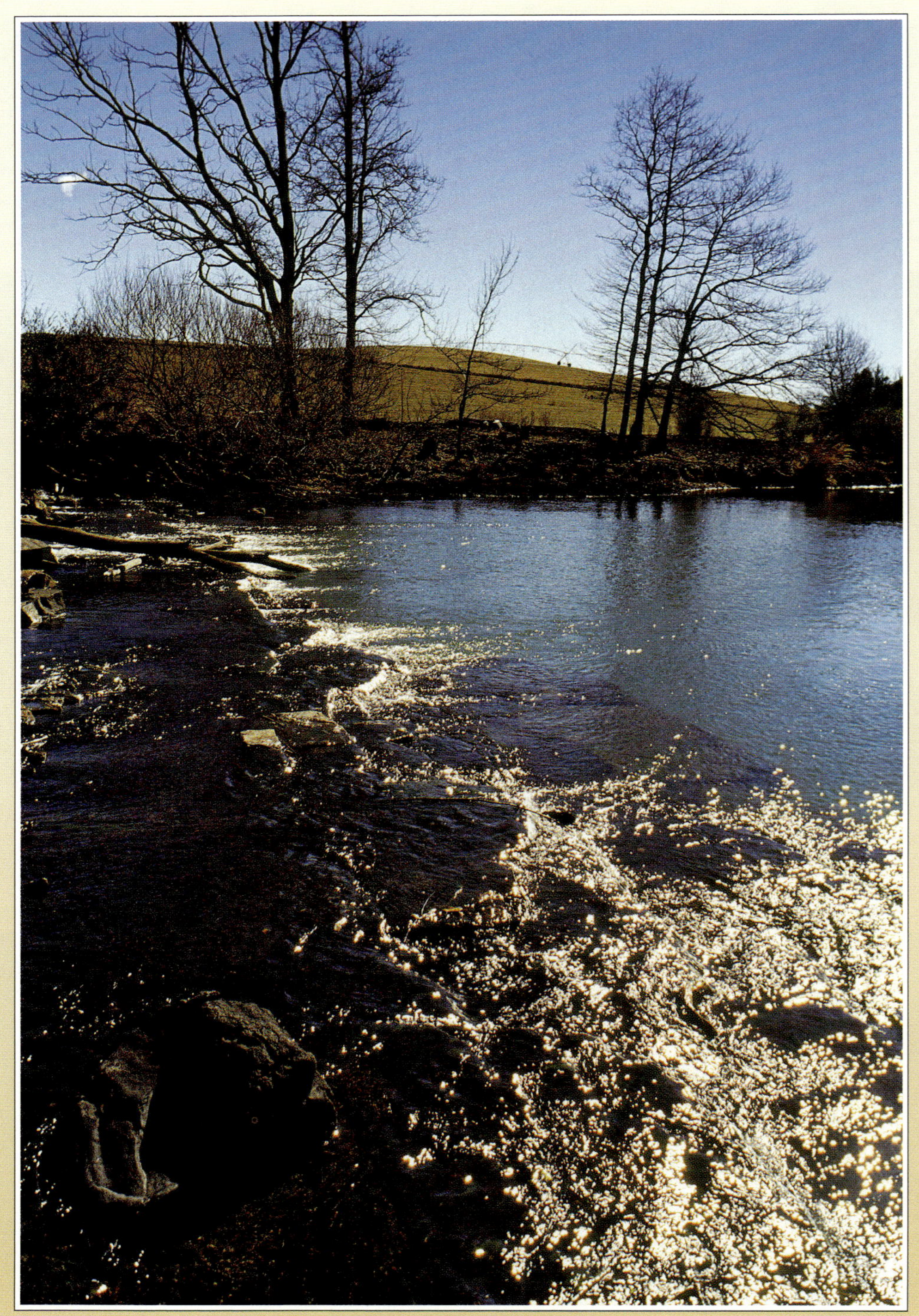

Travellers stopping for something to eat and drink at Mother Goose near Rosetta can watch the Mooi River flow gently past.

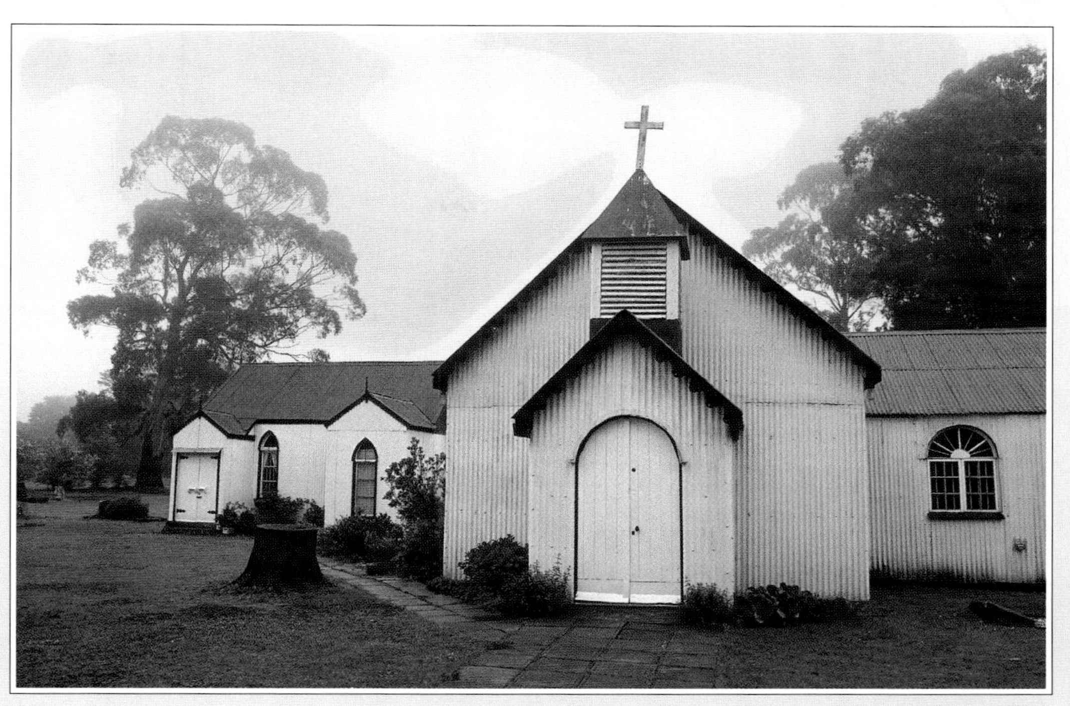

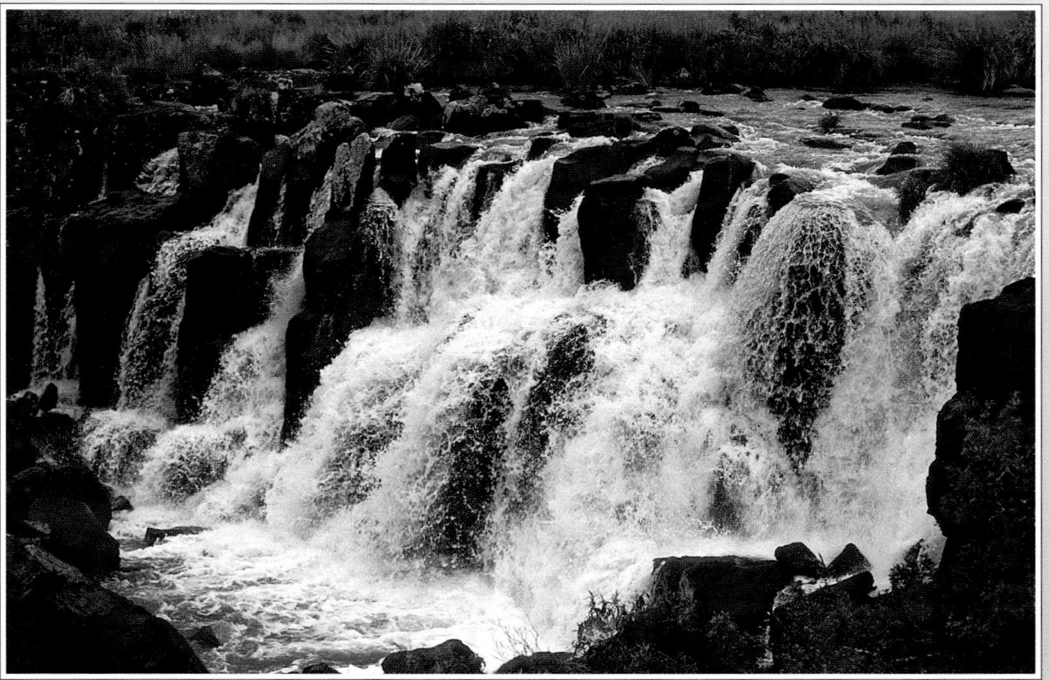

Top:
The historic St. Johns Gowrie Church in Nottingham Road, with its simple wood and iron construction, was built in 1885.

Bottom:
Abundant rains have boosted the flow of water rushing over this attractive waterfall on the Lions River.

DAY 16

Northern Drakensberg

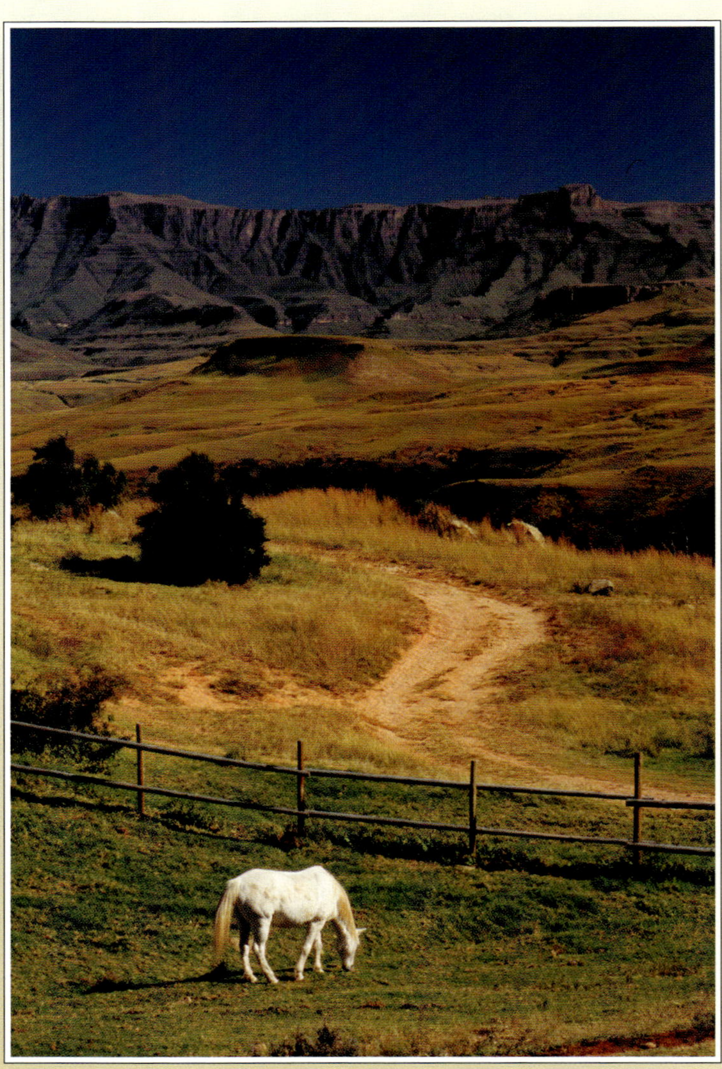

Visitors to the Little Switzerland Hotel (and the resident horses!) have a grandstand view of the Amphitheatre at the northern end of the main Drakensberg range.

Travelling northwards from the Midlands, the majestic Drakensberg mountain range dominates the skyline in the west. The main mountain edifice and much of its foothills fall within the central and northern parts of the uKhahlamba-Drakensberg Park. A large number of holiday resorts, which include hotels, time-share establishments, self-catering cottages and caravan and camping sites, have been developed in this area over the years, mainly concentrated in the Champagne Castle, Cathedral Peak, and Amphitheatre areas. In addition, the KwaZulu-Natal Parks Board offers accommodation in rest camps at Kamberg/Highmoor, Giants Castle, Injasuti and Tendele. In many cases, the roads to these resorts pass through Zulu tribal areas where subsistence farmers and their families, who still live in traditional dwellings, watch over their cattle, sheep and goats grazing on communal land or tend the maize crops growing in small fields near their homes.

The entire Drakensberg area is a mecca for hikers and rock-climbers, but there is more than enough to do and see for those who don't intend heading for the top of the escarpment with heavy backpacks or climbing ropes. For a start, with such magnificent mountains, photographic opportunities abound everywhere. As in the case of the Southern Drakensberg, there are also plenty of attractive dams, rivers and trees to complement the mountain backdrop. The thunderstorms that suddenly appear on most summer afternoons will invariably add a dramatic element to any scene. The occasional winter snowfall will be the ultimate serendipity, provided of course that one is not snowed in for a week in the process!

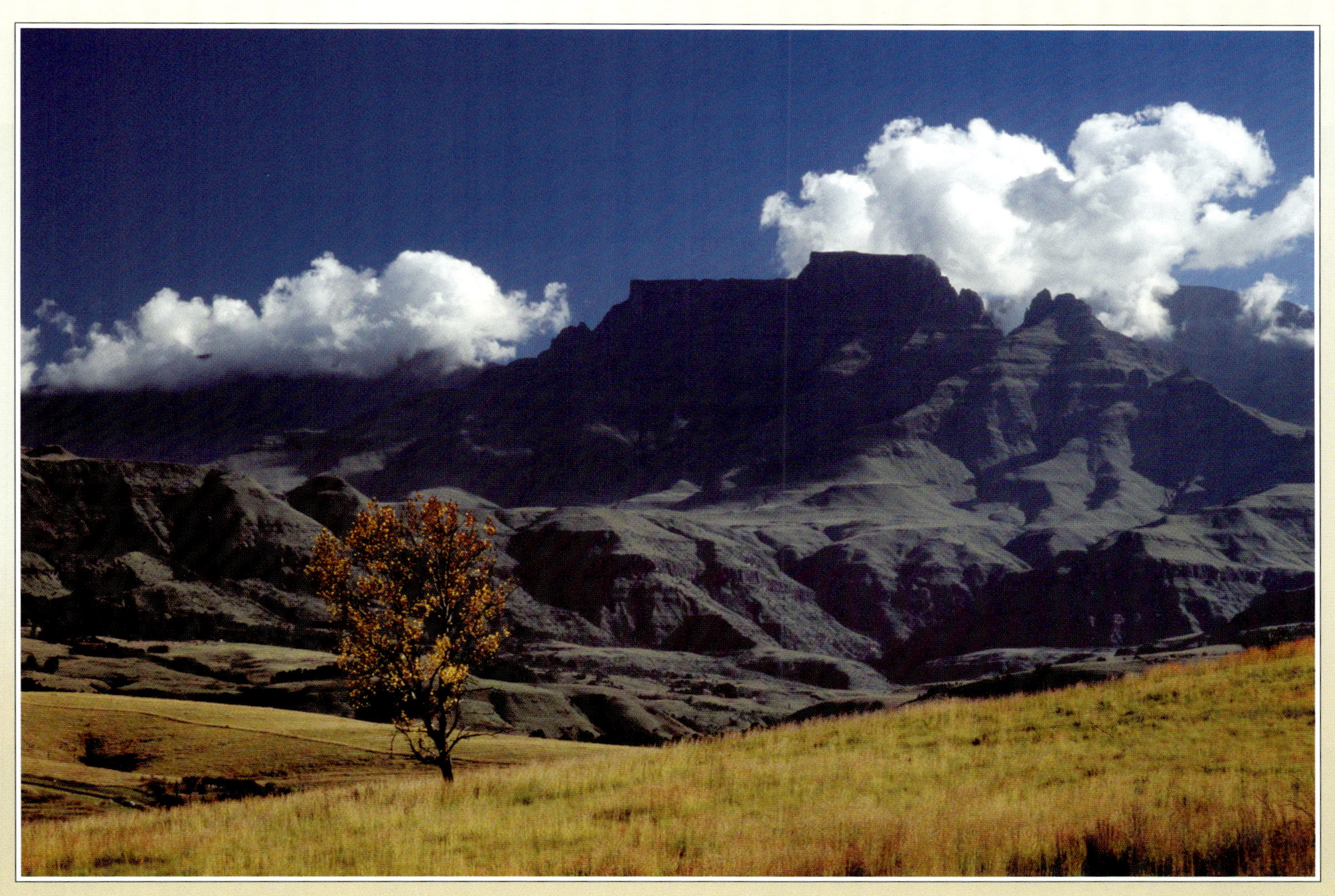

Champagne Castle and its neighbouring peaks will soon be in full shadow as the autumn sun descends behind them.

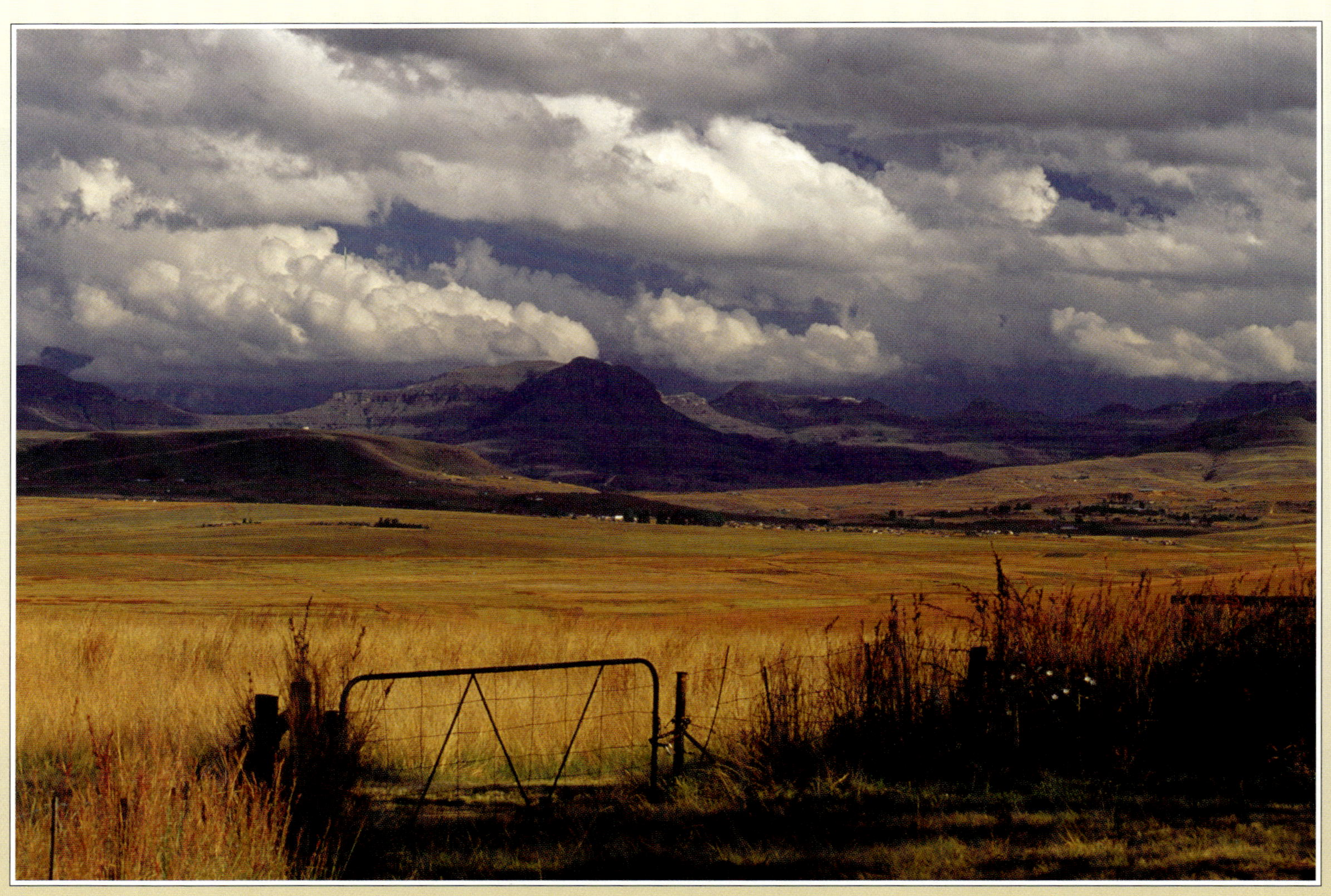

Low clouds and rain often obscure the higher parts of the mountain range, as in this view from the main road north of Bergville.

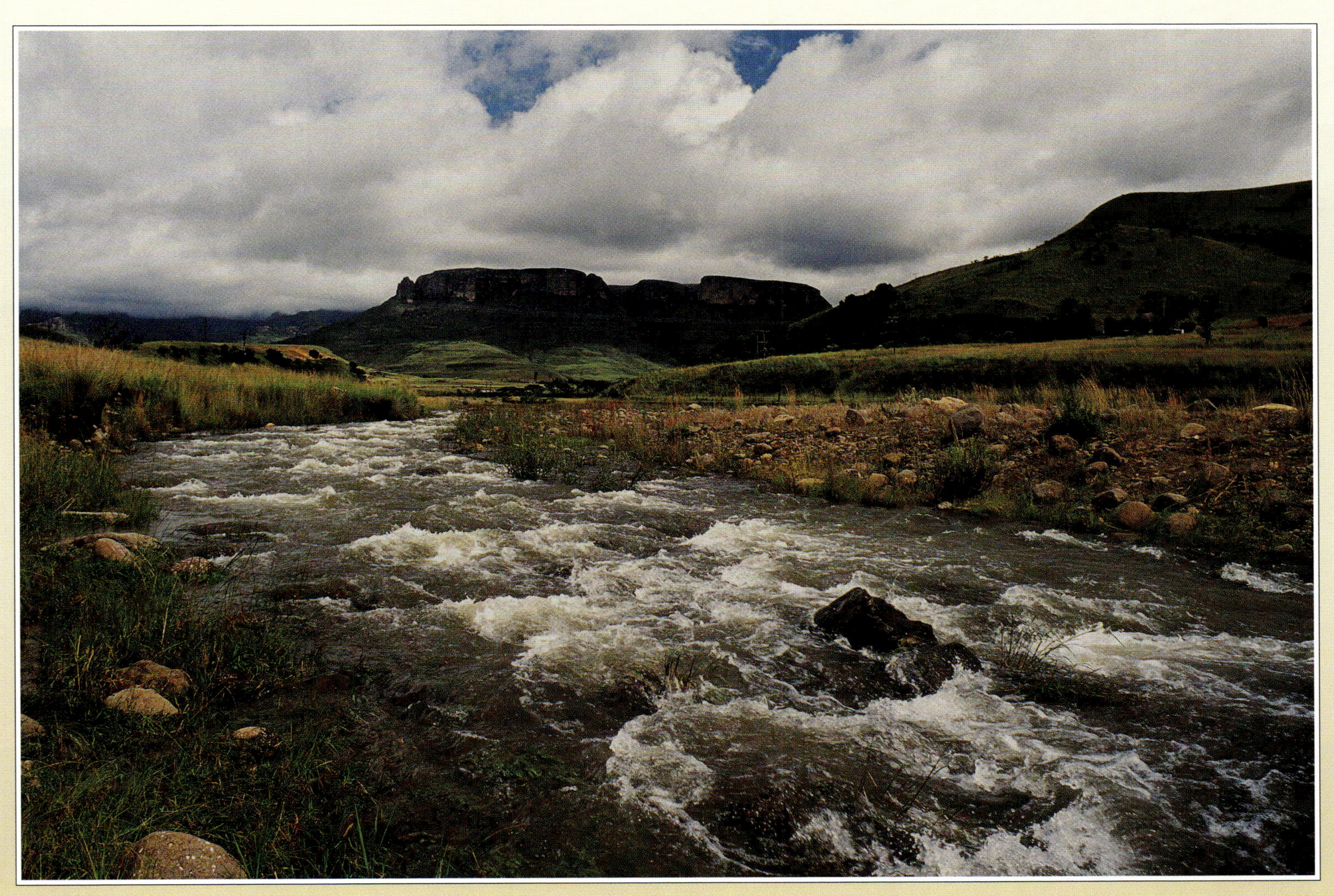

The strongly flowing Tugela River, immediately upstream from the bridge near the entrance to the Royal Natal National Park.

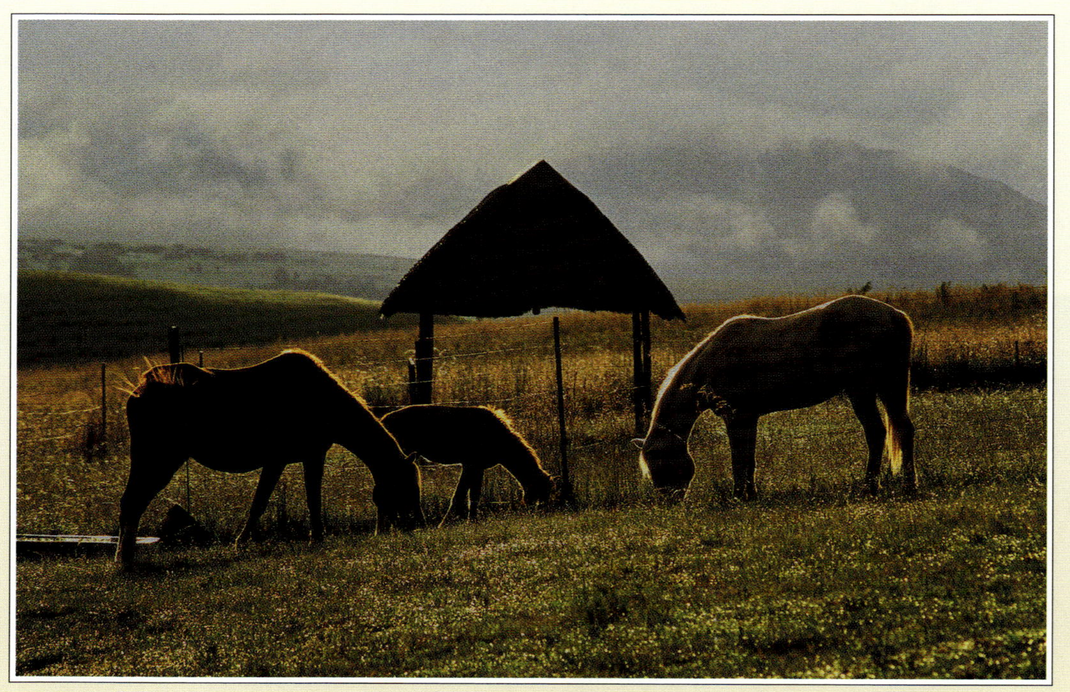

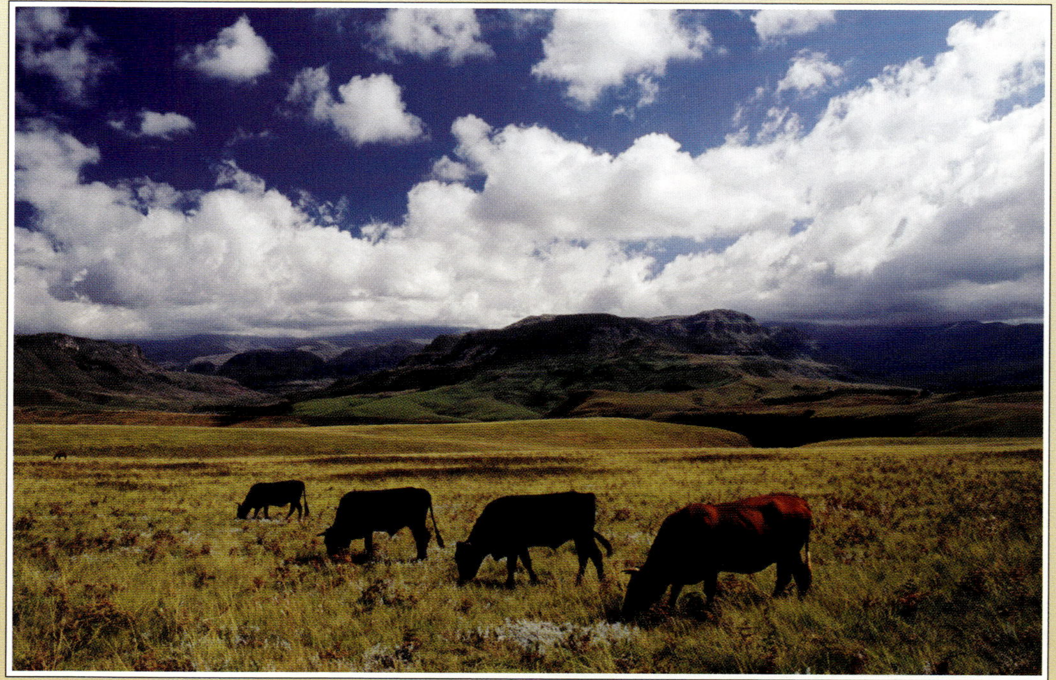

Top:
With the morning dew still thick on the ground, horses nibble the short grass in a paddock on The Ledges guest farm.

Bottom:
Cattle graze peacefully on the green foothills of the Drakensberg next to the road to Injasuti rest camp.

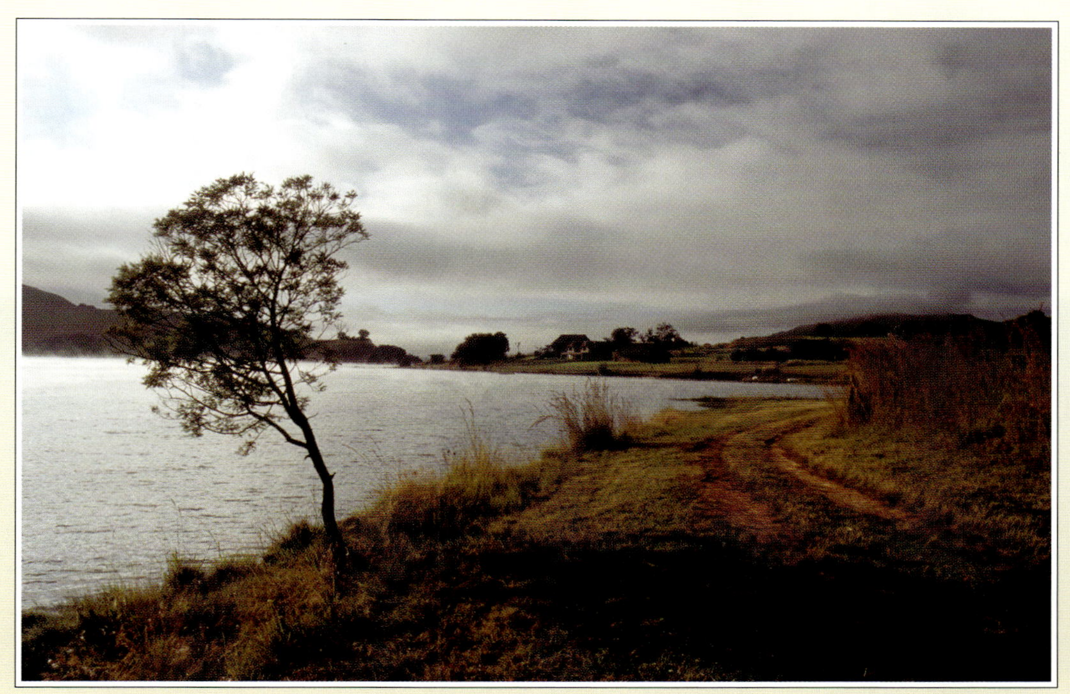

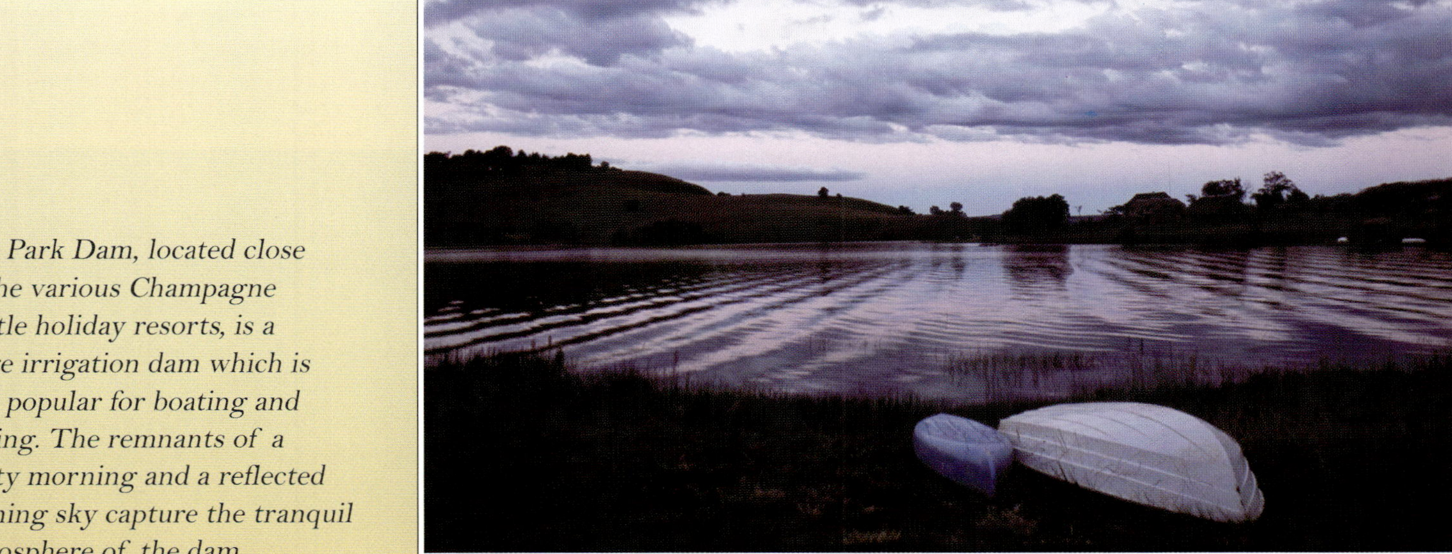

Bell Park Dam, located close to the various Champagne Castle holiday resorts, is a large irrigation dam which is also popular for boating and fishing. The remnants of a misty morning and a reflected evening sky capture the tranquil atmosphere of the dam.

DAY 17

Katse Dam

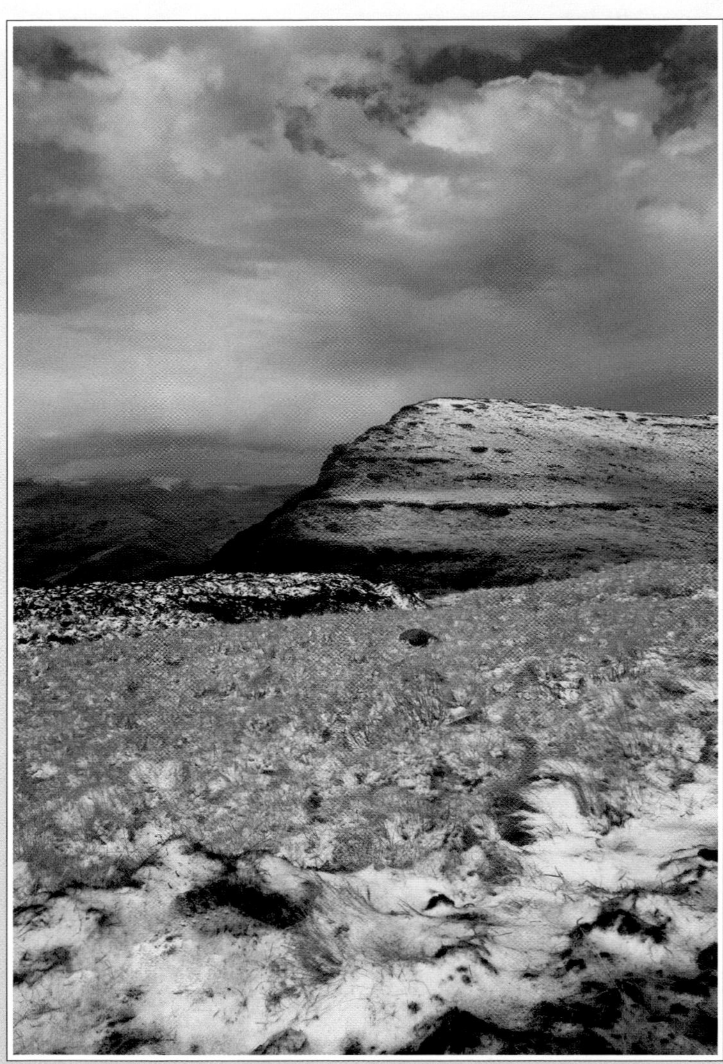

A typical winter landscape near the highest point along the Mafika Lisiu Pass.

The Katse Dam in Lesotho is within easy reach of Clarens and the 400-km round trip there and back constitutes a scenically spectacular day-drive. The Katse Dam is a vast man-made lake in a magnificent mountain setting whose tourist potential has yet to be fully realised. The dam is the centre-piece of the Lesotho Highlands Water Scheme, which generates hydro-electric power as well as supplying water via an 84-km tunnel to the Vaal Dam, thereby helping to avert water shortages during times of drought in the densely populated Johannesburg and Pretoria area.

The closest border post to this part of Lesotho is Caledonspoort near Fouriesburg, southwest of Clarens. The road first traverses typical rural Lesotho countryside before ascending the mountains along the steep Mafika Lisiu Pass, specially built as part of the overall Highlands Water Scheme project. At 3090 m the top of the pass is some 200 m higher than the top of Sani Pass and affords spectacular views in all directions. From the summit the road snakes down again to the level of the dam in the valley below and, after following the western edge of the dam for a few kilometres, crosses over to the eastern side and continues to the wall and nearby tourist lodge.

The dam and its surroundings provide great subject matter for the photographer, particularly if the clouds are co-operative. Once again, thunderstorms in summer and snowfalls in winter add interest to any scene, but the latter can make driving hazardous or impossible. The swiftly flowing streams entering the upper reaches of the dam are attractive in their own right and contrast with the static body of water in the dam itself.

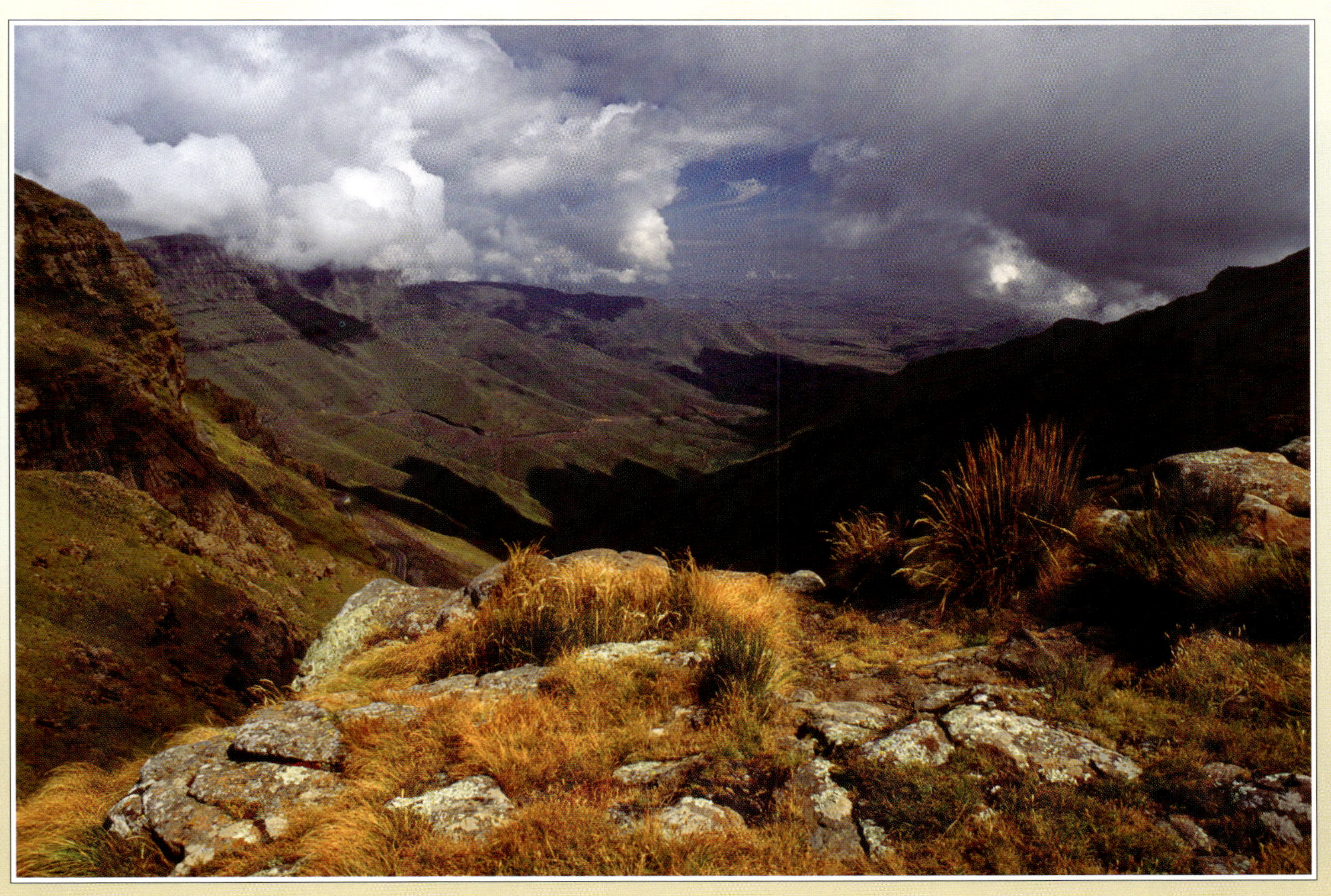

Looking back towards the Free State from the top of the Mafika Lisiu Pass, which links the Katse Dam to the outside world.

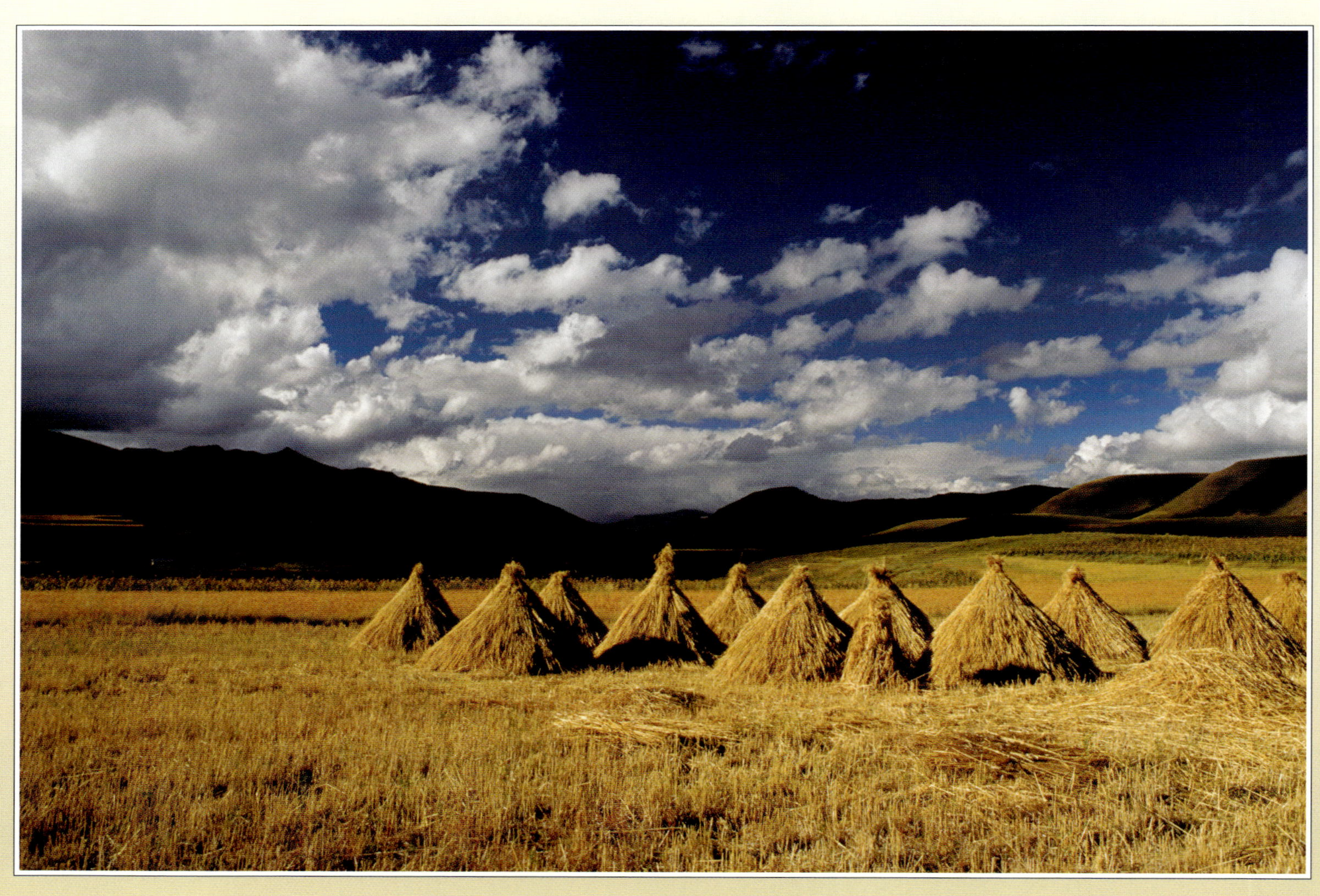

Wheat sheaves stacked in neat bundles in a field near Ha-Lejone village mimic the traditional hats worn by Basuto men.

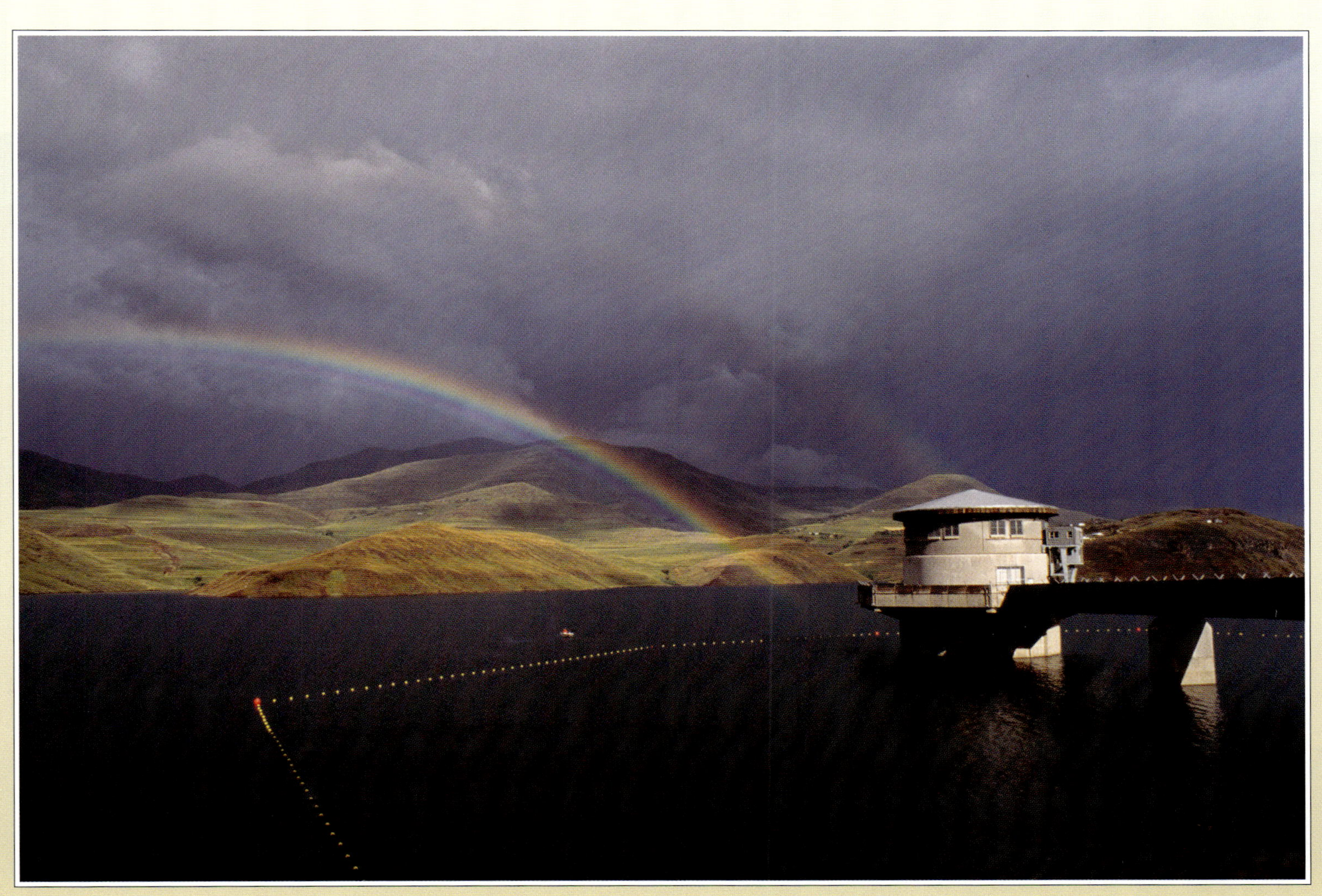

A rainbow near the tunnel inlet marks the end of a thunderstorm over the dam.

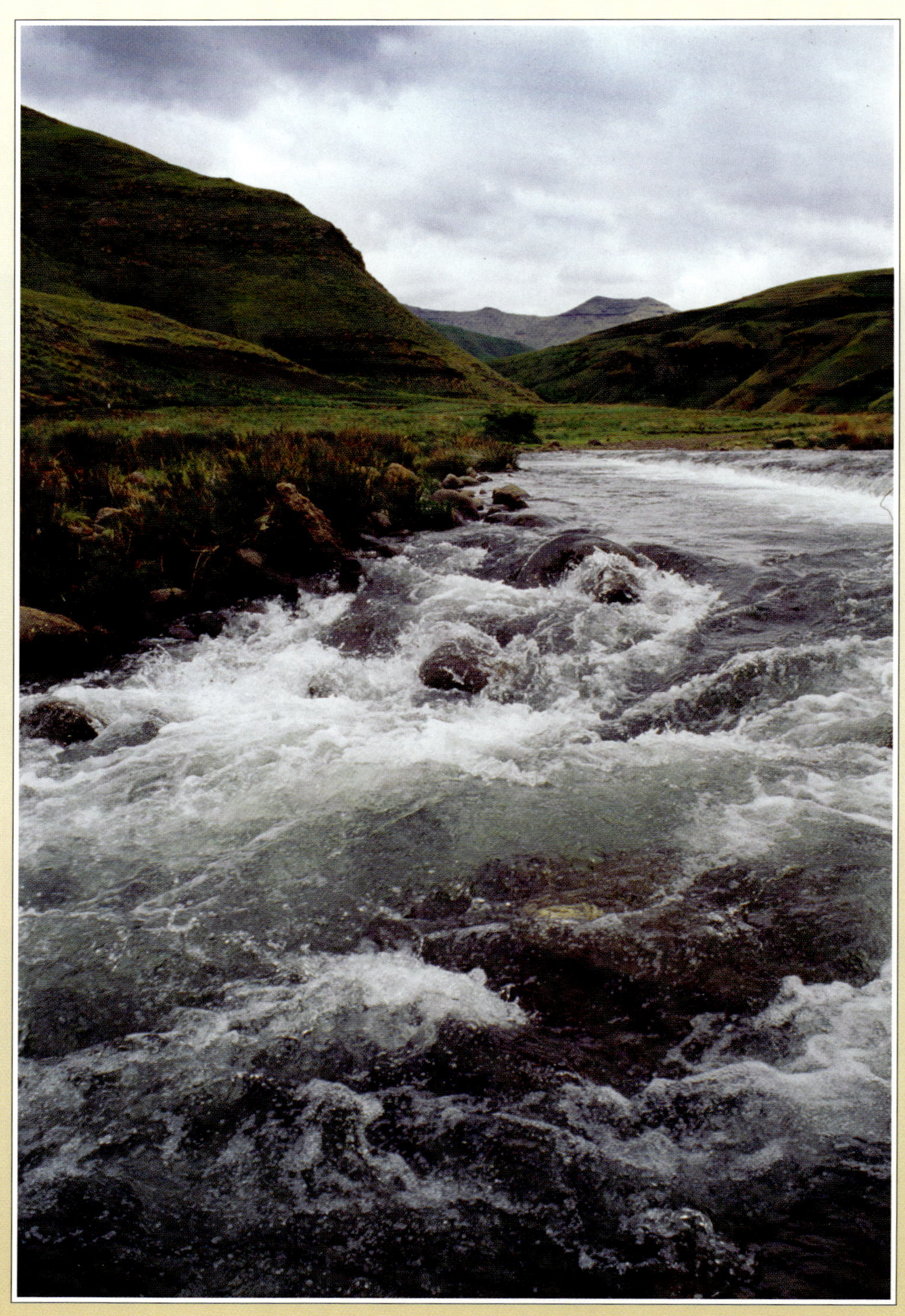

Following good rains, the swollen Pelaneng River feeds yet more water into the Katse Dam.

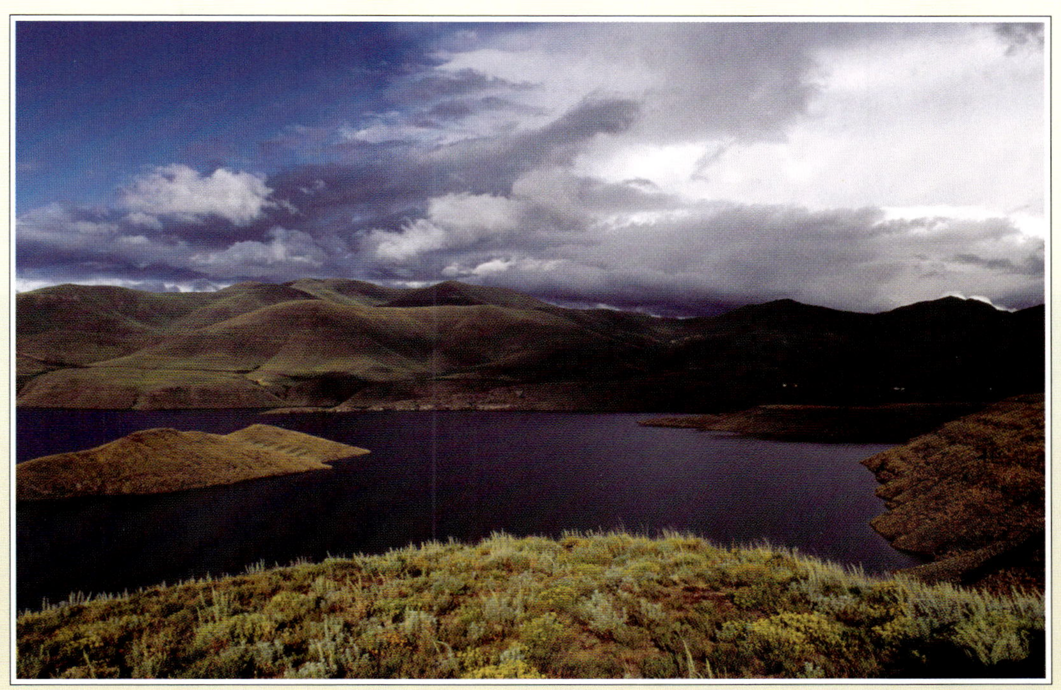

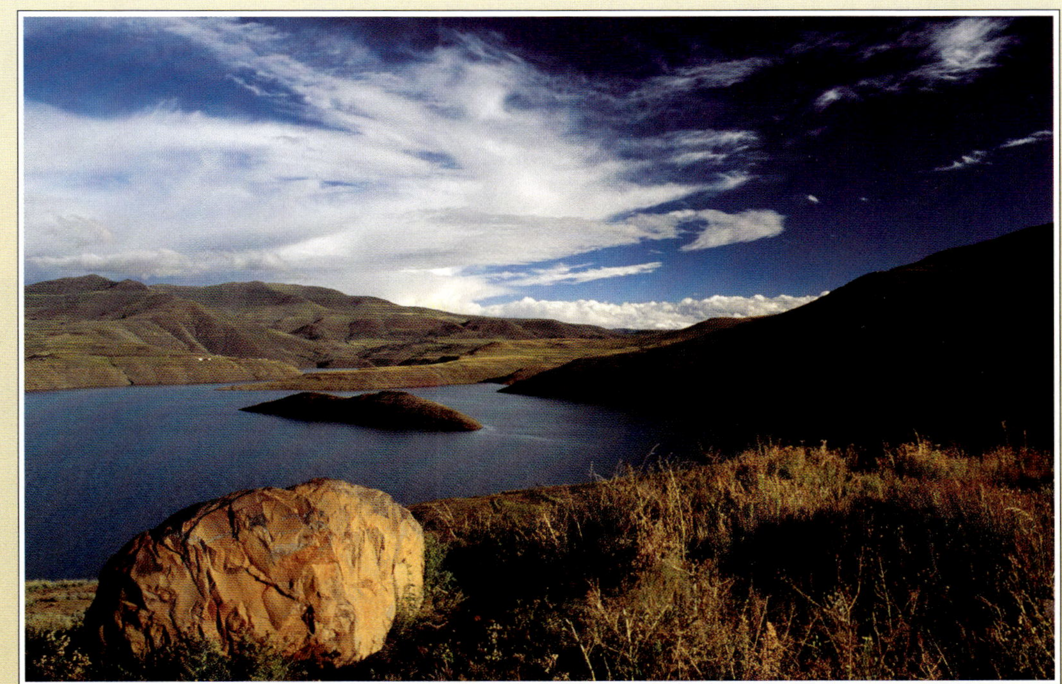

Two views of the Katse Dam and its surroundings, both taken on a particularly clear afternoon —thanks to the unpolluted mountain air—from the gravel road that follows the western shore of the dam.

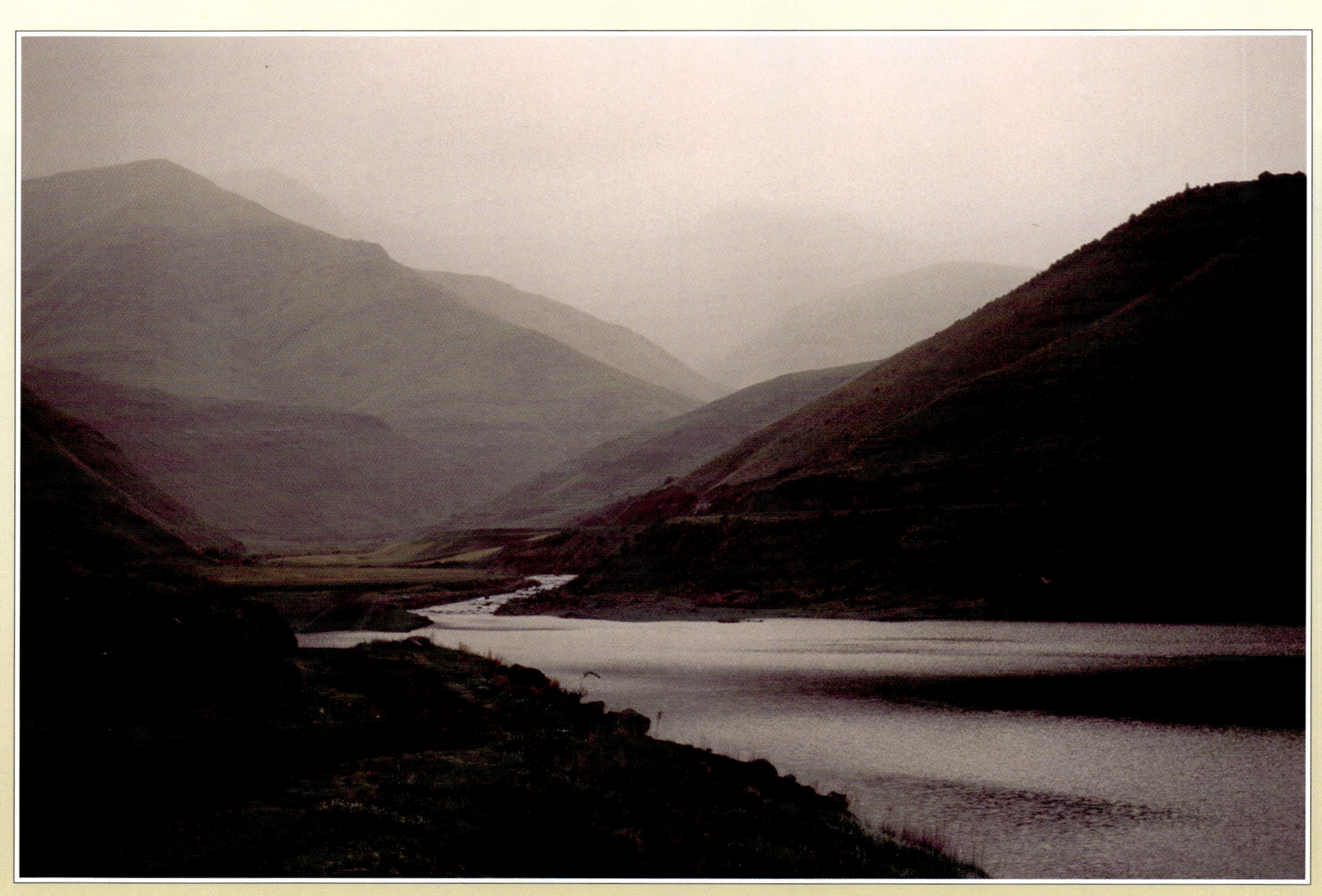

Rain and mist near the top end of the dam create a scene reminiscent of parts of the Scottish Highlands.

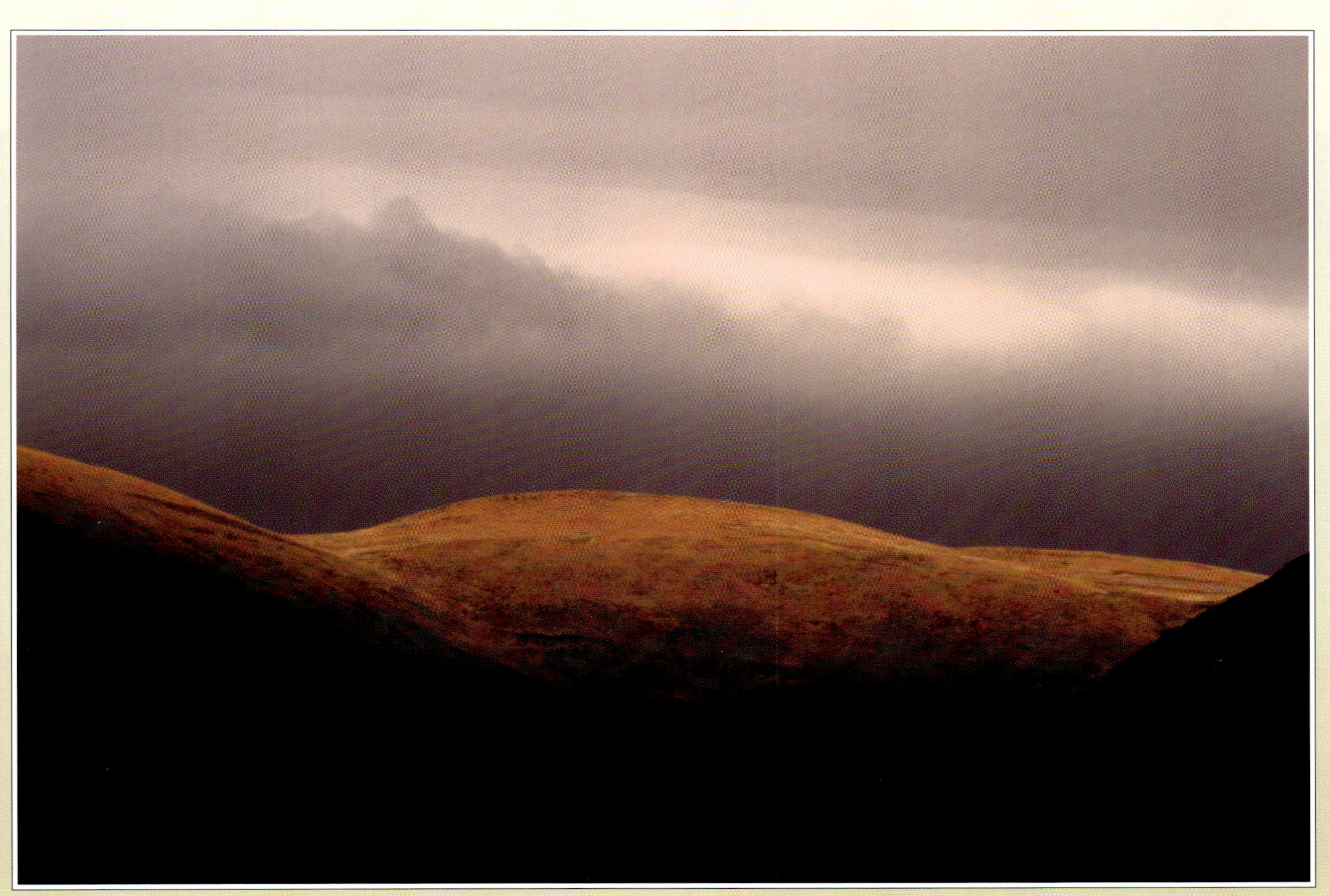

A patch of sunlight briefly touches a mountain top near Ha-Lejone as dark storm clouds gather.

DAY 18

Cosmos Country

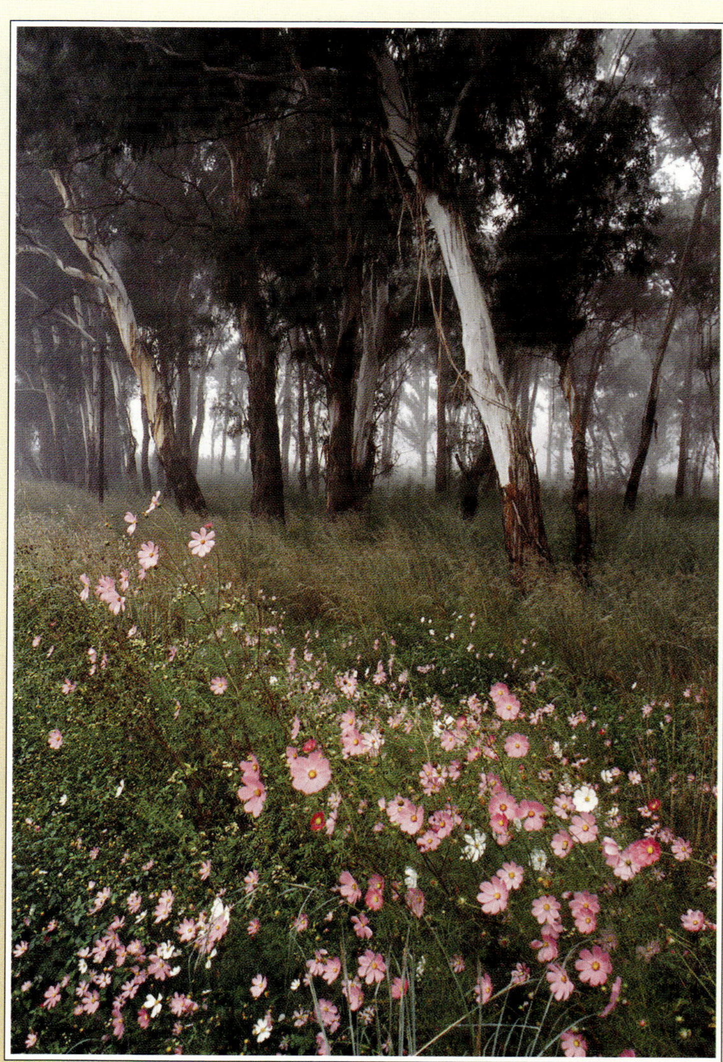

Cosmos flowers are overshadowed by tall eucalyptus trees next to the Pretoria–Delmas road.

As far as this journey is concerned, "Cosmos Country" embraces the countryside stretching from the Clarens—Sterkfontein Dam area northwards as far as Pretoria, traversed by the road from Clarens to Pretoria via Bethlehem, Reitz, Frankfort, Villiers, Devon and Delmas. The name reflects the striking shows of cosmos flowers that brighten the landscape in late summer and early autumn, lining the roadsides and creating massed displays where they have been allowed to grow and flower in fallow fields. This is an essentially agricultural area, with grassy hills dotted with cattle and sheep as well as cultivated fields used for growing maize, wheat, sorghum or sunflowers. The well-known Golden Gate National Park between Clarens and the Sterkfontein Dam is located in an attractive mountainous terrain.

The picturesque village of Clarens is surrounded by sandstone hills belonging to the same geological formation as that which not only forms the frequently photographed reddish cliffs in the Golden Gate National Park, but also the ramparts capping the mountains north of Elliot. The leisurely pace of life and the beauty of the surrounding countryside have attracted most of those who have settled in Clarens. The passing of the seasons is more obvious in this semi-rural setting and is typified by the white and pink fruit tree blossoms in spring, the green hills in summer, the stately yellow poplars in autumn and the brown grass and bare trees in winter. All of these make great subject matter for photographs, as do the attractive stone churches which grace most of the towns in this area, and, of course, the cosmos and sunflowers when they are in season.

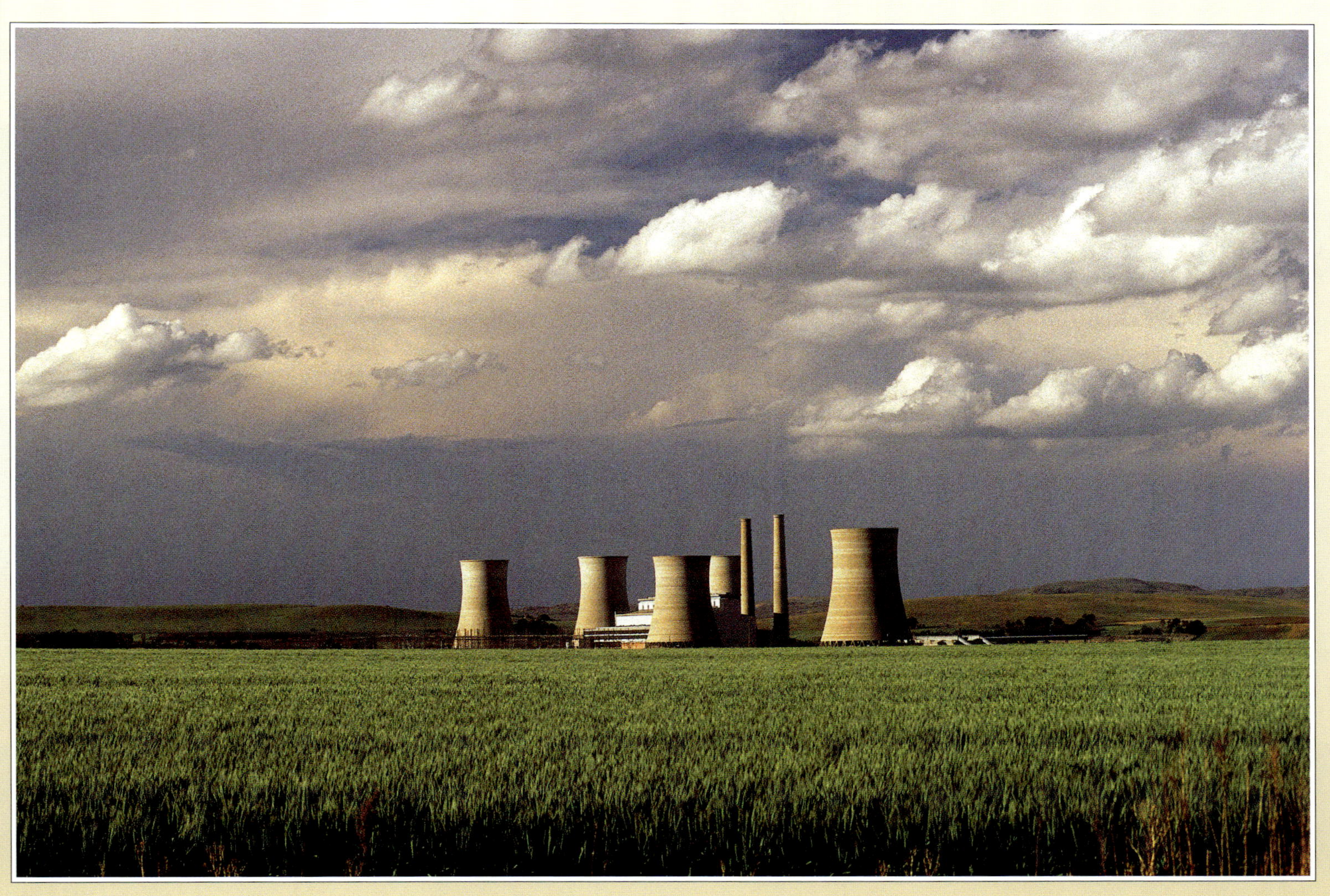

Seen from the southern side, Grootvlei power station near Balfour manages to blend fairly harmoniously into the surrounding countryside.

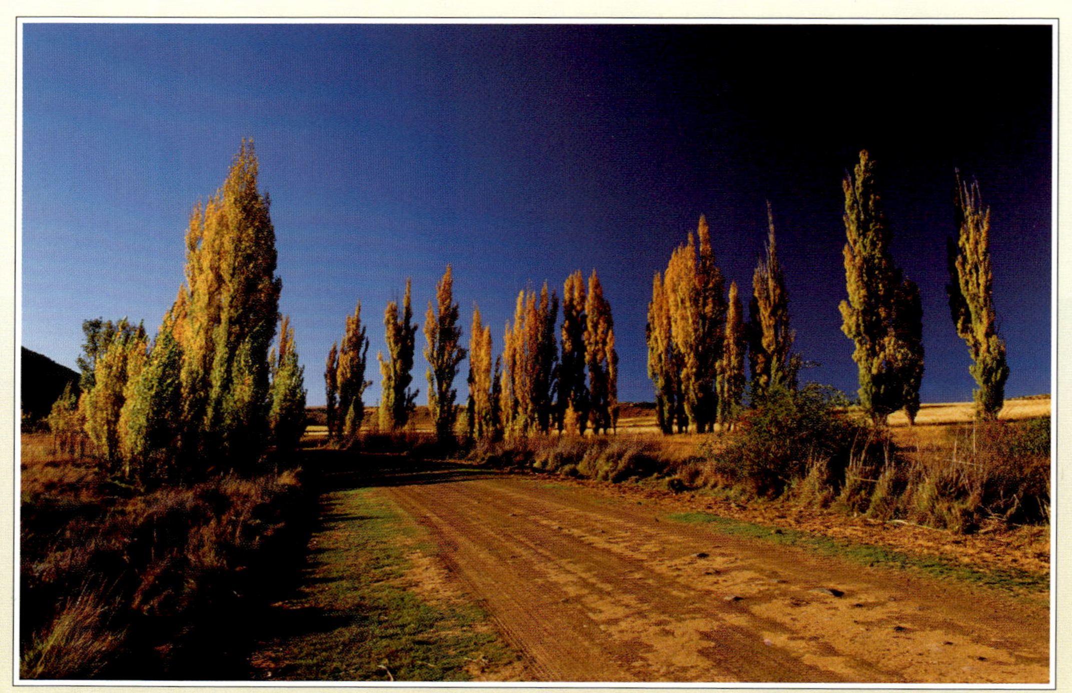

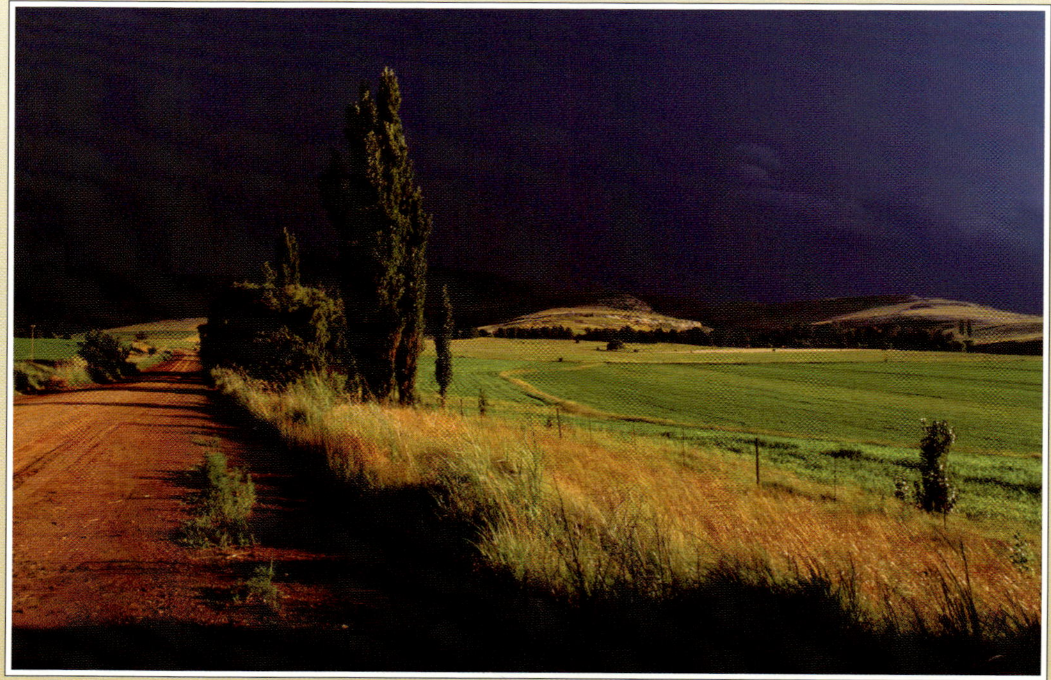

Stately Lombardy poplars are very common in Clarens and the surrounding area, often forming avenues along farm roads. Their bright yellow autumn colours make them particularly attractive during the months of April and May.

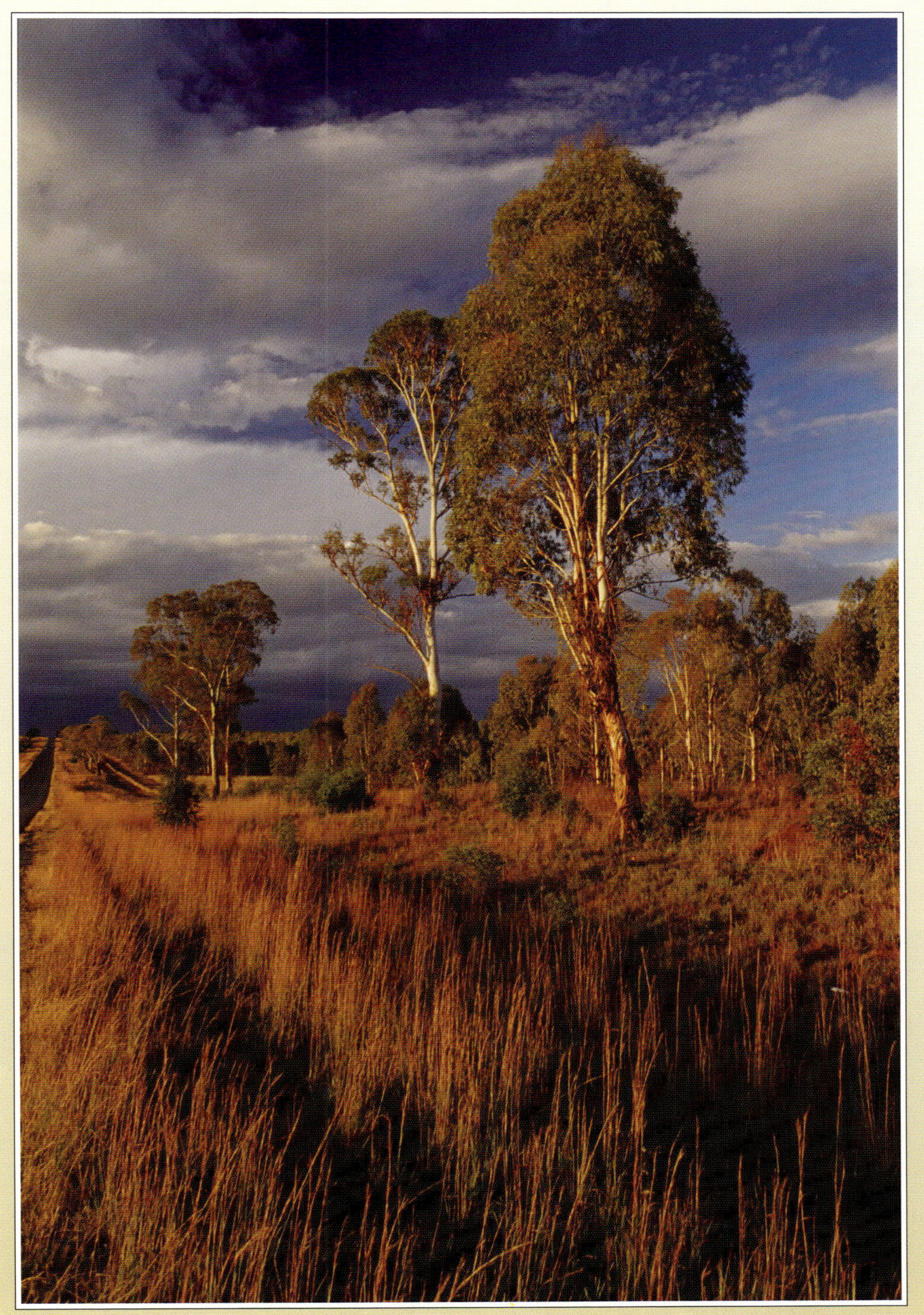

The right lighting can do wonders for the grass and trees that flank the road between Balfour and Devon.

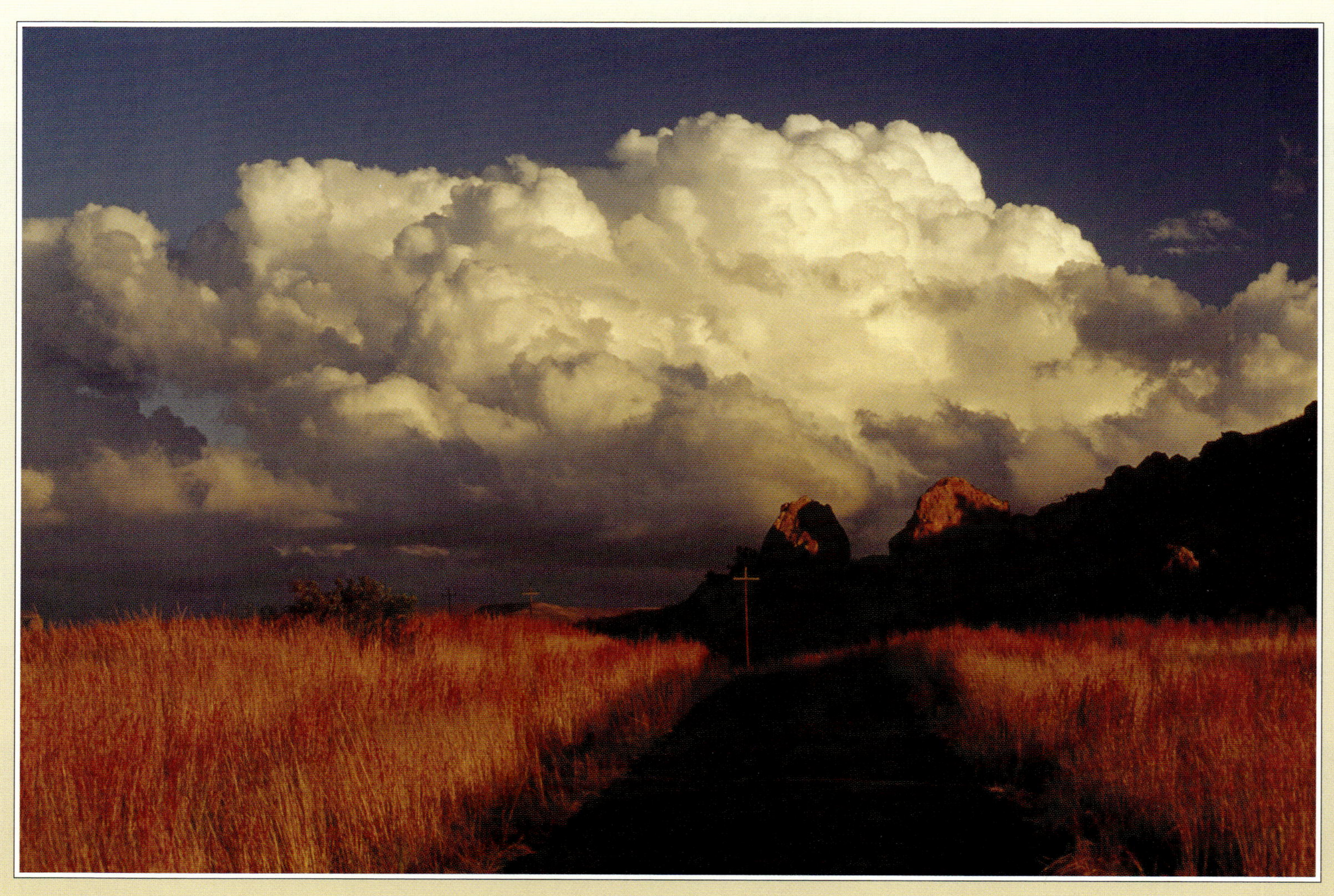

Dark shadows have swallowed up the narrow, winding road to Qwantani Resort on the upper reaches of the Sterkfontein Dam.

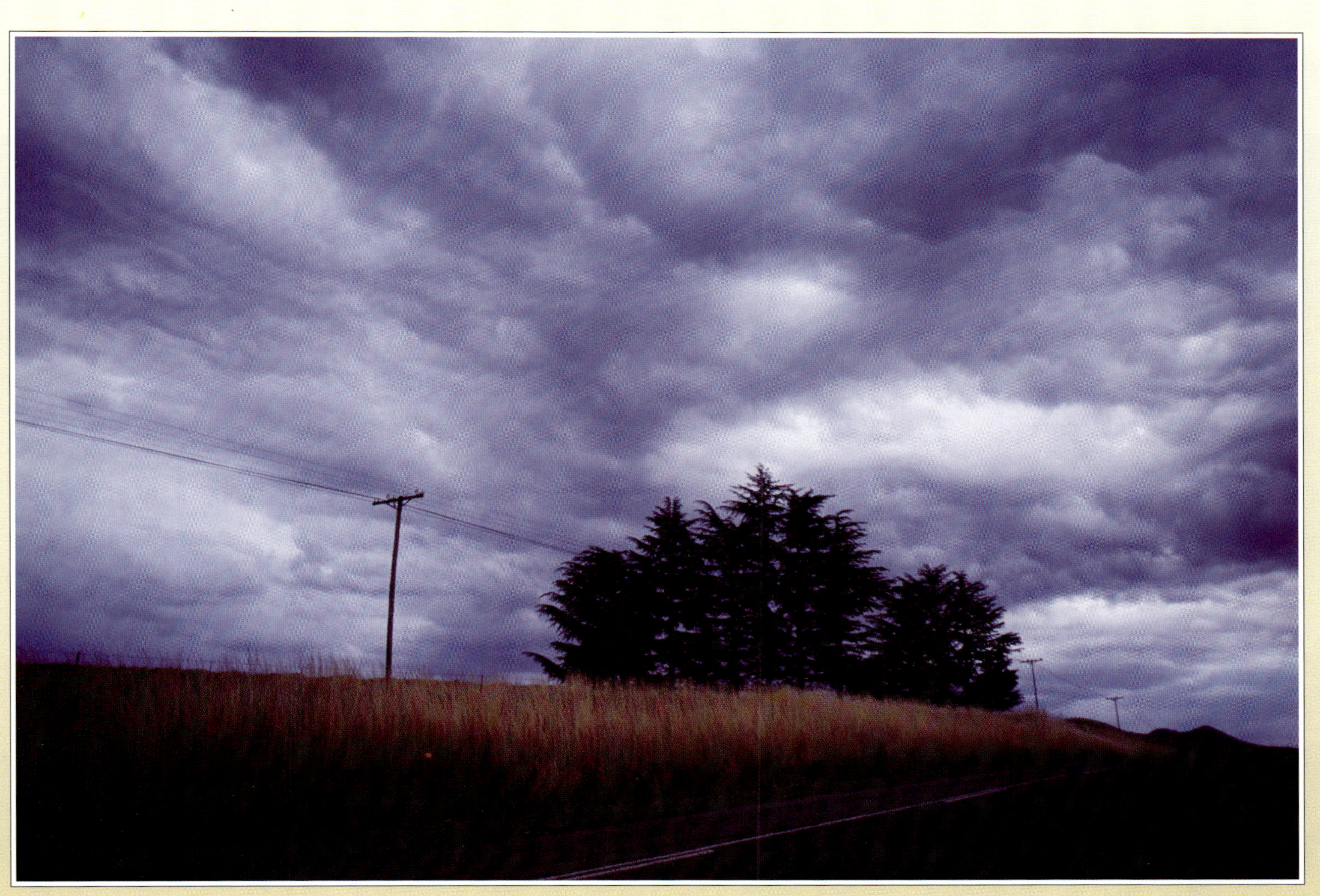

A group of trees on the last hill before reaching Clarens from the Golden Gate side is silhouetted against a dramatic sky.

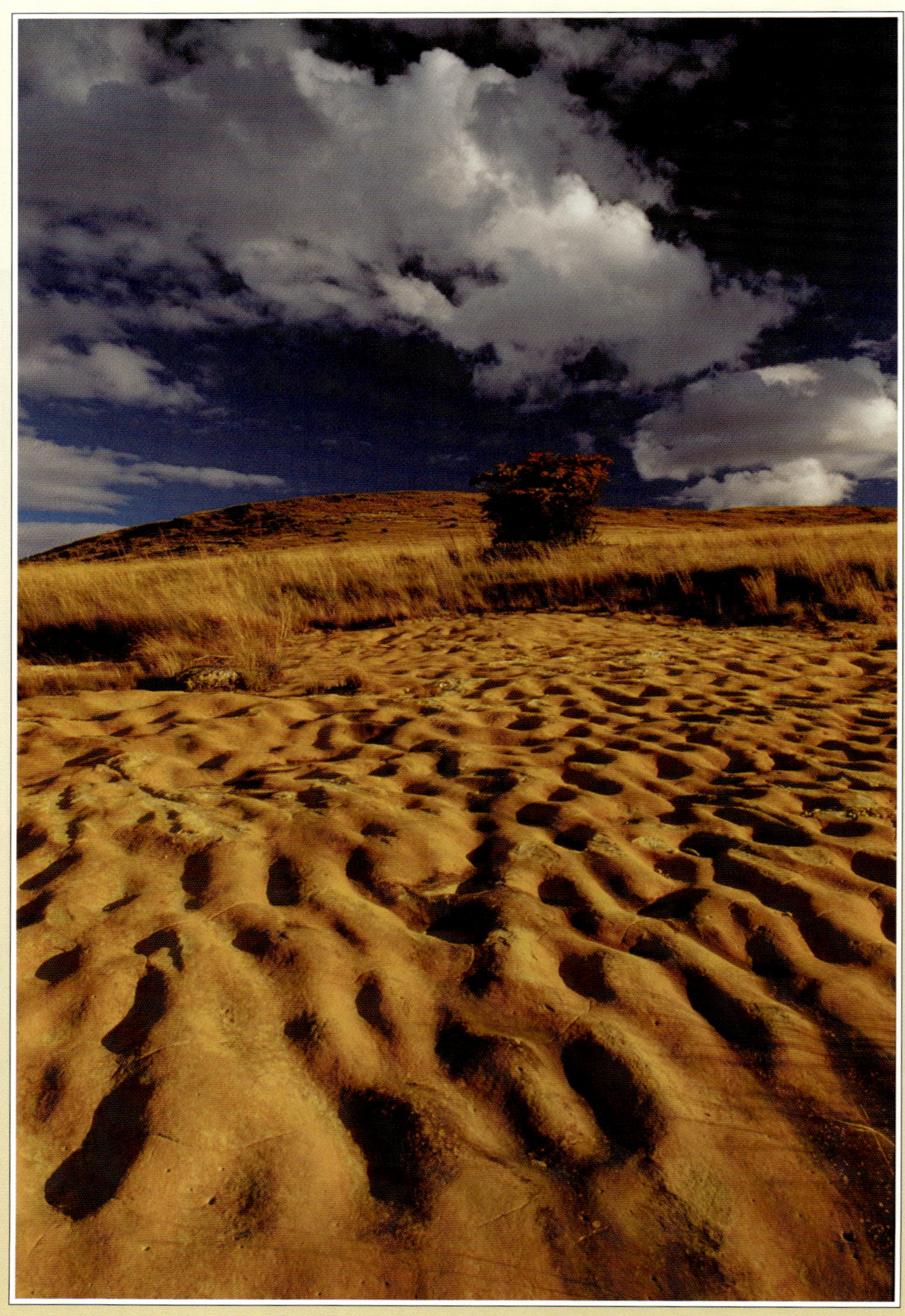

A cryptic pattern on a sandstone ledge in the hills above Clarens is a bit of a geological puzzle but makes for an interesting photograph.

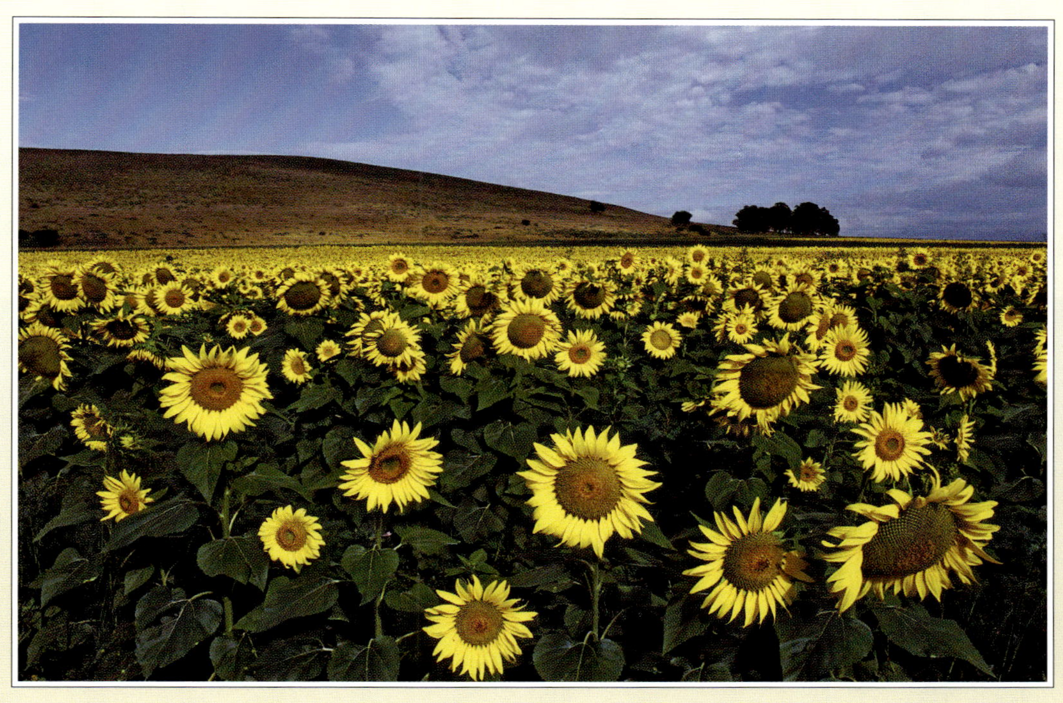

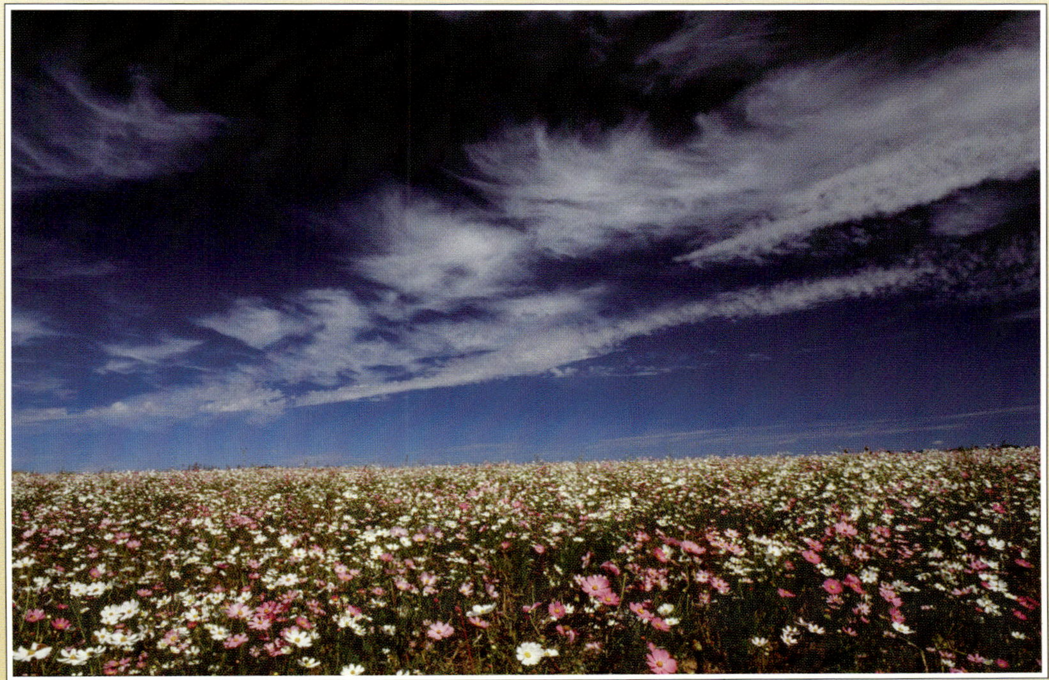

Top:
Sunflowers in full bloom are always an attractive sight; these specimens were growing alongside the road from Balfour to Villiers.

Bottom:
An attractive swathe of cirrus clouds moves sedately across a field of cosmos near Reitz.

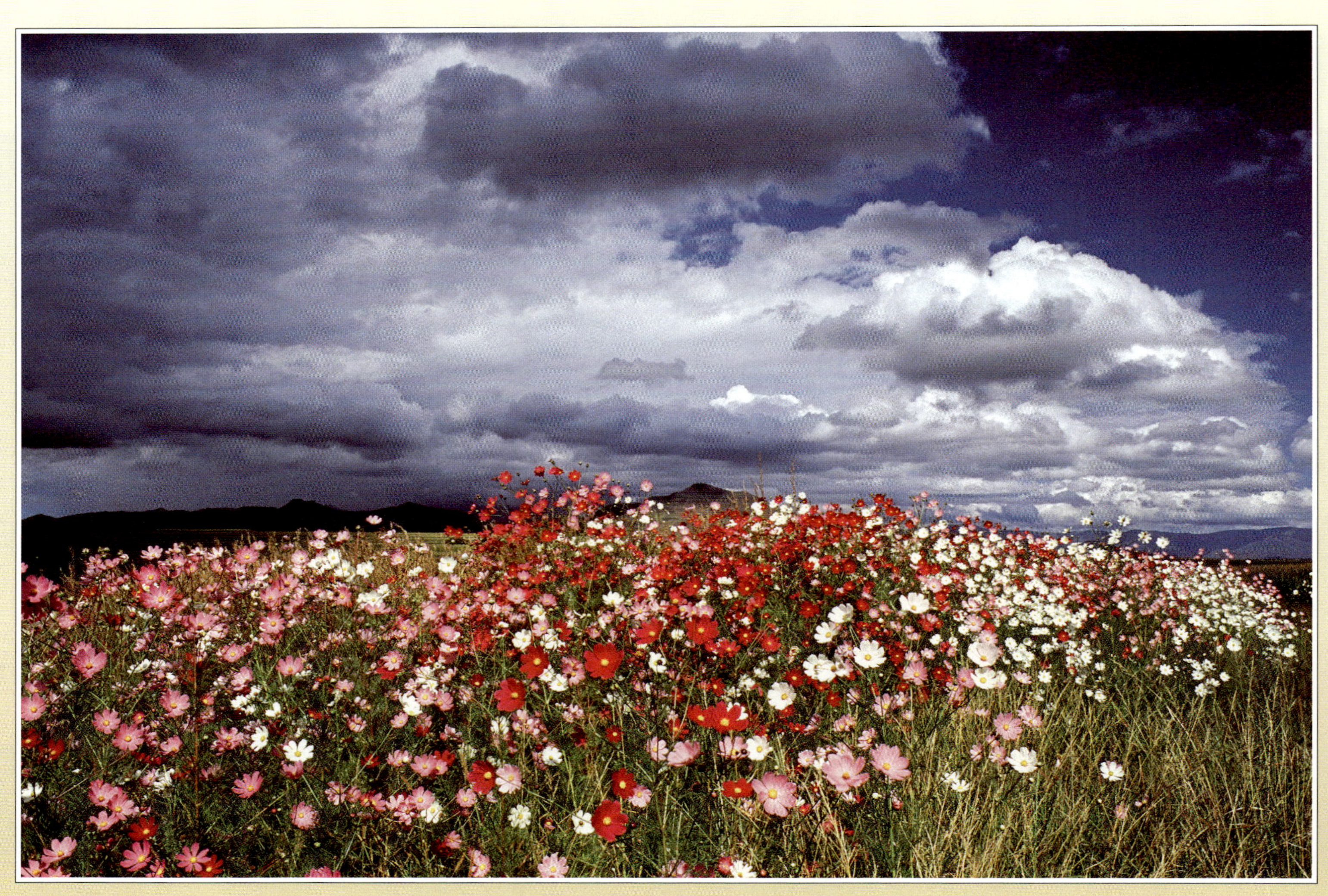

Cosmos displays its full glory along the road from Clarens to Old Mill Drift on the Lesotho border.

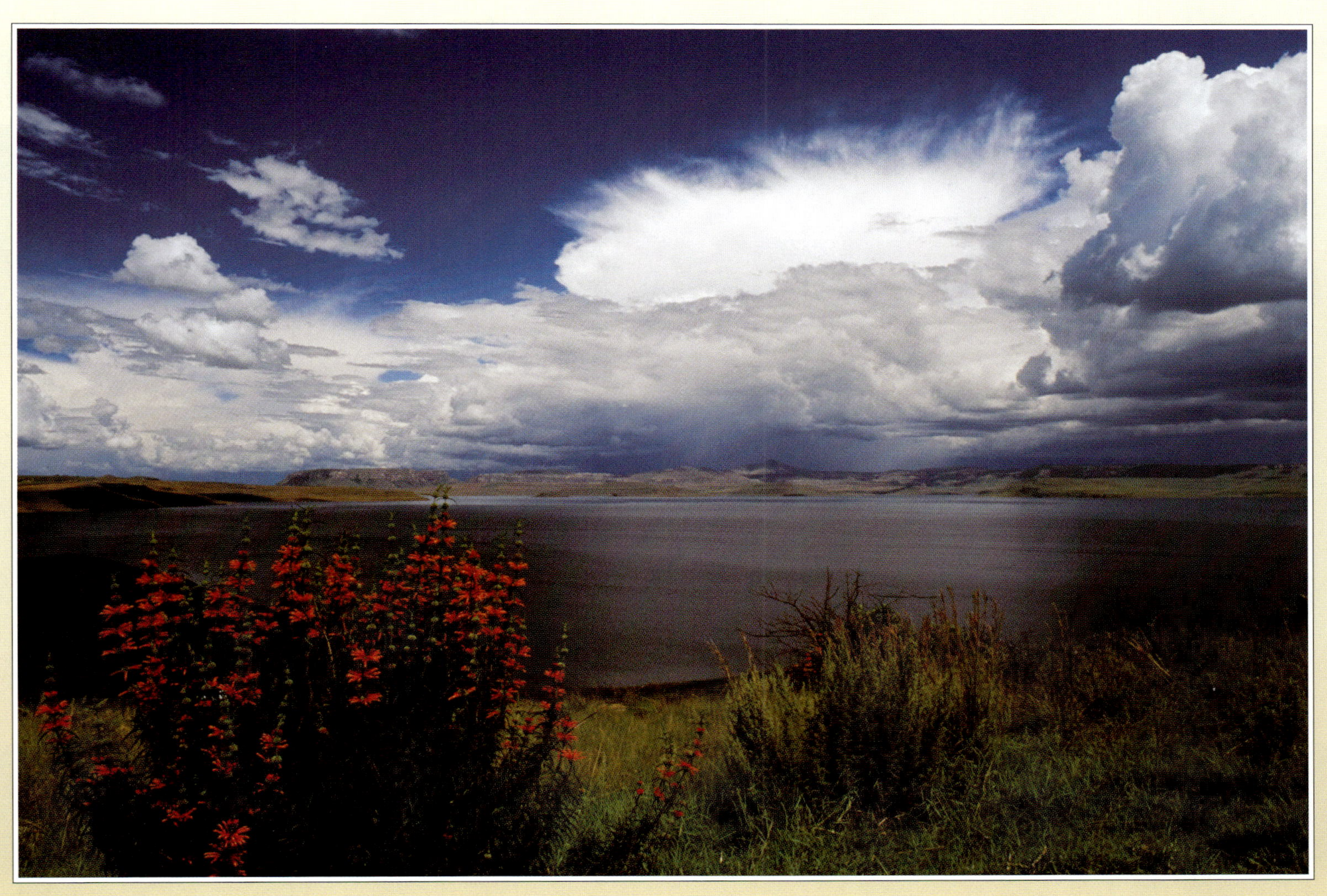

A *Leonotis leonurus* bush adds contrasting colour to this view of the Sterkfontein Dam south of Harrismith.

THE JOURNEY DAY BY DAY

Our 18-day journey is outlined below in terms of photographic opportunities, suggested overnight stops and the approximate distances involved. Those with less than 18 days at their disposal can cut out some legs, such as the Katse Dam excursion, while those with more time can split up some of the longer days. Day 1, for example, could become Pretoria to Kuruman (540 km) followed by Kuruman to Upington via Witsand Nature Reserve (385 km).

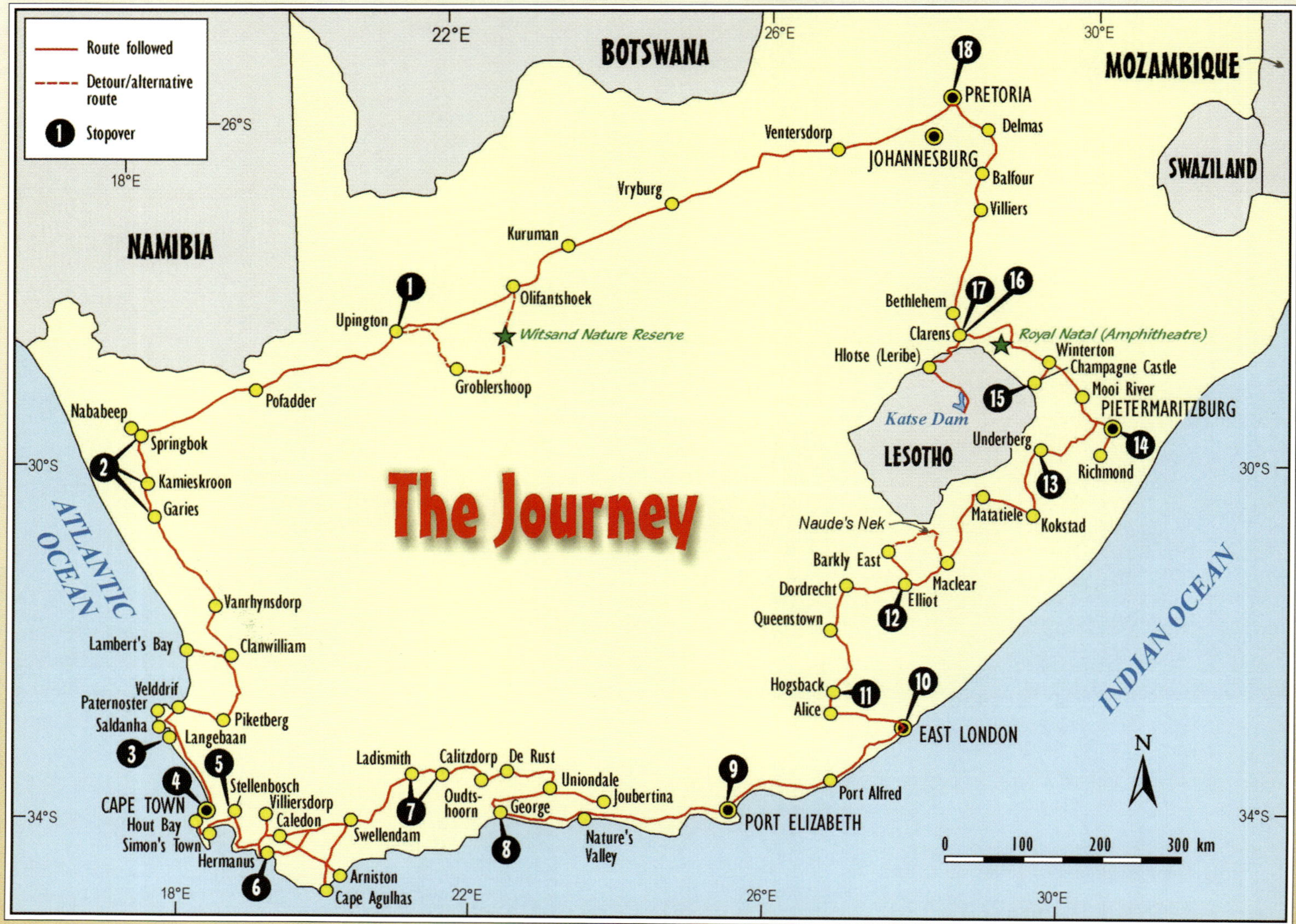

DAY 1 (Pretoria to Upington): Take photos in Pretoria (previous day if possible) and en route (time permitting, via Witsand Nature Reserve) to Upington (800/925 km). Stopover: Upington.

DAY 2 (Namaqualand): Travel to Springbok (early) and take photos in the Goegap Nature Reserve and/or Nababeep area or Namaqualand Nature Reserve (Skilpad Section) or Leliefontein area (440/540 km). Stopover: Springbok or Kamieskroon/Garies.

DAY 3 (West Coast): Travel to Langebaan via Clanwilliam, Velddrif, Paternoster and Saldanha, taking photos en route (600/490 km, starting from Springbok/Garies). Stopover: Langebaan.

DAY 4 (Cape Peninsula): Take photos in West Coast Nature Reserve and travel to Cape Town. Take photos in and around Cape Town, if possible including Cape of Good Hope Nature Reserve (140–240 km). Stopover: Cape Town.

DAY 5 (Stellenbosch): Complete Peninsula photography, travel to Stellenbosch and take photos in and around the town (80–100 km). Stopover: Stellenbosch.

DAY 6 (Kogelberg Coast): Travel to Hermanus via Gordon's Bay and Kleinmond and take photos en route (including local nature reserves) (110 km). Stopover: Hermanus.

DAY 7 (The Overberg): Take photos in the Villiersdorp–Caledon–Cape Agulhas–Swellendam area and travel to Ladismith or Calitzdorp (310–550 km). Stopover: Ladismith/Calitzdorp.

DAY 8 (Little Karoo & Langkloof): Travel to Uniondale via Cango Caves, Oudtshoorn and De Rust (Little Karoo), then to Joubertina and back (Langkloof) and on to George via the Outeniqua Pass, taking photos en route (460 km). Stopover: George or one of the nearby seaside resorts.

DAY 9 (Garden Route): Travel to Port Elizabeth along coastal road, taking photos en route (350 km). Stopover: Port Elizabeth.

DAY 10 (Port Elizabeth): Take photos in and around Port Elizabeth and travel to East London (300 km). Stopover: East London.

DAY 11 (East London): Take photos in and around East London, travel to Hogsback and start taking photos in Hogsback (160 km). Stopover: Hogsback.

DAY 12 (Hogsback): Complete Hogsback photography (early morning), travel to Elliot and take photos along Barkly East road (360 km). Stopover: Elliot.

DAY 13 (Cape Drakensberg): Take photos around Elliot and travel to Underberg via Matatiele and Kokstad (400 km). Stopover: Underberg or nearby Drakensberg resorts.

DAY 14 (Underberg area): Take photos in Southern Drakensberg area and travel to Pietermaritzburg (200 km). Stopover: Pietermaritzburg.

DAY 15 (Natal Midlands): Take photos in Richmond–Mooi River area (Natal Midlands) and travel to Champagne Castle valley (260 km). Stopover: Champagne Castle resorts.

DAY 16 (Northern Drakensberg): Take photos in Champagne Castle-Amphitheatre area and travel to Clarens via Oliviershoek Pass, taking photos en route (250 km). Stopover: Clarens.

DAY 17 (Katse Dam): Travel to Katse Dam, take photos en route and at the dam and return to Clarens (400 km). Stopover: Clarens.

DAY 18 (Cosmos Country): Take photos in Clarens area and return to Pretoria via Villiers, Balfour and Delmas, taking photos en route (400 km). Journey's end: Pretoria.

TOTAL DISTANCE: c. 6500 km.

AVERAGE DAILY DISTANCE: c. 350 km.

ACKNOWLEDGEMENTS

I would like to thank the following who have, directly or indirectly, contributed to the making of this book:
The friendly staff at ProLab, Pretoria, where all my more recent film processing was done.

Henry and Latzi at RadioLens, Pretoria, who have been ever helpful to me as a regular customer for over 30 years.

Nicol Stassen, Jeanette Ferreira and Karen Horn at Protea Boekhuis for the part each one played in bringing the book to fruition.

John Bertram in Pietermaritzburg who translated my preliminary ideas into an attractive and marketable initial product, the general concept of which was retained for the published version.

Elrene Jones who was responsible for the final layout.

Travis McNeill at Wet Ink Design, who expertly scanned most of the original colour slides.

Family and friends who provided accommodation on the numerous occasions that the round trip was done: Brian and Win Johnson in Cape Town, Zelda Botma in Betty's Bay, Dene and Cynthia Sampson in Port Elizabeth, Denzil and Gay Schwulst in Elliot, Steve and Kathy Johnson in Pietermaritzburg, Greg and Lindy Heath in Lesotho and Gideon and Sue Groenewald in Clarens. Without their generous hospitality many of the photos in this book would never have been taken.

Last, but not least, my wife Des who supplied unfailing companionship and support despite having to endure many uncomfortable hours in a hot car parked at the roadside during journeys that were often long and arduous.

TECHNICAL NOTES

Having up to now managed to resist the digital onslaught, most of the photos in this book were taken on Kodak Elite Chrome Extra Color film or, when unavailable, its "professional" equivalent, Ektachrome 100VS. Very basic equipment was used: a late 1970s vintage Canon AT-1 fully manual 35 mm camera or, when it had to be replaced a few years ago, a Canon A-1 of similar age. The vast majority of the photos were taken with a 28 mm Osawa lens, normally with a polarising filter attached. Its ability to bring together in sharp focus the various elements of a scene, extending from nearby flowers or rocks through to the sweeping expanse of an attractive sky, makes a 28 mm lens ideal for landscape photography. Where a telephoto shot was required, I used a 80-200 mm Tokina zoom lens, recently upgraded to a 70-210 mm Canon lens (with the compliments of my son David, who had "gone digital"). I very rarely use the 50 mm standard lens which I only acquired (second-hand) comparatively recently.

I know that serious landscape photographers are meant to keep their cameras on tripods at all times, but setting one up would keep my passenger(s) waiting even longer in the car, or provoke a party of fellow geologists with whom I might be travelling to start hooting impatiently! In addition, working with a tripod can be somewhat restrictive when it comes to moving around trying to find just the right position and height for a photo. Fortunately, with using a wide-angle lens most of the time camera shake is not normally an issue. It goes without saying, of course, that poor light or fitting a long telephoto lens will make the use a sturdy tripod mandatory.